WIDENING THE FAMILY CIRCLE

To our families, both immediate and extended. Thank you for teaching us first about the power of family relationships.

WIDENING THE FAMILY CIRCLE

New Research on Family Communication

EDITORS

KORY FLOYD
Arizona State University

MARK T. MORMAN
Baylor University

SAGE Publications
Thousand Oaks ▪ London ▪ New Delhi

For information:

Sage Publications, Inc.
2455 Teller Road
Thousand Oaks, California 91320
E-mail: order@sagepub.com

Sage Publications Ltd.
1 Oliver's Yard
55 City Road
London EC1Y 1SP
United Kingdom

Sage Publications India Pvt. Ltd.
B-42, Panchsheel Enclave
Post Box 4109
New Delhi 110 017 India

Printed in the United States of America

Library of Congress Cataloging-in-Publication Data

Widening the family circle: New research on family communication/
edited by Kory Floyd, Mark T. Morman.
      p. cm.
Includes bibliographical references and index.
ISBN 1-4129-0921-X (cloth)
ISBN 1-4129-0922-8 (pbk.)
      1. Communication in the family. 2. Interpersonal communication.
I. Floyd, Kory. II. Morman, Mark T.
HQ519.W53 2006
306.87—dc22

                                                        2005015496

This book is printed on acid-free paper.

05   06   07   08   10   9   8   7   6   5   4   3   2   1

Acquisitions Editor:	Todd R. Armstrong
Editorial Assistant:	Deya Sayoud
Production Editor:	Denise Santoyo
Typesetter:	C&M Digitals (P) Ltd.
Cover Designer:	Janet Foulger

Contents

Acknowledgments

Like many significant projects, a book is a journey. It has its genesis in an idea, and it navigates a path along which it requires many forms of help from many different people in order to arrive safely at its destination. It is our pleasure now to thank those who helped this book traverse that path.

The impetus for this volume was our observation that although families are diverse, dynamic structures that encompass a broad range of relationships, the discipline of family communication has focused a large proportion of its research on only two: marriage and parent-young child relationships. There can be little argument that these relationships merit in-depth attention, but we believed that the discipline's understanding of the family would be greatly enhanced by "widening the circle" to include other relationships, such as those with grandparents, adoptive parents, in-laws, aunts and uncles, siblings, and stepparents.

We first engaged this idea in a graduate seminar that we taught together at Arizona State University during the spring of 2002. We called the seminar *Communication in Under-Studied Family Relationships,* and we used it as an opportunity to delve into the literatures of familial relationships other than those between spouses or parents and young children. We were encouraged by the quality of research we found on many of these relationships and we came to believe more strongly that a volume in which much of this literature was brought together would be of use to the field. The graduate students who participated in our seminar offered insightful questions and criticisms about this literature that helped greatly to sharpen our focus for this book, and we are grateful to each of them for their contributions.

Following completion of our seminar, we began to ask our colleagues in the family communication area to contribute their work on family relationships to the book. Many of the contributors we asked were well known to us beforehand, and some we had the pleasure of meeting as a result of this project. We are so pleased to include in this volume the work of such a fine and diverse set of scholars, and we thank each of them for being willing to share their work with us.

Of course, no book sees the light of day without the involvement of a skilled editor, and we are profoundly grateful to Todd Armstrong for his willingness to take our vision, refine it, improve on it, and bring it to fruition. Todd, and his assistant, Deya Saoud, have supported this project in every manner possible, and we thank them both for their commitment and encouragement.

In addition, the contributions of the following reviewers are gratefully acknowledged.

Michael Arrington
University of Kentucky

Nancy J. Eckstein
Bethel University

Jonathan Hess
University of Missouri–Columbia

Michelle Miller-Day
Pennsylvania State University

Barbara Penington
University of Wisconsin–Whitewater

Chris Segrin
University of Arizona

Lynn H. Turner
Marquette University

Amber M. Walker
Pennsylvania State University

Introduction

On the Breadth of
the Family Experience

The family is one of nature's masterpieces.

—George Santayana (1863–1952)

To call the family an important human institution is to understate its value profoundly. Virtually no other relationship engages us socially, genetically, legally, financially, and intimately with the pervasiveness of the family. Families are with us from beginning to end; we are born into familial relationships and we often leave this life with family members at our side. Families protect us, provide for us, and give us an identity and a sense of belonging. They engage the full spectrum of our emotions, from immeasurable joys to our deepest sorrows, and they enjoy a level of permanence unparalleled by almost anything else in our lives. Indeed, one could easily argue that the family is situated at the focal point of nearly *all* relational encounters. It is, truly, a masterpiece of the human experience.

Among the family's many unique attributes is its breadth across the relational landscape. From the nuclear reproductive and parental relationships, the family branches off in nearly innumerable ways to encompass other forms of familial ties. Some relationships, such as grandparents or nieces and nephews, are *vertical ties*, meaning that they span two or more generations. Others, such as siblings or cousins, are *horizontal ties*, meaning they represent contemporaries within one's own generation. Many family relationships are genetically bound, however distantly (e.g., aunts and uncles, great-grandparents, second cousins). Others are formed through legal means, such as adoption (e.g., adoptive siblings), marriage (e.g., parents-in-law), remarriage (e.g., stepfamilies), or divorce (e.g., post-divorce relationships). Still others are formed and maintained purely through social interaction; these fall under the category of "fictive kin," or family-like relationships that are neither genetically nor legally bound (e.g., godparents, neighbors, or longtime friends who are considered "family").

As suggested by the metaphor of the *tree*—often used to explicate family relationships—families exist in both nuclear and greatly extended forms. Any given person is linked, in some form or another, to every person on every other limb, branch, and stem of his or her own tree. Certainly, many of these relationships may seem at times to be socially inconsequential, particularly if they involve relatives who are distant genetically, geographically, or both. There is relevance in these relationships, however, that often goes unacknowledged by family communication scholars but is nonetheless operative. For example, genetic relatives (both within and outside the nuclear family) are often the first to be turned to for emotional or economic support during times of crisis, sometimes being preferred even over close friends (see Burnstein, Crandall, & Kitayama, 1994; Essock-Vitale & McGuire, 1985). Similarly, it is almost always genetic relatives to whom assets are allocated in wills, and in some cultures, nieces and nephews are preferred over children in the allocation of property (Smith, Kish, & Crawford, 1987). People are even likely to communicate regularly with non-nuclear family members through mechanisms such as e-mail (Braithwaite, McBride, & Schrodt, 2003) or holiday cards (Fingerman & Griffiths, 1999).

What We Know and Don't Know About Communication in Family Relationships

Despite their relevance, family relationships other than marriage and parent-child relationships have gone largely unscrutinized in research by many scholars in the fields of family communication, family psychology, and personal relationships. In a content analysis of nearly a thousand research articles published in family and personal relationships journals from 1994 to 1999, family scholars Karen Fingerman and Elizabeth Hay (2002) reported that parental and spousal/romantic relationships were by far the most common topics of the research. Specifically, 16.6% of the articles focused on relationships with parents, and 25.6% focused on relationships with young children. Moreover, roughly a quarter (25.2%) focused on romantic ties, and more than four in ten (44.3%) focused specifically on marriage.[1]

In sharp contrast, many other family relationships received almost no scholarly attention at all. Relationships with aunts and uncles, siblings-in-law, cousins, and great-grandchildren, for instance, were the focus of only 0.1% of the research surveyed. Even siblings, a component of the nuclear family, were studied in only 4.1% of the research. Stepfamilies, grandparents, and parent-in-law relationships were similarly infrequently studied. It appears, then, that relative to marriage and parent-child relationships, all other family relationships can reasonably be described as "understudied."

That marital and parental relationships should so frequently be the focus of academic research is entirely understandable, given their importance in the human social agenda. The marital bond is perhaps the principal and most socially significant of all human attachments. It engages people in nearly every dimension of their lives, including physically, economically, legally, sexually, emotionally, reproductively, in terms of their individual identity, and in terms of their social and personal networks. Married people live longer, happier, and healthier lives than never-married people (Lillard & Waite, 1995; Pinquart, 2003), and the termination of marriage, either through divorce (Kiecolt-Glaser, Kennedy, Malkoff, Fisher, Speicher, & Glaser, 1988) or bereavement (Irwin, Daniels, Smith, Bloom, & Weiner, 1987), brings with it pronounced declines in physical well-being. Indeed, data from national surveys indicate that being happy with one's marriage is far more important to one's ratings of overall happiness than anything else, including satisfaction with careers or friendships (Glenn & Weaver, 1981).

Undoubtedly, many of the same points could be made with respect to the parent-child relationship (at least, to the relationship between parents and young children). Evolutionary psychology suggests that humans (and all sexually reproducing species) have evolved through the pressures of natural selection to give primacy to the health and well-being of their offspring, and that this creates ingrained motivations to love, protect, and provide for one's children more than for nearly anyone else in one's social circle (see, e.g., Workman & Reader, 2004). These motivations manifest themselves in the innumerable ways that parents invest in their children's well-being. One such way is reflected in the considerable economic resources parents willingly provide their children. Indeed, in its most recent annual report on the Expenditures on Children by Families, the U.S. Department of Agriculture's Center for Nutrition Policy and Promotion estimates the cost of raising a single child to age 18 to be as much as $261,270 (Lino, 2005). This figure includes the major child-rearing expenses of housing, food, transportation, clothing, education, child care, and health care, as well as miscellaneous expenses such as entertainment or personal care. The importance of the parent-child bond is also reflected in the magnitude of grief that parents typically experience at the premature loss of a child. Researchers have known for decades that the death of a child is among the most potent of all psychological stressors (Holmes & Rahe, 1967). Indeed, contemporary research indicates that losing a child is associated with pronounced increases in parental post-traumatic stress disorder (Murphy, Johnson, Chung, & Beaton, 2003) and parental morality (Li, Precht, Mortensen, & Olsen, 2003).

However important marital and parental relationships are to the human social agenda, though, they represent only a narrow slice of the family experience. As we noted above, familial relationships beyond marital and parental bonds have been relatively neglected by scholars in the family and personal relationships fields. One of the principal problems with this imbalance in academic attention is that it belies people's actual familial experiences. After content-analyzing the family and personal relationships journals to quantify the amount of focus on each family relationship, Fingerman and Hay (2002) surveyed a sample of adults consisting of relationship scholars, those with advanced degrees in other fields, and those with less education. They asked participants to indicate which family relationships they considered applicable to themselves and then to rate their importance. Although spousal and parent-child relationships were understandably rated highly on both counts, other relationships were also considered highly applicable, including cousins (95%), aunts or uncles (92%), nieces or nephews (85%), siblings-in-law (80%), siblings (75%), parents-in-law (63%), and grandparents (50%).[2] Moreover, participants rated all of these relationships, with the exception of cousins, above the midpoint of the scale for importance.

These findings merely quantify what we suspect many people would say on their own: although spousal and parental relationships are extremely important, they are only two among myriad relationships that make up the experience of family. Indeed, many other relationships engage people in ways that spouses, parents, and children do not. Siblings, for instance, are usually our most longstanding life companions; we typically enter sibling relationships early in life and, barring premature death, they are the people at the end of our lives whom we have known the longest. Moreover, grandparents or aunts and uncles can serve as important allies and confidantes in ways that parents may not. Cousins may serve as surrogate siblings and may be particularly instrumental in the lives of only children. Adoption opens the door to parenthood for those who choose not to reproduce biologically or who are unable to. Still other relationships are notable because they can be tremendously supportive, yet are often the sources of pronounced stress, such as stepfamilies or parents-in-law. Indeed, the diversity of the familial experience is great, and a focus on marital and parental relationships—critical though they are—prevents us from appreciating the rich tapestry that is a *family*.

Widening the Circle of Family Communication

This book represents a coming together of contemporary research on many of these lesser-studied family relationships. The focus of the research covered herein is relational communication, broadly construed to include various patterns of meaning-making. Each chapter details one understudied relationship and offers either a critical review of existing literature, a presentation of original data pertaining to communication in that relationship, or both. The goal of each chapter is to illuminate why the focal relationship is consequential and to describe its important communicative attributes.

Our mission with this collection is two-fold. An immediate objective is to offer a resource for students and scholars of family interaction to learn of the research done on relationships outside the nuclear reproductive and parental unions. Such a view certainly is not intended to replace a focus on marital and parent-child relationships but rather to augment it, allowing students and scholars a broader appreciation of existing knowledge about family communication. Our longer-term objective with this contributed volume is to encourage the additional exploration of communication in these and other family relationships. We believe this will become ever-increasingly important as the continued evolution of the family within the human social experience makes previously unusual familial relationships more mundane.

We have divided the book into three sections, the first of which addresses relationships rooted in the family of origin. This section begins with a chapter on the mother-daughter relationship, which, although it is a parental relationship, is relatively understudied in its adult form (i.e., when the daughters are adults, as opposed to children). The second chapter focuses on the adult sibling relationship, which is understudied in general and is particularly so among young and middle adult siblings. The final chapter in the first section addresses the meaning of "sonhood," or the relationship men have with their parents.

Whereas the chapters in the first section address relationships that are more often studied in other forms (e.g., parent-child relationships with young children), those in the second section address relationships that are beyond the nuclear family configuration. Addressed in this section are the grandparent-grandchild relationship, the relationship of aunts with their nieces and nephews, the parent-in-law/child-in-law relationship, and the relationship of siblings-in-law. These topics represent a mixture of vertical and horizontal ties and a blend of genetic and legally bound relationships. The final section focuses on relationships that are formed through the processes of divorce, remarriage, and adoption. Considered first in this section are the relationships of parents with their adopted children. Next discussed are post-divorce relationships. Finally, stepfamily relationships (which include parent-stepchild as well as other step-relationships) are addressed.

Concluding each of these sections is a commentary by one of three distinguished family communication scholars: Anita Vangelisti, Fran Dickson, and Beth Le Poire. Each commentary reflects on the themes and information addressed in the chapters in that section and identifies important areas of inquiry for future research. Similarly, this volume concludes with a summary and extension provided by family communication scholars Lynn Turner and Richard West, who use the research explicated herein as a starting point to describe what the field of family communication knows—and what it has yet to learn—about communication in family relationships.

To be certain, not all lesser-studied family relationships are addressed in the chapters herein. One evident challenge in offering a collection such as this is that because the focus is on a wide variety of family relationships, many relationships that were potential topics simply had received too little academic attention to facilitate their inclusion in this book. Despite this limitation, we believe there is much to be learned about the family—and about family communication—by broadening our perspective to include relationships outside of those traditionally studied by family scholars. We hope this collection will illuminate the dynamics of family relationships and will provoke scholars toward their continued exploration.

Notes

1. The percentages sum to greater than 100 because some studies focused on more than one type of relationship.

2. Percentages for siblings, parents-in-law, and grandparents are averaged between the two sexes. For example, Fingerman and Hay asked separately about grandmothers (48%) and grandfathers (52%); we averaged these to report a 50% figure for grandparents.

PART A

Family-of-Origin Relationships

The first section of this book focuses on three relationships that exist within the family of origin but have received less attention from communication scholars than the relationships between spouses or between parents and young children. These include the relationships of mothers and their adult daughters, the relationship of adult sons with their nuclear family members, and the relationships between adult siblings. We grouped these chapters together because they share similar characteristics within the family dynamic. For one, they are often genetically bound (unlike some of the other relationships covered in this book), which can have the effect of binding people emotionally even during contentious or conflictual times in their relationships. These relationships also tend to be extraordinarily long standing. For example, the sibling relationship is often the longest and most enduring of all human relationships, lasting throughout the entire life cycle, and the role of son or daughter is literally the only universal and permanent role a person will occupy throughout his or her lifetime. The chapters in this section discuss these and many other unique and important attributes of these family-of-origin relationships.

In the first chapter, authors Carla Fisher and Michelle Miller-Day explore the unique strengths and challenges of the mother–adult daughter dyad in their effort to examine both women's perceptions of this relationship across time. Using both turning point and dialectical theory in their analysis, they offer new research on the distinctive communication patterns of mothers and daughters over the life span. The second chapter, by Alan C. Mikkelson, examines what is known about adult sibling relationships in

1

this comprehensive review of the extant literature on sibling communication behaviors. The final chapter of this section, by Mark T. Morman and Kory Floyd, investigates the role and experience of being a son. These authors present new research on the nature of sonhood and what it means to hold the role of son within the family structure. All three chapters are reviewed and summarized in an insightful commentary written by Anita L. Vangelisti of the University of Texas at Austin.

1

Communication
Over the Life Span

The Mother-
Adult Daughter Relationship

Carla Fisher and Michelle Miller-Day

. . . the daughter is for the mother at once her double and another person.

—Simone de Beauvoir (1974, p. 38)

In her 1992 book *Lives Together, Worlds Apart*, Suzanna Danuta Walters discussed how television and films have represented the mother-daughter relationship as one of never-ending conflict, with mothers either being martyrs or malevolent beings. Walters argued that this image of mothers might be seen as necessary for daughters in American culture in order to justify their fight for independence from their mothers. In one contemporary television show, *The Gilmore Girls*, three generations of mothers and daughters are represented, with Emily Gilmore depicted as the martyred and controlling mother/grandmother and Lorelai Gilmore as her misunderstood adult daughter who has vowed never to make the same mothering mistakes when rearing her own daughter. In this television series, the audience follows the travails of Lorelai, who is five parts friend and three parts maternal figure to her young adult daughter, and witnesses her challenged relationship with her own mother; not surprisingly, we discover that gaining independence from one's mother is not an easy task. Indeed, it may not be the task at hand at all for daughters.

Within sociological and psychological research of the mother-daughter relationship, daughters are often depicted as extensions of their mothers. Jung and Kerenyi (1969) claimed "every mother contains her daughter within herself, and every daughter her mother" (p. 162). This close mother-daughter bond is the centerpiece to Freud's (1917, 1923) classic theories, asserting that separation from mother is a necessary step in a daughter's developmental process (Surrey, 1993). The idea here is that if a daughter is to become a woman in her own right, she must separate from mother and establish her own unique identity. However, in the early 1990s, other scholars challenged this idea and, instead, argued that women's development is not dependent on separation from mothers but on staying relationally connected to mothers throughout adulthood while developing a unique personal identity (Jordan, 1993; van Mens-Verhulst, Schreurs, & Woertman, 1993). Van Mens-Verhulst et al. (1993) in particular advocated a movement toward a communicatively developed relational self, indicating that the mother-daughter relationship holds a curious fascination for women because it promises *a key to the understanding of self.*

According to this relational perspective, men and women experience issues of dependency on their mother differently. This contemporary view contends that boys' separation from their mothers is essential for the development of masculinity; yet, for girls, femininity is defined through attachment, *not* separation. Therefore, the mother-daughter relationship is central to women's lives and not merely an obstacle in a daughter's development (Jordan, 1993). A relational framework for viewing mothers and daughters is essential to analyze patterns of communication that link women across generations. It foregrounds women's lives as lived in relation with others, with communication as the lifeblood of that connection.

Communication and Connection in Mother-Adult Daughter Relationships

Understanding the strengths and challenges of the mother-adult daughter relationship requires a review of research in this area. As Miller-Day (2004) wrote, "each mother-daughter relationship has a *story*. Across the years the cast of characters change, the settings are altered, and the stories evoke a range of unresolved contradictions, joys, hopes, and tensions" (p. 4). Surprisingly, few scholars have examined mother-daughter stories as they unfold into adulthood. Much of the research of the mother-daughter relationship has focused on two developmental time periods: when the daughter is in adolescence and when the mother is elderly and needs a caregiver (Kroger, 2000). This lack of research attention to what goes on in the mother-daughter relationship *in between* a daughter's adolescence and her mother's infirmity creates an unfortunate gap. This developmental period is very important because this is when a woman moves into adulthood, renegotiates her identity as a unique person with her own interests and life, sometimes falls in love, and often becomes a mother herself. Throughout all of this, most mothers and daughters remain bound together by "velvet chains"—chains of security, love, and devotion (Miller-Day, 2004).

Jones and Nissenson (1997) contended that "a mother-daughter friendship can surpass other relationships because it incorporates all the years spent intimately studying each other and learning to interpret each other's behavior, because of shared memories . . . because of mutual experience as women" (p. 326). Many scholars, such as Fischer (1991) argue that the mother-adult daughter dyad may have the highest level of intensity in terms of bonding, interdependence, and emotional connectedness among all potential family relationships. The mother-daughter bond has the potential to intensify as daughters transition from adolescence into adulthood, providing both women with a lifelong means of emotional support. Further evidence of the importance of the bond between mothers and daughters in their adult years is the potential for this relationship to affect entire family systems. Women in families are typically considered the "kinkeepers"; that is, they are the glue that tends to hold family members together, keeping extended family connected across time and distance (Hagestad, 1986). Even though the mother-adult daughter relationship has been understudied, there is no need for it to be overlooked. The remainder of this chapter reports on contemporary research of mothers and adult daughters, focusing on three areas of interest: unique patterns of communicating, relational dialectics, and relational turning points.

Unique Patterns of Communicating

In her 2004 book *Communication Among Grandmothers, Mothers, and Adult Daughters*, Miller-Day examined patterns of communication that linked mothers and daughters across three generations. Drawing on eight months of field research, Miller-Day lived with and closely examined the relationships of six sets of middle-income Caucasian grandmothers, mothers, and adult daughters. She conducted hundreds of hours of in-depth semi-structured interviews, informal unstructured interviews, and observations of interactions, and she documented field notes and audio recordings of mothers and daughters interacting and talking about their maternal relationships. Women aged 18–82 participated in the study, thus providing the opportunity to present detailed descriptions of women managing the tensions of growing together, growing apart, and negotiating intimacy during different developmental periods in the mother-adult daughter relationship. In this book, Miller-Day reminded readers that "every grandmother-granddaughter relationship is connected by two mother-daughter bonds" (p. 216).

Miller-Day (2004) reported that two different levels of closeness emerged among the mothers and daughters of Elkwood, USA. Among the 18 mother-adult daughter relationship pairs in this long-term study, 9 mother-daughter pairs lived in close proximity and were emotionally connected, but they each lived their own independent lives; these mother-daughter relationships were termed *connected*. The other 9 mother-daughter pairs were characterized as *enmeshed*; that is, they were physically and emotionally close, made high demands on each other for loyalty, and often enacted the image of "my mother/my self," with few boundaries between the mother and daughter. It was not only interesting that these two distinct levels of closeness appeared in this study, but unique patterns of communicating emerged within each of these levels of closeness.

The communication pattern that emerged among the mother-daughter dyads that were in connected—but autonomous—relationships was characterized by highly adaptable relationship scripts that were adjusted as the relationship changed across time.[1] Over time, family members develop a number of scripts that guide them through different kinds of interactions in their relationships with each other (Duck & Wright, 1993; Tracy, 2002). In the connected mother-daughter relationships in Miller-Day (2004), as daughters moved into adulthood and became mothers themselves, the women moved from treating one another as dictated by their family role as "mother" or "daughter"—a positional orientation—to orienting themselves toward the other woman as a unique person—a personal orientation. When enacting the revised relational script, these women tended to contribute equally to the communicative interaction, both offering directives,[2] requests, and challenges to the other. Discussion between mother and daughter was characterized as open and direct, rather than closed and indirect, and included a tolerance for debate or negotiation. Non-evaluative, descriptive language was used increasingly as daughters got older, with less occurrence of positive or negative judgments and less defensiveness.

The script in the enmeshed maternal relationships, by contrast, was firmly entrenched across time and rather inflexible. In these relationships, developmental changes in the daughter's life were often perceived as threatening by the mother. For these women, a pattern of scripted interaction emerged that Miller-Day (2004) called *necessary convergence of meaning*. Within this script, a daughter's continued acceptance in the enmeshed mother-daughter relationship was conditional on meeting her mother's high expectations. Thus, from adolescence into later life, she would converge her meanings with her mother's and over-accommodate maternal perceptions for relational maintenance purposes. For instance, one daughter stated, "If I see it as black and she says it's gray, then I say, 'Oh yeah, it must be gray'" (Miller-Day, 2005, p. 70). Instead of negotiating or coordinating their differing perceptions of the world, any novel meaning in these relationships was seen as relationally threatening. As a result, daughters almost inevitably demonstrated a skewed deference to their mothers' values, beliefs, and interpretations. The term *necessary* suggests convergence is perceived as essential to achieve a certain result, and *convergence* indicates a tendency to one point. Therefore, to obtain maternal approval and avoid rejection, daughters would adopt the interpretive frame of mother. Convergence was viewed as relationally adaptive by the women in these enmeshed mother-daughter relationships. Daughters from the ages of 18–65 reported that they learned this relational script in childhood and that no re-scripting or adjustment of the script occurred as they moved into or throughout adulthood.

The women in these enmeshed mother-daughter relationships tended to maintain a positional orientation rather than a personal orientation with one another across the life course of the relationship. Talking with daughters who were 42, 54, and 65, Miller-Day (2004) reported that this characteristic of their interactions with their mothers did not change much through middle age. Moreover, when a daughter issued any directive to her mother, she would most frequently present it in a guarded fashion, often offering directives as questions or hints. Faced with a directive from her daughter, the enmeshed mother would then respond in a manner that served to reinforce her positional status in that relationship. If the daughter's directive honored her mother's higher status, then her mother's response would be to acknowledge her daughter, and resources, such as positive regard and respect, would be freely offered. If the directive was interpreted as conveying disrespect for her status, then her response would be evaluative or defensive, invalidating the request or threatening the withdrawal of emotional resources.

To illustrate a sampling of some of these differences, compare the following examples drawn from Miller-Day (2004, pp. 200–201):

> Lois and Barb are in a connected mother-daughter relationship. In this scene Lois is helping Barb shuck corn for a barbeque that was to occur later that afternoon:
>
> Sitting in Barb's kitchen with a pile of 20–30 unshucked ears of corn at her feet, Lois sat concentrating on her work. Without looking up from the task at hand, she made a direct request of Barb: "Please pass the bucket over here when you get a chance."
>
> Barb, who was busy loading dishes into the dishwasher, responded, "Yep, just a second and I'll be right there." However, the telephone rang and Barb left the room to answer the phone. When she returned 10 minutes later, her mother had already finished loading the dishes and was back to shucking the corn with the requested basket in hand.
>
> Barb murmured, "Thanks," and smiled at her mother. Lois smiled back and proceeded to shuck her corn while Barb moved on to making some coffee.

When I asked Lois and Barb about the request, the noncompliance, and what they were thinking during this episode of request and response, Lois did not say she was upset with Barb for not honoring her direct request. In fact, Lois said, "She had her hands full, too. I thought maybe I could just help her out." Barb also did not express any guilt about not honoring her mother's request right away and did not believe that their relationship was compromised in any way by her noncompliance with the request. Moreover, although appreciative of her mother's assistance with the dishes, this too was taken as a common exchange of assistance and not as a secret test of their relationship.

Consider the following exchange between Kelly and Kendra, who were in an enmeshed mother-adult daughter relationship (Miller-Day, 2004, p. 184). This exchange is similar to the one between Lois and Barb, but note how the nature of the request is more positional than personal and how the response is reacted to on the relational level:

> Kelly was sitting in Kendra's living room, folding cloth diapers. Kendra was in her kitchen, sterilizing baby bottles and listening to the radio. Kelly and I were chatting about a local band that was scheduled to play that weekend, which Kelly hoped to go see. Her lap was filled with unfolded diapers and I was nursing my son, so she raised her voice and called into Kendra, issuing a directive: "Ken, hon, bring in two glasses of water."
>
> Kendra replied, "Just a minute, okay, I've gotta go to the bathroom."
>
> Kelly chatted with me a few more minutes, then with a huff of frustration flung the unfolded diapers from her lap, knocked over one pile of folded diapers,

and hurried into the kitchen, getting two glasses of water to bring into the living room.

When Kendra emerged from the bathroom about 5 minutes later, she noticed that her mother had already gotten the water. She remarked, "I was gonna get those in just a few minutes."

Kelly responded, "No, I know. Since I'm the mom, I can come over and help you with your laundry but you can't even take the time to get me a glass of water. Whatever."

"Sorry," replied Kendra. "Can I get you anything now that I'm out? Are you hungry?"

The two scenarios are similar, yet this discourse illustrates some differences in relational scripts. For Barb and Lois, the use of a personal appeal engaged the other person as an individual who faces unique contingencies. Their identities were connected by mutual respect, allowing the other her personal space and needs. In Kelly and Kendra's exchange, however, Kelly initially used a personal appeal, but she quickly adjusted to a positional orientation when her request was not honored and her status of mother was presumably not respected. Kendra handled this by ingratiating herself to her mother with the queries "Can I get you anything now that I'm out? Are you hungry?" In doing so, she accepted her mother's evaluation and attempted to repair the situation by reaffirming her mother's status. The communication patterns differed between connected and enmeshed mothers and adult daughters, with a defining characteristic of the less satisfied relationship being a resistance to orienting toward one another as *women* rather than as one's mother or daughter.

In addition to distinct communication patterns, the mother-adult daughter relationship must manage a variety of relational dialectics. This next section introduces the concept of dialectics by discussing a few dialectics that mothers and daughters manage in their adult relationship.

Dialectics

All relationships are constantly changing and fraught with contradictions. These contradictions are social rather than cognitive phenomena and are referred to in dialectical theory as relational *dialectics* (see Montgomery & Baxter, 1998 for a complete discussion of dialectical theory). A description of dialectics in the mother-adult daughter relationship begins to capture the dynamism of this relationship, with mothers and daughters continually managing opposing interdependent forces that stand in dialectical association with each other. For the purposes of this chapter, we discuss two dialectics that most clearly show the communication behavior and developmental changes over time: openness-closedness and stability-change.

Openness-Closedness

Dialectical theory argues that all relationships negotiate levels of privacy—what information to disclose and what to keep secret (Montgomery & Baxter, 1998). This balancing act is difficult for many mothers and daughters as sharing information entails both benefits and risks. Disclosure and secrecy are related but separate constructs. Secrets are kept when risks associated with disclosure are too great and the tolerance for such vulnerability is very low (Derlega, Metts, Petronio, & Margulis, 1993). Thus, secret-keeping may be conceptualized as located at the closed end of the self-disclosure continuum, while secrets themselves may be viewed as information that would be disclosed under usual conditions but concealed if it is too threatening or shameful to reveal (Derlega et al., 1993). However, the word "secret-keeping" may not adequately represent what occurs in many mother-adult daughter relationships as many would rather "edit" information and experiences (Kraus, 1989).

Previous research on mother-adult daughter relationships reveals that daughters report a greater desire to obtain support from mothers than sons (Trees, 2000). While daughters are open about some topics (e.g., sexuality; Raffaelli & Green, 2003), they tend to withhold information about others, including pregnancy (Miller-Rassulo, 1992), health (Fingerman, 2001), and risky behaviors (Miller-Day, 2004). However, disclosure of information is not always a good thing. Koerner, Wallace, Lehman, and Raymond (2002) discovered that mothers' disclosures to daughters regarding topics such as financial concerns, negativity toward ex-husband, and personal concerns were clearly associated with greater daughter psychological distress rather than greater feelings of closeness. In this case, information increased the level of stress and daughters' worry about their mothers. Furthermore, Vangelisti (1994) pointed out that withholding information serves many functions. Two recurrent functions of secret-keeping in mother-adult daughter relationships have been identified: (1) a relational maintenance function—withholding information to maintain the status quo so as not to threaten the bond with change, and (2) a protective function—withholding or managing information so as not to harm or upset the other person or for fear that it might be used against her (Miller-Day, 2004).

In the Miller-Day (2004) study, there were differences between the connected and the enmeshed mother-daughter dyads in terms of how they managed openness-closedness in their relationships. As with the relational scripts, for the women in connected relationships, managing openness and closedness was a process of adjusting to the daughter as an autonomous adult while maintaining relational intimacy. For example, a daughter in this study said, "I've always been very open with my mother; I can tell her anything about everything. But, I'm at a stage in my life where I want to do things on my own and not depend on her so much to do things for me." Her mother added, "Just because [my daughter] is exploring the world on her own doesn't mean that we are less open and honest with each other. I think I know pretty much what she feels about things and what she does during the course of any given week" (pp. 79–80). This is in contrast with mothers and daughters in enmeshed relationships who made demands for disclosure but practiced "awe-inspiring amounts of secrecy" (p. 142). Miller-Day (2004) reported, "the processes of maintaining secrets, disclosing secrets, and baring the wounds left by secrets were intimately tied to relational communication in these enmeshed relationships" (p. 127). There was also a mantra used among the sisters in these enmeshed families— "don't tell Mom!"

While the openness-closedness dialectic is helpful in understanding communication between mothers and daughters, changes in communication are evident when examining transitions in the relationship. Across the adult life course, the changing nature of life events and relationships present unique challenges to mothers and daughters. This next section discusses some of the most significant changes mothers and adult daughters may experience and how they manage the stability-change dialectic across the adult years.

Stability-Change

Stability refers to maintaining constancy or familiar patterns whereas *change* refers to variation and unfamiliar patterns. Indeed, as women move through their life course, their maternal relationships experience periods of stability and change. While certain aspects of their relationships may be undergoing change, others may exhibit constancy. Fingerman (2001) aptly points out that as daughters become women, things change for both daughter and mother and role functions are less clear. Across the life span many salient moments of change result in the recalibration of maternal relationships, and communication constitutes this recalibration. Relationship evolution itself is, in part, a function of the stability-change dialectic, and it is common to acknowledge that nonfamilial relationships require variation and changes across time (Gottman, 2000). However, scholars know little about how variation and change affect parent-adult children relationships.

Miller-Day (2004) discovered that when change was *resisted* and women did not adapt to the change, the relationship experienced a period of "growing pains." For example, when one daughter in this study divorced and moved back in with her mother, her mother remarked, "When you got married, in my heart I felt that I had lost you. Now I feel like I have you back" (p. 85). Later, the daughter shared the following reaction:

> that comment really shocked me. I don't think she ever lost me. My God, I just lived a little bit away. What happened was that someone else had my full attention, and she didn't want to share me. She never lost me, we just had to figure out a way that she could share me. (p. 85)

Yet, for others, change is a catalyst for closeness. One mother commented on how her daughter's battle with cancer initiated increased closeness.

> [my daughter's] husband was on the way out at that time. He showed his true colors through her illness because he was not supportive. So, I took her for treatments and stuff, and I also took her to the [regional] clinic to get a second opinion. We kind of put down our boxing gloves and dealt with each other a bit differently during that time [in her life]. (Miller-Day, 2004, p. 112)

These *points of change* in mother-adult daughter relationships may be considered relational "turning points" and often require minor adjustments to the relationship. Both Miller-Day (2004) and Fisher (2004) discovered that these relational turning points are particularly consequential for understanding adult mother-daughter relationships.

Turning Points

Past research has identified several turning points in mother-daughter relationships. In addition, a recent turning point analysis of the mother-adult daughter relationship (Fisher, 2004) produced new insights, specifically in the way the daughter's adult development affects the bond as well as the way recent social changes may have altered the course of the relationship's growth.

Turning points in adulthood identified in past research include changes in proximity when the women are separated geographically by choice or necessity (Golish, 2000), a daughter's marriage (Miller-Rassulo, 1992), or her pregnancy and childbirth (Miller-Day, 2004). For grandmothers, the birth of a grandchild is often "a defining moment—a grand passage" (Sheehy, 2002, p. 7); for a new mother, the birth of her own child allows her to see her mother in a new way, reinforcing the bond between the two women. This is also considered a significant point of change in the mother-daughter relationship, when a younger woman begins to see her mother as a person rather than just in her role as mother. This change has been called *seeing the woman behind the role* (Miller-Day, 2004) and *filial comprehending* (Nydegger, 1991).

Relationally, turning points are also reported when mother or daughter either positively or negatively violates relational expectations. Mothers and daughters expect their maternal relationships to provide them with both emotional (e.g., expressing love, providing encouragement, empathizing, and offering and accepting advice) and instrumental support (e.g., household help, assisting with errands, or financial aid) (Miller-Day, 2004). Given this, it is not surprising that another key turning point in mother-adult daughter relationships occurs when the daughter assumes caretaking responsibilities for her mother (Fingerman, 2001), which is one of the most commonly represented caregiving relationships in Western culture (Cicirelli, 1992). This relationship is often referred to as a "role-reversal," as the daughter shifts into the caregiver role for a frail mother; however, as Bromberg (1993) argued, mothers will always remain the parent and the daughter the child. A loss of the quality of the previous relationship exists but does not mean it is a "reversal." It merely requires a framework of mutuality where both mother and adult daughter provide for each other's needs as necessary.

Fisher's (2004) recent examination of the mother-adult daughter bond over the life span adds to this research by examining transitions during an understudied age period of the daughter—her transition into adulthood. Daughters between the ages of 21–34 were sought, and both mothers and their daughters were interviewed individually to more closely examine transitional and communication changes according to both mothers' and daughters' perceptions. Fisher sampled women across the United States in both rural and urban areas and interviewed them using Retrospective Interview Technique, the most prominent tool used in turning point analysis. In accordance with this approach, participants were asked to recall changes that affected the relationship over time.

In this sample of 21 dyads, women did identify some of the same turning points as previous research on both the mother-daughter and parent-child relationships, including the daughter's marriage and changes in proximity (Fischer, 1981; Golish, 2000). However, other previously unidentified turning points also emerged that reflect significant communication changes in the relationship as the women transitioned into an adult relationship. Moreover, some turning points indicated that the mother-daughter bond may now evolve differently in light of recent social changes.

Several turning points identified by both mothers and daughters centered on the daughter's adult development, and most of these transitions yielded positive effects on the bond. These transitions highlighted a reconnection between mothers and daughters that generated a new dynamic. For instance, 15 mothers (71%) reported changes when they could "see a real growth" in their daughters. This change usually occurred during the daughter's 20s. Mothers recalled that daughters were now less dependent, had gained a sense of individualized self, and had lost the teenage attitude. Similar to the findings in the Miller-Day (2004) study, mothers in this study reported that relational dynamics changed by progressing slowly from a relationship built on family roles into a friendship. Positive communication changes resulted from this shift into friendship, with mothers reporting more open and frequent communication with their daughters because the relationship was perceived to be less "one-sided." As one mother put it, "I mean, now it's not just about her." Mothers also recalled finding "common ground" and "relat[ing] a lot better" with their daughters, which "started to draw [them] back together, [because of] the maturity, kind of growing out of that attitude and kind of realizing."

Likewise, 52% of the daughters also recalled a similar turning point when their mother began to treat them as an adult, or as one daughter described this point in time, "[when] a light switch got flipped [in our relationship]." Daughters indicated that this change of perspective was evident to them when their mothers supported their decisions or independence. Again, this change was reported during the daughter's 20s. One daughter said, "She treats me as an adult. I'm not a little child anymore. She actually respects my decisions." Often this support manifested in communication changes.

> She plays more devil's advocate, I think, than just kind of sounding off what she thinks would be best for me. She kind of gives me various options and points of views to consider and . . . [lets] me make decisions for myself.

The mother's changed perception of the daughter during this turning point was parallel to the daughter's new perception of her mother found in another transition. When daughters matured, 33% reported that they had "got enlightened" about their mother. In other words, their perspective of their mother changed. This tended to occur post–age 18. Again, closeness increased as a result of this turning point. In this sample, one daughter recalled,

> You start to realize the things your parents gave up for you, and the things they sacrificed for you . . . I started to recognize . . . she is a person; she's not just my mom. She's not trying to make my life miserable. She actually wants to try and help me get ahead in life so you start to do more mutual respect things.

In addition to transitions that coincided with the daughter's development, both mothers and daughters also reported transitions that involved one of the women's romantic partner. Unlike the previously noted changes, these transitions challenged the relationship, which often manifested in communication changes. As in past research, mothers and daughters reported the daughter's marriage as a turning point. For instance, 29% of mothers and 19% of daughters recalled that the daughter's engagement, wedding planning, or marriage increased closeness, although some experienced confusion about new relational boundaries. Some mothers reported feeling less close because their daughter now had a "new best friend." Many realized that the relationship was redefined; thus, they gave their daughters space: "I was smart enough to know to try and stay away"; "I had to butt out . . . I didn't know how to be close to her and try to affect her now that she had a husband." At least in one instance, the mother's struggle was misinterpreted by the daughter: "She was very distant. And so my feelings were kind of hurt . . . I almost felt like she wasn't supporting me." However, other daughters seemed to understand their mothers' actions and forged a new bond.

> That brought us closer because now it's like I'm stepping into a new part of my life and she's totally there for me to support me and to listen. But she's also realizing that she kind of has to let go after that . . . we won't have the same kind of relationship.

However, this study also showed that a mother's marriage might affect the mother-adult daughter bond. When moms started dating or got remarried, negative effects were evident and often seemed more salient to the daughters (reported by 14% of mothers, 43% of daughters). Mothers reported that they believed their daughters felt like "somebody was coming in between [them]." Mothers described this as a time when they had to again set new "parameters" in the relationship. Daughters also remembered feeling like someone was coming in between them. As one daughter stated, "I was afraid I was going to lose that closeness that I had with my mom because this new guy was coming in." Also, often communication was strained; as one mother remarked, "I couldn't talk to her about anything. There were certain things I just knew I better not say because I knew it would just upset her." Like the mothers, daughters also reported communication changes in the relationship. Daughters reported increased arguments because they voiced their dislike of their mother's partner. Ironically, this negative communication change also occurred when daughters reported having a boyfriend, as mothers voiced their dislike of the daughter's partner.

Social changes over the past few decades also serve to explain some of the unique turning points that emerged in this study. Like Golish's (2000) findings, divorce was commonly mentioned as a critical event in the mother-daughter relationship, likely due to high rates of divorce. In addition, two turning points prominent in previous research (the daughter's marriage and pregnancy) were not reported with much frequency in Fisher's (2004) study. Of the 21 daughters interviewed, only 10 were married or engaged. All but 1 daughter reported it as a turning point, and about 60% of these daughters' mothers reported it. Of the 21 daughters sampled, only 2 had children (all of these daughters/mothers reported it as a turning point). This is contrary to previous studies that reported marriage and childbirth as highly salient in the relational lives of mothers and daughters (Fischer, 1986). These findings suggest that perhaps among contemporary women, these two turning points may occur later in the life span of the relationship. Various societal changes during the last part of the 20th century have affected patterns of courtship, marriage, and childbearing, which likely have affected the timeline for changes in maternal relationships and the developmental course of the mother-daughter relationship. For example, the Women's Movement in the 1970s drastically expanded opportunities and roles for women. Furthermore, sociological studies during the early 1990s indicate that both men and women are marrying at a later age compared to earlier generations and that many married couples are choosing to remain childless (Rindfuss, 1991). Thus, women may be delaying (or forgoing) getting married or having children as they now have the opportunity to pursue higher education and have more career opportunities.

While Fisher's (2004) exploratory study confirmed turning points similar to those found in previous studies, such as movement toward filial comprehending, it ultimately revealed some new relational turning points for mothers and adult daughters, such as a mother's remarriage. Clearly, the mother-adult daughter relationship is one that dynamically changes over time. In addition to its unique development, it is also important to recognize the need to reevaluate this relationship over the adult life span because social and developmental changes can impact the nature of women's experience, and thus the mother-daughter bond.

Conclusion

Clearly, the mother-daughter bond is one that continuously evolves while facing challenges throughout the relationship's life span. Miller-Day's (2004) examination of mothers and adult daughters indicated that mothers and adult daughters who exhibit different levels of closeness may enact unique patterns of communication. These communication patterns were characterized by relational scripts that were either adaptable over time or inflexible and interpersonal orientations that were personal or positional. These findings indicated that those women in close mother-adult daughter relationships who also maintained independent lives seemed to respect the other woman and adapt to the way the relationship evolved over time. As a result, communication tended to be open and negotiable. In contrast, enmeshed mother-adult daughter relationships, though emotionally close and physically close, demonstrated less flexible communication that was more controlled by family roles and status. Thus, "too" close mother-daughter relationships in adulthood may exhibit less positive interaction patterns. More research is needed to uncover the specific dynamics of these communication patterns and how they might affect mother-daughter relationships across the life span.

Dialectical tensions of openness-closedness and stability-change were also discussed in this chapter, noting that while all relationships manage these dialectical tensions, mothers and adult daughters manage them in unique contexts. Moreover, just as all relationships are characterized by change, the particular turning points experienced in mother-adult daughter relationships are distinctive. As past research has shown, mothers and daughters experience turning points in their relationship that can both increase and decrease closeness. Additionally, these changes over the life span alter mothers' and daughters' roles and perceptions of one another. Communication behavior continuously evolves in response to such transitions, yet this behavior can be instrumental in either facilitating positive transitions or impeding the bond's development. Recent research findings indicate that transitioning into an adult mother-daughter relationship seems to be a defining moment for women and provides an opportunity for women to develop a personal orientation, increasingly egalitarian woman-to-woman bond (Fisher, 2004; Miller-Day, 2004). As Miller-Day indicated, mothers and daughters have expectations of each other for emotional and physical support. It is likely that these expectations begin to merge as the daughter becomes an adult and her mother perceives her as independent.

Further study is required to fully understand the complexities of the mother-adult daughter relationship. It was interesting that Fisher (2004) reported that few daughters reported that childbearing affected their relationship with their mothers, yet fewer than 10% of the daughters had children. The average age of the daughters in Fisher's study was 25 years of age; this coupled with sociological changes delaying marriage and childbirth explain the finding more completely. However, her finding that only 60% of mothers perceived their daughter's engagement or marriage as affecting the mother-daughter relationship, while all but 90% of the daughters who had been engaged/married defined this as important, illustrates the need for research that collects both mothers' and daughters' perceptions and at different phases of the relationship's life span. What is deemed significant at one point for a person might likely change over time. Conducting studies in this fashion will likely produce a more refined portrayal of relational development for mothers and adult daughters.

Though past research on the mother-daughter relationship tended to focus on daughters in adolescence and pick up again with caretaking and elderly mothers, it is clear from the more recent research such as Fisher (2004), Miller-Day (2004), and Fingerman (2001) that the mother-adult daughter relationship constantly evolves across a lifetime. The studies highlighted within this chapter add to the limited body of research on mothers and adult daughters by examining relational patterns, interaction, and development and by emphasizing the central role communication plays in sustaining maternal relationships.

Future research on the mother-adult daughter relationship might focus on nonbiological maternal relationships (e.g., adopted daughters-mothers or stepmothers-daughters) to determine differences or similarities between biological and nonbiological relationships. Furthermore, cultural groups beyond Caucasian American women should be included and compared across groups. Previous studies show that mother-daughter dyads of different cultures have different expectations (Rastogi & Wampler, 1999), yet a gap remains in mother-daughter research across cultures.

In addition, more research is needed on change processes in maternal relationships (role, boundary, and communication changes) that are central to relationship evolution in order to better understand patterns of change and how women respond and adapt to them. It is important to consider that though the mother-adult daughter bond is often reported as long-lasting and intimate, this is not necessarily so. As not all mother-daughter bonds remain emotionally connected across the life span, studies on mothers and daughters who are disengaged or emotionally disconnected are needed. At times, as is seen in Fisher's (2004) study, mothers and daughters who are emotionally close may be more easily recruited to participate in research and may be more willing to discuss the nature of their relationship. Utilizing alternative methods (e.g., longitudinal studies tracking change in intimacy levels) or creative sampling techniques (e.g., sampling in ways that ensure anonymity such as using Internet chat rooms or the use of experience-sampling methods with digital technology) might enhance the probability that researchers include both connected and disengaged mother-daughter relationships in their samples (Barrett & Barrett, 2001; Floyd, Hess, Miczo, Halone, Mikkelson, & Tusing, 2005).

Finally, we believe it is crucial to translate any new knowledge about how mothers and daughters successfully and unsuccessfully negotiate their adult relationship so that this knowledge might be used by clinicians, community-based educational and intervention program developers, and support group members. Such application would provide women with information on what transitions they might expect in their relationship and with skills to manage relational adjustment to transitions, tensions, role changes, or boundary adjustments. In the end, we encourage researchers to challenge themselves to collaborate with practitioners, disseminate findings to the general public, and make connections within their communities because mother-daughter relationships are consequential. We wish to end with a quote by Carol Shields from her book *Swann* (1987):

> Women can never quite escape their mothers' cosmic pull, not their lip-biting expectations or their faulty love. We want to please our mothers, emulate them, disgrace them, outrage them, and bury ourselves in the mysteries and consolations of their presence. When my mother and I are in the same room we work magic on each other. . . . It's my belief that between mothers and daughters there is a kind of blood-hyphen that is, finally, indissoluble. (p. 127)

Notes

1. Relational scripts are scripts we follow with our partners that guide and direct our interactions with them. These scripts are based on previous interactions and experiences we have with our relational partners and are overlearned through repetition (Sillars, 1995).

2. Directives are communicative acts that seek compliance from a partner to do or not do something (Tracy, 2002).

2

Communication Among Peers

Adult Sibling Relationships

Alan C. Mikkelson

The novella *A River Runs Through It* is a story about brothers, fishing, and why we often struggle to help those we love the most. In the story, the older brother, Norman, and the younger brother, Paul, experience conflict over Paul's self-destructive drinking and gambling problems. Although Paul's problems go generally undiscussed throughout the story, Norman nevertheless attempts to do what he can to help Paul, from bailing him out of jail after a fight, to offering to cover his gambling debts, to inviting him to come to Chicago to escape his problems. The story illustrates the idea that even though Norman does not agree with or even understand his younger brother's behavior, he does whatever he can to help his brother. Although this beautiful story ends in tragedy, it nonetheless demonstrates much of the variety of the adult sibling relationship, particularly how conflict and love, anger and support, and frustration and caring are not mutually exclusive experiences within the sibling bond.

Many of us who have siblings have, on one occasion or another, probably experienced similarly contradictory feelings. At times we might say that we love our siblings but don't especially like them. We might also experience competition, conflict, and rivalry while simultaneously feeling love, care, and support. Some siblings might share extremely close and satisfying relationships that rival the closest of friendships, whereas other siblings fight constantly and others barely speak to each other. Certainly the experiences siblings share vary widely, often making them difficult to characterize and understand. The goal of this chapter is to shed some light on these issues by examining research related to communication in adult sibling relationships.

A good deal of research has been conducted on siblings, but a great proportion of it has focused on issues of the effect of birth order, family size, and sex differences on intellect and personality characteristics (Cicirelli, 1995). More recently, research in the social sciences has focused more on the interpersonal relationships between adult siblings and the factors that influence those relationships.

In general, sibling research has progressed relatively slowly in comparison to research on parent-child relationships and marriage relationships (Fingerman & Hay, 2002). With regard to research specific to adult siblings, the topic is even more understudied. Some researchers have proposed that the lack of research on adult siblings is due to the assumption that siblings have little contact with or little influence upon each other in later stages of life (Cicirelli, 1995). However, studies examining the topics of contact, closeness, and support have found this assumption to be false and have demonstrated the significant influences of adult sibling relationships.

While these studies exploring adult sibling contact, closeness, support, and rivalry are inextricably communication related, little is known about actual communication patterns within adult sibling relationships. That being said, the goal of this chapter is to review what is known about the interpersonal relationships of adult siblings, link that literature to communication practices, and finally pose some possibly fruitful areas of future research.

This chapter will begin by exploring the unique characteristics of the sibling relationship that make this an important and intriguing focus of research for family communication scholars. Next, some of the commonly studied interpersonal variables in adult sibling relationships such as contact, closeness, rivalry, and support will be examined. Then I will review literature specific to communication in adult sibling relationships and conclude with future suggestions for communication research on adult sibling relationships.

Unique Characteristics of the Sibling Relationship

The first unique characteristic of the sibling relationship is its pervasive nature. The sibling relationship is the longest-lasting relationship in many people's lives (Bedford, 1993). Researchers have estimated that around

80% of the population spends at least one-third of their lives with their siblings (Fitzpatrick & Badzinski, 1994). Furthermore, few relationships affect as many people as the sibling relationship does. In fact, a 1998 General Social Survey reported that 96% of American adults have at least one sibling (National Opinion Research Center, 1998).

Second, the sibling relationship is involuntary and permanent; it is not chosen like friendships. In fact, the sibling relationship is difficult if not impossible to end. Although there may be dissolution of an active relationship, there is no dissolution of the sibling status (Cicirelli, 1995). When an active relationship has ended, siblings still keep informed about one another indirectly through third parties, typically their parents (Allen, 1977). This presents a situation where siblings always have an opportunity to revitalize their relationship because it is not possible to sever all the sibling ties. However, for most adult siblings the dissolution of an active relationship is rare. In fact, most siblings have a commitment to their relationship that extends well beyond just sustaining obligatory family relationships (Cicirelli, 1991). The permanence of the sibling relationship due to the inability to dissolve the sibling status allows siblings to experience and survive many major problems other types of relationships would not be able to survive.

Third, the sibling relationship is similar to friendships in that it is more egalitarian than other family relationships, such as the parent-child relationship (Cicirelli, 1982). In the sibling relationship there is more of an equal power distribution, especially as the siblings move into adulthood. Siblings typically have similar feelings of acceptance for one another, which allow siblings to interact as equals (Cicirelli, 1995). In fact, some sibling relationships are as close and supportive as many of the best friendships.

Fourth, sibling relationships are influenced by a long, shared family history, and this shared history with siblings is different from the shared history with friends. Aspects of shared family history that influence the sibling relationship include such things as the parent's treatment of the siblings, the specific parent-child relationships, and management of sibling conflict during childhood (Brody, 1998; Stocker & McHale, 1992).

Fifth, the sibling relationship can be a source of paradox. Some people would probably express the fact that they love their siblings but cannot stand to be around them. Thus, a great deal of competition, conflict, and rivalry may exist within the sibling relationship as well as love, care, and support. Cicirelli (1994) affirmed that many siblings compete for their parents' resources, and this can be a source of rivalry into later adulthood. Thus, siblings can experience conflict while at the same time experiencing a great deal of closeness and cohesion (Mikkelson, 2004).

These factors combined create an entirely unique relationship compared with any other relationship that people experience. Sibling relationships can rival the best friendships that people may experience, or siblings can be completely indifferent of one another. Because of the difficulty in dissolving the relationship and the inability to dissolve the sibling status, sibling relationships can sustain major problems that many friendships could not. The sibling relationship is one of the few relationships in which people can interact relatively infrequently yet still feel extremely good about the relationship and extremely close to their sibling. These unique characteristics in comparison to other relationships make communication in the adult sibling relationships complex and interesting to examine.

Different Types of Sibling Relationships

Sibling relationships come in many different forms. Siblings either share some degree of common biological origin or share a relationship that is defined legally. Sibling relationships that occur due to common biological origin are the full biological sibling relationship (both biological parents in common) and half-sibling relationships (one biological parent in common). Furthermore, the amount of genetic relatedness between these siblings changes with the type of sibling relationship, with identical twins sharing 100% genetic relatedness, full siblings sharing approximately 50% genetic relatedness, and half siblings sharing approximately 25% genetic relatedness.

Sibling relationships that occur due to some feature of the law include stepsiblings, who are siblings as the result of one biological parent marrying the biological parent of another, and adopted siblings, whereby sibling status is attained when one child is legally adopted into the family. Consequently, sibling relationships can come in many different forms.

Most of the research on adult siblings has primarily examined only full biological siblings. This is an unfortunate oversight considering that only 56% of children live in traditional nuclear families (Usdansky, 1994). Moreover, around 11.8 million American children now live in blended families (Fields, 2001). Thus, the importance of studying the stepsibling and half-sibling relationship in both childhood and adulthood has become increasingly important. For example, a large national study on adult siblings indicated that participants did keep in touch with their step and half siblings, but saw them significantly less than full siblings (White & Riedman, 1992b). However, having no full siblings increased contact with step and half siblings. Furthermore, a higher percentage of conflict and rivalry was reported when relationships involved half siblings and stepsiblings than when relationships involved only full siblings (White & Riedman, 1992b). Moreover, adult sibling closeness was lower in blended families compared to nuclear families, not only for relationships with half siblings and stepsiblings, but for full sibling relationships in blended families as well (White & Riedman, 1992b). Although blended families are becoming more prevalent, there is still much that is unknown about communication patterns between adult half and stepsiblings.

Communication in Adult Sibling Relationships

This section will explore some of the commonly studied interpersonal variables in adult sibling research. Included in this section will be discussions of contact patterns, closeness, support, and rivalry. The discussions will address some of the primary influences on these variables, how these variables change over the life span, and how sex differences (sister-brother, sister-sister, and brother-brother relationships) influence these four variables.

The specific variables of contact patterns, closeness, support, and rivalry were picked for review due to the amount of existing research and its relationship to communication behaviors. For example, contact patterns are explicitly communicative. The problem with most research on contact patterns is that it examines only the frequency of contact between siblings; it does not explore the other aspects of contact patterns such as the channel of contact (e.g., phone, in person), length of contact, or quality of contact. Closeness, support, and rivalry are more implicitly tied to communication in that communication influences feelings of support, closeness, and rivalry while at the same time these feelings influence communication patterns. Unfortunately, while this research is linked to communication practices, little research has actually explored how communication influences these variables. Consequently, after discussing these variables, I will turn to what researchers know explicitly about communication in adult sibling relationships. Finally, I will conclude by exploring some fruitful areas of future research.

Contact

One variable that research on adult siblings has thoroughly investigated is contact patterns between siblings. Contact patterns between adult siblings can vary greatly; some siblings interact every day through phone calls, e-mail, and in-person visits, while other siblings might interact once or twice a year.

As siblings move out of the household to attend college or to live on their own, frequency of contact between siblings is greatly reduced due to the fact that siblings do not share a living space (Leigh, 1982). As siblings move out of the family home and into their own residences, continued contact with siblings not only becomes more difficult, it becomes more of a personal choice. This reduction in contact between siblings continues into the middle portion of the life span as siblings often become busy with their own marriages and families. However, in the latter stages of the life span, Leigh (1982) found that contact between siblings increases. Furthermore, Scott (1983) found as siblings move toward late adulthood, contact tends to increase. Consequently, most researchers have found a curvilinear relationship between contact and age. However, in a large national study, White and Riedman (1992a) found a decline in contact between siblings into late adulthood.

Mikkelson (2004) found that the most frequently used methods to keep in contact with adult siblings were the telephone, personal visits (which included spending time with family and friends), e-mail, instant messenger (IM), letters, indirect third-party communication through family members and friends, and sharing activities both siblings enjoyed. Siblings varied a great deal in the amount of use of each of these methods. For example, some siblings kept in contact primarily through e-mail and IM, others used the telephone, whereas others still only interacted with their siblings when they saw them in person.

Lee, Mancini, and Maxwell (1990) found that emotional closeness, sibling responsibility, expectations, and geographic proximity were the most important variables in explaining adult sibling contact patterns. Similarly, emotional closeness was positively related with the frequency of contact and the desire for additional contact between adult siblings (Ross & Milgram, 1982). Other researchers have also found a link between adult sibling contact and geographic proximity (Connidis, 1989b), with the general trend being that siblings who live closer to one another contact and interact with each other more, due to greater accessibility.

Life events also influence sibling contact patterns. Connidis (1989a) found that getting married and having children often reduced adult sibling contact, whereas those who were single, divorced, or widowed had increased sibling contact.

Although contact patterns vary greatly among adult siblings, most siblings keep in touch with each other through some method. However, some adult siblings share little or no contact with each other. Sometimes this is because siblings share especially negative feelings for each other, but in other cases siblings share neither positive nor negative feelings for each other. These sibling relationships experiencing neither positive nor negative affect and having little or no contact can be characterized as being indifferent, apathetic, or disinterested (Cicirelli, 1985b; Gold, 1989b). According to research, indifferent relationships occur in 5–11% of all sibling pairs (Cicirelli, 1995).

Research has also examined sex differences in the contact patterns of siblings. Generally, sisters make the most contact with their siblings (White & Riedman, 1992a). Furthermore, sister-sister dyads are more likely to see each other in person compared to sister-brother and brother-brother dyads (Connidis, 1989b). Thus, sister-sister dyads usually sustain the most contact, followed by sister-brother dyads, with brother-brother dyads making the least amount of contact.

Closeness

Much of the research on adult sibling relationships has focused on closeness. Closeness between adult siblings is contingent upon a number of issues. Scott (1983) found that closeness between siblings as adults was not as likely if the siblings were not close when they were children. In adulthood, siblings often consider their brothers or sisters to be close friends. In fact, Connidis (1989b) reported that 77% of participants considered at least one of their siblings a close friend. However, Pulakos (1989) found that subjects still often felt closer to their friends than to their siblings. Most topics of conversation were discussed more frequently among friends than with siblings. Subjects also participated in joint activities more with friends than with siblings. Thus, although many siblings are close friends, they are often not as close with siblings as they are with their chosen friends.

Other variables that influence closeness between siblings are commonalities. In an interview study, Folwell, Chung, Nussbaum, Bethea, and Grant (1997) found that closeness between adult siblings was influenced by the number of similarities in interests, opinions, beliefs, and attitudes between siblings. Additionally, they found that those siblings who were close in age felt closer than those with a great difference in age. McGhee (1985) suggested that in adulthood, closeness may be felt between siblings of a similar age due to mutual aging concerns.

Different life events can also influence levels of closeness felt between siblings. According to a qualitative study by Connidis (1992), modal responses for life events indicated that marriage caused siblings to feel less close, whereas having children, divorce, or a family member's death or poor health all caused siblings to feel emotionally closer. Moreover, widowed or single siblings are often closer than married siblings (Connidis, 1989b).

The level of closeness felt between siblings can also have positive mental effects. Ponzetti and James (1997) found an inverse relationship between feelings of loneliness and closeness between siblings. Furthermore, with respect to closeness, rivalry, and conflict between siblings, closeness was the most significant predictor of feelings of loneliness.

The level of closeness between siblings oftentimes changes over the life span. One of the largest changes the sibling relationship faces is the change from everyday contact in the household to the greatly reduced contact after siblings are living on their own. Although it might appear that reduced contact would reduce feelings of closeness between siblings, results have been mixed. Bedford (1990) argued that because contact decreases in adulthood and increases again in late adulthood, closeness also decreases in early adulthood, drops to its lowest point in middle age, and then increases again in late adulthood. This argument is based on the findings that contact patterns are a major predictor of emotional closeness among siblings (Lee, Mancini, & Maxwell, 1990). With respect to their most frequently contacted sibling, 65% of older adults reported feeling close or very close to their sibling (Cicirelli, 1980). Although contact with siblings is reduced, older adults reported greater feelings of closeness with their siblings than did younger adults with their siblings (Cicirelli, 1980, 1985a). Cicirelli (1982) compared his results with those of Adams (1968) and found that closeness tended to increase with age. However, White and Riedman (1992a) found that there was no change in feelings of closeness between siblings into middle and late adulthood. Consequently, the results of sibling closeness are mixed, with some studies indicating a curvilinear relationship, others indicating an increase in closeness across age, and other studies indicating no change in closeness. These mixed results are probably due to the variance in the sibling relationship itself in addition to variation in operational definitions of closeness and the methodologies.

Research has also examined sex differences in the closeness of siblings. Results have been somewhat inconsistent, as some researchers have found significant sex differences, whereas other researchers have not. Some studies have reported that same-sex sibling dyads (brother-brother and sister-sister) are closer than sibling dyads of different sex (brother-sister) (Gibson & Mugford, 1986). A possible explanation for these findings is that same-sex siblings have more common interests and are more comfortable sharing intimate matters with one another. Further research suggests that adult same-sex sibling dyads are more likely to consider their same-sex sibling a close friend compared to opposite-sex siblings (Connidis, 1989b; Scott, 1983). However, most research suggests that women are closer to their siblings than are men (Goetting, 1986). Ross and Milgram (1982) found that the relationship between sisters grows closer throughout adulthood. Other studies have shown that sibling dyads with at least one female are closer than male sibling dyads (Cicirelli, 1982, 1989). In addition, Pulakos (1989, 1990) found that women felt their sibling relationships were closer and more important than men did and females were closer and more involved with siblings than were males. Consequently, research examining closeness in sibling dyads is mixed, making it difficult to make concrete conclusions about the nature of these differences.

Rivalry

Rivalry between siblings often starts in childhood or adolescence (Cicirelli, 1995). Although one would think that childhood sibling rivalry would decrease in adulthood, there is conflicting research as to whether sibling rivalry decreases with age or stays relatively stable (Cicirelli, 1995). Some research has found that rivalry declines over time, so as siblings move into late adulthood sibling rivalry is minimal. Cross-sectional age trends for feelings of rivalry between siblings indicated that rivalry decreases as siblings age (Cicirelli, 1985b). Furthermore, rivalry appears to be low throughout adulthood and old age and in general, lower for older siblings as compared to younger siblings. However, evidence from clinical interview techniques suggested that sibling rivalry may be greater than indicated in self-report studies. Bedford (1989a) found that 71% of individuals reported feeling sibling rivalry at some point in their lives, with 45% still feeling sibling rivalry into adulthood. Ross and Milgram (1982) reported that for some siblings, rivalry persists even into old age. In addition, there were no differences between older adults and younger adults in the amount of feelings of rivalry. Ross and Milgram (1982) reported that when siblings do have feelings of rivalry they often repair their relationship by later adulthood and old age.

Sibling rivalry has a negative influence not only on the closeness of the sibling relationship but on the emotional well-being of the siblings as well. Ponzetti and James (1997) found an inverse relationship between feelings of loneliness and rivalry between siblings. Furthermore, siblings who feel greater amounts of rivalry interact less (Ponzetti & James, 1997).

Again due to the permanence of the sibling relationship, siblings are able to experience rivalry and yet still maintain their relationship. Cicirelli (1995) argued that if older adults do still have underlying feelings of rivalry with their sibling, they have developed ways of interacting where the rivalry and conflict do not become overt. As a result, siblings in old age rarely experience great amounts of hostility and aggression due to feelings of rivalry.

Research has also examined sex differences in the feelings of rivalry. Rivalry was found to be greatest between pairs of brothers and lowest between cross-sex siblings (Cicirelli, 1980, 1985b). Ross and Milgram (1982) found that brothers reported more competitiveness, ambivalence, and jealousy in their relationships than did any other sibling combination. Furthermore, they found that sibling rivalry is most often initiated by a brother and less frequently by a sister. However, Bedford (1989a, 1989b) found that sisters reported more conflict and competitiveness than brothers. Consequently, these relationships need further examination before any conclusions can be drawn concerning rivalry and sibling sex differences.

Support

The frequency of sibling contact through early and middle adulthood suggests that siblings continue to stay supportive after moving out of their parents' house (Goetting, 1986). According to Goetting (1986), the primary developmental task of siblings during early and middle adulthood is to provide companionship, emotional support, and direct aid to one another. The importance of providing companionship through reminiscence, emotional support, and direct aid continues into old age (Goetting, 1986). Generally, siblings who are emotionally closer and interact more provide more emotional support for each other (Cicirelli, 1995).

Evidence exists that siblings serve as important sources of support for people who are unmarried or childless (Connidis & Campbell, 1995; Heinemann, 1985), older widowed individuals (Matthews, 1987), and individuals who are divorced (Connidis, 1989a). Specifically, Connidis (1989a) found that getting married and having children often reduced sibling support, whereas those who were divorced or widowed had an increase in sibling support. Consequently, siblings often responded positively toward one another's loss with increased support.

Sibling helping and support behaviors have been more expansively studied during old age than in early and middle adulthood (Bedford, 1995; Cicirelli, 1995). During early adulthood sibling support is relatively infrequent (Adams, 1968). However, in middle age siblings are relied on more frequently for support, especially in times of crisis (Troll, 1975). Research indicates that sibling support increases in old age, as siblings sometimes provide a great deal of help (Cicirelli, 1995). The most common type of support that siblings offer in old age is psychological support (Avioli, 1989). In a study of family relationships of the elderly, Cicirelli (1979) found that most siblings were seen as a source of help to be called on in a time of crisis. Wellman and Wortley (1989) found that siblings comprise

24% of all emotionally supportive relationships, and siblings together as a group comprise 21% of all instrumental support.

The difference between instrumental help and psychological support in elder siblings is illustrated by Cicirelli's (1990) study of hospitalized elders. In this study, instrumental support from siblings was second only to support from spouses. About 20% of the hospitalized elders received instrumental help from siblings, whereas only 6% wanted or expected instrumental help from siblings. In contrast, about 50% of the hospitalized elders wanted psychological support from their siblings. Consequently, support becomes an important aspect of the adult sibling relationship, especially as siblings move towards old age.

Research has also examined sex differences in sibling support. Similar to the research on closeness, research generally finds that females are more supportive of their siblings than males (Cicirelli, 1995). Dolgin and Lindsay (1999) found that sisters were more likely to disclose information for the purpose of seeking emotional support than were brothers. Furthermore, both men and women were more likely to confide in their sisters than their brothers (Connidis & Campbell, 1995). According to Adams (1968), emotional support occurs most between pairs of brothers and pairs of sisters. Other research has found that sisters both gave and received the most help (Gold, 1989a).

Communication Behaviors Among Adult Siblings

Although contact patterns, closeness, rivalry, and support are four of the most studied subjects in adult sibling literature and their relationship to communication is undeniable, a perusal of the literature demonstrates the lack of understanding of how actual communication behaviors influence these subjects. Consequently, it is important to develop a more complete understanding of how communication influences each of these areas specifically and how they influence the adult sibling relationship in general. This section will explore studies that have made explicit links to communication behaviors and the relational outcomes for adult siblings.

Much of the adult sibling research in communication has examined how different communicative strategies and skills have influenced the adult sibling relationship. For example, studies have examined the use of functional communication skills (Myers & Knox, 1998), relational communication messages (Myers et al., 1999), verbal aggression (Teven, Martin, & Neupaurer, 1998), self-disclosure (Floyd, 1996b; Martin, Anderson, & Mottet, 1997), willingness to communicate (Rocca & Martin, 1998), interpersonal solidarity (Myers,

1998), and relational maintenance behaviors (Myers & Members of COM 200, 2001).

Results from this line of research have indicated that affectively oriented functional communication skills were perceived to be used more frequently by adult siblings than nonaffectively oriented skills (Myers & Knox, 1998). In addition, female siblings were perceived to use comforting, ego support, and conflict management skills more than male siblings. Finally, in contrast to research finding differences in adult siblings across the life span, there were no significant differences in perceived use of functional communication skills across age groups (Myers & Knox, 1998). With respect to self-disclosure, Martin, Anderson, and Mottet (1997) found that self-disclosure was positively related to perceived understanding. Specifically, the honesty of self-disclosure was of particular importance to ratings of perceived understanding. Floyd (1996b) found that women believed that self-disclosure was more important for increasing closeness with their sisters compared to brother-brother dyads and brother-sister dyads.

Floyd (1996b) also noted that the friendship-like relationship between siblings becomes common when the relationship is more voluntary in nature, as it is in the early adult years through old age. Due to the more voluntary nature of the relationship, siblings' willingness to communicate becomes important in understanding adult sibling interaction. Rocca and Martin (1998) found that people's willingness to communicate with their siblings was positively related to their frequency, breadth, and depth of communication with their siblings.

Myers and the Members of COM 200 (2001) found that five relational maintenance behaviors (positivity, openness, assurances, networks, sharing tasks) were related to sibling liking. They also found that the task-sharing relational maintenance strategy was used most by adult siblings and the openness relational maintenance behavior was used least. In fact, female siblings used all five relational maintenance behaviors at higher rates than did male siblings.

Other research has focused on one specific sibling dyad. For example, Floyd (1996a, 1997) has examined closeness in the fraternal dyad. Floyd (1996a) reported that men often see their relationship with their brother as the most intimate male-male relationship they have. Although Floyd (1995, 1996a, 1997) noted that some research has found the brother-brother dyad to be the least close of the three sibling dyads, he argued that this is due to equating self-disclosure with closeness. He noted that relationships between brothers might not, in fact, be less close than other sibling dyads; it might be that the experience of closeness is different for brothers than it is for sisters. Floyd (1996a) found that five themes emerged to characterize the experience of closeness between brothers: shared conversation, solidarity, companionship, shared perceptions and memories, and surviving shared adversity. In another study, Floyd (1997) found that love between brothers was predicted by relational qualities such as self-disclosure, whereas liking and closeness were predicted by commitment and interdependence.

Although these studies represent a good start to understanding the role communication plays in the oftentimes complex sibling relationship, there is much left to investigate and understand. The next section will discuss some of the future directions that adult sibling research in communication could take.

Learning More About Adult Siblings

In general, the research examining the adult sibling relationship has excelled in its coverage of many different and important aspects of the sibling relationship. However, methodologically there are two areas in which adult sibling research could improve. First, although the research has examined adult siblings at different points in the developmental process and at different ages, almost none of the research has used longitudinal data. Another methodological possibility for understanding the changes that occur over the life span of adult sibling relationships is turning point analysis. Second, much of the sibling research has examined reports from one sibling only instead of utilizing dyadic data, which gives a more complete and representative portrait of the relationship.

Another area of concern in adult sibling research is the fact that there have been few advances in adult sibling research in the past five years. A few recent studies have examined how adult siblings manage care of their elderly parents (see Ingersoll-Dayton, Neal, Ha, & Hammer, 2003), but little new research exists examining the nature of the adult sibling relationship itself.

Although the most studied variables in adult sibling research (contact patterns, closeness, rivalry, and support) are communication related, little communication-related research exists focusing on adult siblings and these variables. Specifically, some researchers have examined how certain communication patterns influence closeness or related constructs, but little is known about rivalry and support. Siblings provide support for one another throughout the life span; however, how is that support provided and communicated? Furthermore, if rivalry is communicated between adult siblings, what is its form? How do siblings manage and resolve rivalry in adulthood? Thus, there are many places that communication researchers could make significant contributions to this area of study by examining how different communication behaviors influence feelings of closeness, rivalry, and support.

Similarly, although researchers know that particular developmental events change the dynamics of adult sibling relationships, researchers do not know how communication patterns and strategies change due to those events. For example, siblings who are married are less close than siblings who are not. However, how do communication patterns and strategies change after marriage, if at all? What do siblings who maintain their relationships and closeness with other siblings do differently from those who do not maintain their relationship and closeness? Consequently, longitudinal studies would be a preferred method of analyzing these questions, as they would be able to ascertain the state of a sibling relationship before, as well as after, these developmental changes.

Another aspect that would intuitively appear important for sibling relationship research is that of affectionate communication. Unfortunately, very little research has explicitly examined how siblings express affection to one another and how those expressions of affection influence the relationship between adult siblings. Affection could have important implications for sibling support, which includes physical and physiological health. Furthermore, there might be important differences in the way affection gets expressed to adult siblings in comparison to friends.

Given the increasing trend in America for divorce and remarriage, more research is needed in the area of step and half siblings. Around 11.8 million American children live in blended families (Fields, 2001). Thus, an even greater percentage of children and adults have step and half siblings that they do not live with. Consequently, as the number of blended families increases in our society, understanding the dynamic between step and half siblings becomes even more important. Understanding how these relationships are similar and different from full sibling relationships could prove useful in helping blended families deal with their new circumstances.

Previous research of siblings, especially siblings in old age, indicated a benefit to the physical and mental health of those with strong sibling ties (Cicirelli, 1977, 1989). Although the research has suggested that those who are close with their siblings, especially a sister, have fewer mental and physical problems than those who are not, little is know about the specific communication patterns that lead to improved health. For example, do feelings of closeness improve health alone, or is the communication of affection and love needed? More specifically, studies could examine the use and amount of supportive communication between siblings to determine its effects.

Another line of questioning surrounds genetics. Full biological siblings share between 33% and 66% of their genes, with identical twins sharing

100% of their genes (Cicirelli, 1995). How do biological or trait similarities and differences influence sibling interaction? Clearly, both differences and similarities can undermine the formation of a positive relationship between siblings. For example, if both siblings are hostile and aggressive during conflict, these similarities could prove problematic for the development of a constructive sibling relationship. Thus, how do individual differences and similarities, either biological or trait, account for differences in the communication patterns of siblings and consequently the positive or negative nature of their relationship? Furman and Lanthier (1996) conducted a study on childhood siblings that examined how personality differences accounted for differences in the sibling relationship. However, this type of work has not been conducted on adult siblings.

Conclusion

The sibling relationship may take many different forms and serves many different functions. It can be a source of joy and support or frustration and hostility. Siblings can sustain long periods without interaction yet still feel close. The sibling relationship can also sustain great amounts of hostility and rivalry due to its permanence. Other adult siblings can be as close as the best of friends. In addition, strong adult sibling relationships may provide many positive benefits throughout the life span, including instrumental and emotional support and improved physical, emotional, and psychological health.

Researchers have demonstrated that adult sibling relationships are not inconsequential, as sibling relationships can have both positive and negative effects on people's health and happiness. Thus, researchers wishing to study communication in adult sibling relationships have many avenues to take their research as the adult sibling relationship is still generally understudied. Hopefully, future research will dig deeper into some of the issues discussed in this chapter and as a result, family communication scholars and students alike will have a greater understanding of adult sibling relationships and the important role of communication in these relationships.

3

The Good Son

Men's Perceptions of the Characteristics of Sonhood

Mark T. Morman and Kory Floyd

O f the many roles men play during the course of their lives, the only universal relational position that all men hold is that of son. Some men may never become brothers, boyfriends, husbands, uncles, fathers, or even grandfathers, but all men are sons. Furthermore, the role of son is a role inherently created as a result of the relationship a male has with his mother or father; it does not exist without the family context and only exists because all men are someone else's son. As a result of this universal and relational nature, the role of son holds a prominent place within the ethos of society, a significance apparent in almost every aspect of our culture. For example, the Judeo-Christian narrative is replete with powerful examples of the role of son; from the fratricide of Cain killing Abel, to the return of the prodigal son, or even to Jesus Christ as the son of God, stories of sons fill the Biblical text. Whether it is Oedipus marrying his mother Jocasta in great literary works from the ancient Greeks, or Luke teaming with his sister Leia in a heroic pursuit of their father Darth Vader in great works of modern American film, the son's struggle to understand and embrace his role in life has been the topic of much epic fiction. In U.S. politics, the role of son has received renewed attention as the Presidents Bush have been forced to publicly negotiate their relationship on the world's political stage. From an economic perspective, sons routinely take over the family business from retiring elders, and in sports, sons often follow in the footsteps of their athletic parents.

Perhaps more significantly, the role of the son, particularly the first born son, continues to hold major importance in the lives of families all over the world. In China, for example, the desire to have a son has led to the death or abandonment of unknown numbers of baby girls, born to families with no interest in raising a daughter in a culture that in almost every manner privileges the male role (Litke, 2003). Currently, the royal family of Japan is in distress due to the fact that Crown Prince Naruhito and his wife Princess Masako have "failed" to produce an heir to the throne. Under Japanese law, only a son may assume the throne upon the death of the emperor. Currently, the prince and princess have a little girl, Princess Aiko (Brooke, 2004). Thus, whether in literature, politics, business, religion, family life, or even sports, the role of the son receives considerable attention within our culture.

However, one area where it has not received much attention is in scholarly research. Despite the centrality of the role of son in the lives of men, we actually know very little about the nature and structure of the son role itself or what men believe makes a son a good son. Moreover, we also appear to have almost no direct research probing what men themselves consider to be important or relevant characteristics of sonhood. This is ironic because not only is every man someone's son, no man ever transitions out of the structure of the son role. Clearly, men perform the role of son differently as they age and transition into various stages of life, and yet from a family structure perspective, the role is always present in the lives of every man. Furthermore, the developmental literature establishes an overwhelming argument that the quality of the relationship between a son and his parents, particularly when the son is a boy or adolescent, is critical for a vast array of psychological, emotional, and relational issues that in many ways dictate the trajectory of the son's future. Clearly, these are vital issues for literally *all* men, and yet the literature on the culture of sonhood itself is incomplete at best, totally neglected at worst.

Therefore, the current project is designed to address this gap in the academic literature. This study is dedicated to directly examining the role of the son within the family context. As such, we will first provide a review of the extant literature focusing on the son and his relationship to other family members and then report findings from our research conducted to provide answers to the questions of what men think about the role of son and what they believe it means to be a good son.

The Role of Son

While foundational to the lives of all men, critical to a host of psychological and developmental variables, and prominent in multiple areas of cultural life, curiously, the role of son apparently is not a part of most men's self-concept. Salmon and Daly (1996) asked a group of adolescent men and women (average age under 21 years, 96% single, 99% childless) to generate 10 different statements in response to the simple question, "Who are you?" Men and women were equally likely to reference familial or kinship status in their answers; however, women were more likely to mention family roles, whereas men were more likely to mention their surnames as aspects of their identity. The study reported that 44% of the women characterized themselves as a daughter, while only 12.5% of men characterized themselves as being a son. When asked to reveal to whom they felt closest, only 7% of the total participant group referenced their fathers, with women noting their mothers and men their sisters as their closest family relationships. As the authors noted, these findings lend support to the arguments of some (e.g., Cousins, 1989) that the modern American sense of identity is more concerned with personal, physical, or attributive traits rather than social or relational roles. Therefore, a possible explanation for the finding that most men do not incorporate the son role into their overall personal identity is that the role of son is perceived as relational in nature. Furthermore, the son role is perhaps most pertinent primarily during the time in many men's lives (i.e., adolescence) when they are attempting to establish a sense of an individual self, not a relational self. Traditional masculinity demands that men be independent, and conversely, not overly dependent on others, particularly other men (Wood, 1999). The exclusion of the sonhood role as a central part of any male's self-identity may stem from his embracing the more traditional aspects of the masculine gender role (i.e., independence) and rejecting any sense of dependency or connection to others in the developmental process of transitioning from boy to adolescent to man, a progression described by some as adolescent separation-individuation (Blos, 1987; see also Mahler, Pine, & Bergman, 1975).

But even if the male self concept minimizes the relational nature of the role of son in forming a sense of personal identity, what is clear is that most of the extant research in both the popular and scholarly press attempting to analyze sonhood as part of the lived male experience is crafted from an inherently relational perspective. In fact, very little research exists that focuses directly on the role of son *exclusive* from any other familiar relationship, leading us to contend that our current understanding of the role of son has been constructed through the lens of other relationships, drawn primarily from father-son, mother-son, or sibling research efforts. Like parenthood or siblinghood, sonhood is inherently relational; thus, it makes sense to investigate it from a relational perspective. However, the result of taking such a relational perspective is that, in a sense, we appear to have an indirect or "back-door" understanding of the role of the son, an understanding shaped in an almost exclusively dyadic manner.

In most popular literature, for example, the role or described experience of being a son is almost always framed in relationship to other family members and spans a wide array of experiences associated with holding the role of the son within the family dynamic. Without question, the largest category of popular press books on the role of being a son is framed within the father-son relationship, a category search topic that generated over 105,000 hits on a recent Amazon.com search. A huge number of books on the father-son relationship focus on a wide array of activities or action-adventure type experiences, featuring topics like playing golf together (Dodson, 2003), scuba diving (Chowdhury, 2000), baseball (Stanton, 2001), sailing (Hays & Hays, 1995), football (McGraw, 2000), bicycling (Lind, 1993), fly fishing (Plummer, 2000), and hiking (Patton, 1999). Other action-oriented titles involved traveling together (McKeen & McKeen, 2003), doing construction projects together (Marchese, 2002), and even going to war together (Takiff, 2003). The lessons of life learned from a father is the subject of another large category of books, best represented by NBC newsman Tim Russert's (2004) best-selling book *Big Russ and Me: Father and Son—Lessons of Life.* Other father-son categories include historical father-son relationships (Gullan, 2004; Skemp, 1994); reconciliation with fathers (Ilardo, 1993); dealing with the death of a father (Veerman & Barton, 2003); living with famous fathers (Reagan & Hyams, 1988); religion and faith-based teaching from fathers (Clark, 2002); "how to" fathering books (Poulter, 2004); prose, poetry, and drama about the father-son relationship (Friel, 1999; Gerrold, 2003; Shinder, 1984); the father, son, and brother triadic relationship (Lott, 2000); and gay sons writing about their straight fathers (Shenitz & Holleran, 2002) or straight sons writing about their gay fathers (Gottlieb, 2003). Finally, a smaller category of popular books focuses on the mother-son relationship (Caron, 1995) or providing insight for women concerning the father-son relationship (Jampolsky & Jampolsky, 1998). In our review of the popular press, we were unable to find a single example of a book that assesses or describes the role of a son independent from any another family relational dyad.

Furthermore, very little scholarly research directly focuses on the conception or meaning of the son's role within the family. Even fewer works attempt to describe the characteristics associated with sonhood separate from other familial relationships. Much like the popular press, most academic research on sons is conducted in association with a family dyad—most notably father-son, mother-son, brother-brother—or by analyzing the psychological components of the culture of boyhood. A brief overview of each area follows.

Sons and Their Fathers

For the last 60 years, the father-son relationship has been the focus of a number of studies related to the interaction between pre-adolescent or adolescent sons and their fathers. The advent of World War II inspired an interest in the effects of father absence on the developmental processes of children left behind when Dad went off to war (e.g., Bach, 1946). Subsequently, other researchers became interested in the significance of the father's role in the lives of his children once he returned home (e.g., Glueck & Glueck, 1950). Today, those early research efforts continue to frame investigations into the unique ways a son is influenced by his father, research that, for the most part, substantially maintains its focus on the important issues of father absence and father involvement.

Overwhelming amounts of research support the argument that many important developmental processes regarding the son are significantly mitigated by his father; in fact, few other relationships will have more influence, whether positive or negative, on the trajectory of a man's life than the relationship between son and father (see Day & Lamb, 2004, and Peters & Day, 2000, for excellent reviews of the extant research). The quality of a son's relationship with his father has been found to be an important predictor of a son's future success or failure in a host of important variables like educational achievement (Singer & Weinstein, 2000), relational involvement (Beatty & Dobos, 1993), income level (Duncan, Hill, & Yeung, 1996), gender identity (Horsfall, 1991), and parenting styles (Simmons, Beaman, Conger, & Chao, 1993). A son's relationship with his father has also been linked to attitudes and behaviors associated with physical and emotional violence directed towards women (Dick, 2004). Moreover, decades of research have found sons to be adversely affected as a direct result of father absence, with the son's cognitive (Juby & Farrington, 2001), moral (Daum, 1983), and social development (Angel & Angel, 1993) negatively influenced due to the lack of a father's presence in his life. Furthermore, father absence has been found to negatively affect a son's peer relationships (Mitchell & Wilson, 1967), self-concept (Parish & Taylor, 1979), self-esteem (Miller, 1984), and masculine development (Beatty, 1995), and appears to predict increased levels of delinquency (Juby & Farrington, 2001), drug and alcohol abuse (Brook, Whitman, & Gordon, 1985), psychiatric problems (Beck, Sethi, & Tuthill, 1963; Seligman, 1974), and a host of other antisocial behaviors

(Peterson & Zill, 1986). A complete review of the developmental research associated with sons and their fathers is well beyond the scope or purpose of this section; however, without question, the quality of the father-son relationship is a strong predictor of sons' overall well-being (Lamb, 1997). As Wallerstein (1984) noted, whether physically near or distant, and regardless of how much or how little time a father spent with his children, he is a significant psychological presence, particularly in the life of his son.

At the beginning of the 21st century, evidence is mounting that a "changing culture of fatherhood" (Morman & Floyd, 2002, p. 395) is well underway, as men attempt to reject such negative titles as "the disqualified dad" (Kindlon & Thompson, 1999) or the family's "weak link" (Larson & Richards, 1994) in favor of a more positive perspective on their roles as fathers. This has created what Furstenberg (1988) has called the "good dad-bad dad" phenomenon, in which men are recognized for their increased involvement in the lives of their family while simultaneously criticized for increasing rates of father neglect, absence, and disengagement from family responsibility (i.e., the "dead-beat dad," Corneau, 1991). For example, data reveal that one in four American children lives in a single-parent home, 88% of which are headed by a woman (U.S. Bureau of the Census, 1996). On the other hand, studies have reported that fathers are now spending more time with their children. The amount of time an American father spends with his children has increased over the past few decades to an average of 3.48 hours per day in 1997 (Bond, Galinksy, & Swanberg, 1998; see also Fuligni & Brooks-Gunn, 2004 and Pleck & Masciadrelli, 2004 for detailed reviews of this literature). Reports from the United Kingdom also note that the average British father assumes a third of the total time spent in parental childcare (O'Brien & Schmilt, 2003). Adler (1996) reported that 70% of the men in his survey claimed to spend more time with their children than their fathers spent with them. These findings are particularly relevant because fathers are more likely to increase their proportion of caregiving if the children in his family are boys (Wood & Repetti, 2004), with sons engaged with their fathers in playful, rough-and-tumble type interactions involving emotional arousal and learning how to get along with peers. Further, sons benefit from this type of father play in that it appears to provide opportunities for fathers to model and reinforce turn-taking, affect regulation, acceptable ways of competing with peers, and other gender appropriate behavior (DeKlyen, Speltz, & Greenberg, 1998). However, paternal engagement and accessibility decreases with advancing levels of pubertal development, limiting the amount of time fathers spend with their adolescent sons by about 50% (from two to three hours a day to .5 to one hour a day) (Doherty, Kouneski, & Erikson, 1998; see also Ogletree, Jones, & Coyl, 2002).

While much research into the father-son dynamic reflects the "bad dad" approach with emphasis on conflict (Comstock, 1994) or dysfunction (Lee, 1987), we believe that good fathering performed within a loving, affectionate, supportive, warm, structured, and empathic environment (Morman & Floyd, 2003) results in a host of positive outcomes for sons, ranging from stronger self-esteem (Biller, 1993) and emotional stability (Brody, 1996) to a more even perspective on balancing the demands of the masculine gender role (Pollack, 1998; Pruett, 1989). In many substantial ways, the culture of sonhood is significantly shaped and influenced as a direct result of the contributions of the father to his son.

Sons and Their Mothers

While we clearly appear to know much more about the nature of sonhood as it is played out within the father-son dyad, that does not mean that the mother-son relationship lacks significance within the culture of sonhood. Compared to fathers, mothers spend up to three times as much time alone with their children and continue to hold responsibility for the majority of the planning, organizing, supervising, and scheduling of their activities (Baruch & Barnett, 1996; Pleck & Masciadrelli, 2004). A son's relationship with his mother has been investigated in a number of ways, from the influence of mothering on son's social outcomes (Maccoby & Martin, 1983; Rothbaum & Weisz, 1994) to the effects of marital conflict (Lindsey, Lewis, Campbell, Frabutt, & Lamb, 2002), maternal depression (Burke, 2003), influence on son's peer relationships (Boyum & Parke, 1995), son's levels of emotional reciprocity (Kerig, Cowan, & Cowan, 1993), and mother-son conversation patterns (Beaumont, Vasconcelos, & Ruggeri, 2001). Another small line of research deals with the paradoxical situation of adolescent sons being raised by lesbian mothers, women facing the unique challenge of instilling certain forms of masculinity within their sons' self-identity while at the same time rejecting other patriarchal attitudes that have traditionally prevented equality between the sexes (Chrisp, 2001; Davis, 1997). Other research has assessed the effects of a son disclosing his homosexuality to his mother and the impact such a revelation has on trust in their relationship (Miller & Boon, 2000; see also Saltzburg, 2004).

Contrary to the large amount of research purporting father-son conflict, Matthews, Woodall, Kenyon, and Jacob (1996) found it is more often the son's relationship with his mother that predicts sons' hostility and anger, and that sons in their study, while desiring greater father involvement, wanted their mothers to leave them alone, let them dress their own way, let them stay out late, and let them make their own decisions. Their research supports other studies reporting higher rates of disagreement between a son and his mother as opposed to the father-son relationship (Laursen, 1995). Sons have been found to be more withdrawn in conversations with their mothers than are daughters (Whalen, Henker, Hollingshead, & Burgess, 1996), and sons tend to interrupt their mothers in conversations significantly more than do their sisters (Beaumont et al., 2001). Sons spend less time than daughters talking with their mothers about emotions (Dunn, Bretherton, & Munn, 1987), and sons receive fewer directives or commands from their mothers during typical conversations (Leaper, Anderson, & Sanders, 1998).

While more limited in scope than the research on sons and their fathers, the quality of a son's relationship with his mother, nevertheless, has a significant effect on the son's social, psychological, and cognitive well-being. In fact, Diamond (2004) argues, "a securely rooted male identity is largely built upon a boy's identification with his mother's unconscious attitudes toward his maleness" (p. 367). For example, adolescent sons of working mothers report that they believe they will be doing more housework and spending more time in child care than sons of stay-at-home moms report, with 86% of the sons of working mothers agreeing that husbands and wives are equally responsible for child care, compared to 66% agreement from the sons of stay-at-home mothers (Riggio & Desrochers, 2004). A recent study by Jones, Kramer, Armitage, and Williams (2003) found that a positive relationship between a son and his mother helps a son to achieve a healthier acceptance of his dependent strivings, a more trusting perspective toward others in regard to those related needs, and a lessened fear that connectedness and the meeting of one's needs would result in a loss of self or independence. Their findings argued that sons are substantively and positively helped by the critical role a mother plays in helping them regulate the anxieties associated with the transition from boyhood to manhood.

Sons as Brothers

Logically, the brother-brother dyad should reveal the most about the nature and role of sonhood within the family unit because not only are both male siblings performing the role of brother, they are also simultaneously performing the role of son. The brother-brother dyad creates the space for brothers to co-create the sonhood experience as they live life together not only as brothers, but also as sons. By doing sonhood together, the brother-brother dyad clearly provides the potential for additional insight into the sonhood experience, and yet family researchers have generated more information on the brother-brother dyad specifically and comparatively little information on the sonhood experience that is also being manifested within the male sibling relationship. Floyd (1996a, 1997), Avtgis (2003), and a few others have focused attention on the unique characteristics of the fraternal dyad, analyzing issues of closeness, affection, self-disclosure, and social/emotional support. For example, the experience of closeness within the brother-brother dyad was found to be characterized by shared conversation, solidarity, companionship, shared perceptions and memories, and surviving shared adversity (Floyd, 1996a). Other variables, such as interdependence, commitment, predictability, and the breadth and depth of the fraternal dyad, have been found to predict closeness, liking, and love between brothers (Floyd, 1997). However, no study has been located to date that addresses the simultaneous performance of both the brother and son role within the family dynamic.

The Culture of Boyhood

An additional and notable path toward understanding sonhood in our culture is derived by taking yet another indirect approach to the subject. A sizable area of academic research has directed its attention toward understanding the emotional and psychological condition of the pre-adolescent and adolescent male. Through analyzing the current culture of boyhood in our society, we are allowed another indirect look at the current state of sonhood, since for a while in the developmental process, at least, they are similar. And yet, sadly, most of the scholarly research focused on pre-adolescent or adolescent males paints a disturbing portrait of the emotional lives of boys and young men in our culture (see Titus, 2004 for a critical review). Framed by some as an "underachieving boys' moral panic" (Titus, 2004), this body of research claims that the boys and young men of today are "under siege" (Eberstadt, 2000), a problem so bad that it is now taking on the characteristics of an "epidemic" and is quickly reaching the level of "a national crisis" (Daley, 1999). Others describe a "culture of cruelty" that forces boys to deny and stifle their emotions (Kindlon & Thompson, 1999) or adopt the "boy code" that promotes risk taking, violence, and emotional suppression (Pollack, 1998). Claiming it's a bad time to be a boy in America, Sommers (2000) and others (e.g., Faludi, 1999) describe boys and young men as being at risk, behind, lost, hurting, and as victims of schools that are inherently anti-male, stifling, neglecting, and failing the boys of our country. Boys are four times more likely than girls to be diagnosed with attention deficit hyperactivity disorder and placed on medication (Kleinfeld, 1998), and three times as likely as girls to be enrolled in special education classes (Sommers, 2000). Further, constant media coverage of "the decaying morality of American youth" (Titus, 2004, p. 151) has apparently created a national consensus that adolescent males are dangerous, threatening, uncontrollable, violent, and criminal, resulting in the belief of many professionals that the American culture is full of the world's most violent population of male children (Gurian, 1997; Levine, 1999). Moreover, youths between the ages of 12 and 24 are more likely to be victims of violent crimes compared to persons in other age groups (U.S. Department of Justice, 2002). Statistics reveal that American adolescents are both the principal perpetrators and primary victims of violent acts (Duncan, 1996; Fitzpatrick & Boldizar, 1993). Most shocking, homicide is the leading cause of death among African American males age 15 to 19, and the second leading cause of death for all other teens in the same age range (Centers for Disease Control & Prevention, 2002a). American adolescents also witness a disproportionately high rate of violence (Centers for Disease Control & Prevention, 2002b; Pastore, Fisher, & Friedman, 1996). Chronic exposure to violence has been linked to a host of adverse psychosocial problems in teens including depression (DuRant, Getts, Cadenhead, Emans, & Woods, 1995); anxiety (Lipschitz, Winegar, Harnick, Foote, & Southwick, 1999); suicide ideation (Pastore et al., 1996); and feelings of loss, stress, and isolation, all of which are described in one study as manifesting themselves in the form of post-traumatic stress disorder (Paxton, Robinson, Shah, & Schoeny, 2004). Virtually none of the research we have uncovered directly relating to the adolescent experience of boyhood describes this developmental time period in a positive or highly functional manner. The lives of many pre- and adolescent boys in this country, and therefore, the lives of many pre- and adolescent sons, appear to be far from ideal, presenting significant challenges to their ability to develop into functional members of society as they transition from boyhood to manhood.

As the family research literature has firmly established, the adolescent period is a significantly challenging time for most families, particularly for mothers and fathers as conflict increases within the family and their parenting skills are pushed and stretched in their attempts to parent their adolescent boys/sons (Arnett, 1999; Laursen, Coy, & Collins, 1998). Low self-esteem, depression, drug abuse, and delinquency have all been associated with parent-adolescent conflict (Montemayor, 1983), as well as parents' experiences of midlife stress (Julian, McKenry, & Arnold, 1990). Decades of research supports the argument that ineffective parenting is an important determinant of delinquent behavior among adolescent males (Hirschi, 1969; Jackson, Henriksen, & Foshee, 1998; Jessor & Jessor, 1977). Poor parenting in the form of lax supervision and monitoring, disciplinary practices that are harsh or inconsistent, infrequent communication between parent and adolescent, and poor interpersonal relations between parent and the adolescent child have been found to be associated with higher levels of delinquency and aggression among adolescents (e.g., Clark & Shields, 1997; Mason, Cauce, Gonzales, & Hiraga, 1994). More specifically, perceived low levels of both agreeableness and conscientiousness between parents and adolescent boys was found to be related to antisocial behavior in the adolescent male (Robins, John & Caspi, 1994).

On the other hand, effective parenting in the form of warmth, support, open communication, and monitoring of the child's activities has been associated with reduced illegal substance usage in children (Li, Stanton, & Feigelman, 2000) and with less association with other adolescents who do engage in illegal substances (Gibbons, Gerrard, Cleveland, Wills, & Brody, 2004). More specifically, parent-son communication and interpersonal relationship quality have been found to be associated with the son's cognitive development and psychological well-being (Jackson et al., 1998), while fathers' monitoring of sons' behavior was found to be inversely associated with sons' subsequent delinquent behavior (Paschall, Ringwalt, & Flewelling, 2003). Parental social support has been determined to predict high self-esteem in sons (Newcomb, 1990), and while adolescent females have been found to have a greater number of supportive friends and to receive more social support from them (Colarossi, 2001), adolescent males perceived significantly more social support from their fathers than female adolescents did (Colarossi & Eccles, 2003). In fact, some studies have reported that in general, males receive more support from both parents and non-familial adults than do females (Frey & Rothlisberger, 1996; Scheirer & Botvin, 1997).

Despite several decades of academic research into the relational and developmental processes of the adolescent male, and despite mountains of research probing into every conceivable variable affecting his cognitive, social, emotional, psychological, and physical growth, we still know very little about what it actually means to be a son within the family unit or how men themselves perceive this role and what they would claim it takes to perform it well. Most of the research concerning the nature of sonhood is indirect and tangential, and most of what is known is gleaned from studies of the whole family or dyads within the family, not from direct and specific inquiries into the structure and substance of the role of son. A considerable amount of information exists concerning a man's ability to negotiate the role of father (e.g., Doherty et al., 1998), husband (e.g., Cutrona, 1996; Dindia & Baxter, 1987), and to a lesser extent, even brother (e.g., Avtgis, 2003; Floyd, 1997). Additionally, male-male friendship roles have received an increased level of attention over the past decade (e.g., Morman & Floyd, 1998); however, almost no research exists on how to establish, maintain, and negotiate the one role that every man is born into and that every man occupies, at least structurally, his entire life.

In many ways, sons learn how to become men (i.e., forming the masculine identity, shaping the male self-concept, developing the masculine gender role) by modeling their fathers (Farmer, 1991; Miedzian, 1992; Lee, 1991; Pease, 2000), but also by differentiating from their mothers (see Diamond, 2004 for an extensive overview and critique of this line of research). Most mothers and fathers work hard to teach their boys how to become men, a learning process that apparently does not necessarily entail or encompass incorporating the role of son into the male self-image (Salmon & Daly, 1996). The *role* of son, perhaps, is being confused with the developmental *stage* of being a boy or adolescent; thus, like boyhood, sonhood is perceived as only temporary, a phase to endure and quickly transition out of in order to move toward the achievement of the actual goal of most parental efforts, successful entry into manhood (Diamond, 1997, 2004). And while most men do developmentally transition out of boyhood, no man will ever transition out of sonhood. Thus, to whom does a man look for a role model on how to be a son? Who teaches a boy how to be a son before he also becomes a husband or father? How do men negotiate the role of the adolescent or adult son? Or simply, at any age, what do males believe makes a son a good son?

The rest of this paper will directly address the question of sonhood; more specifically, what are the qualities and characteristics surrounding the issue of being a good son? What follows is a descriptive report of our investigation into the character of sonhood. Exploratory in nature, our study was primarily designed to discover what adolescent and adult men believe to be the most important characteristics of the role of the good son.

The Good Son Study

Method

The participants in the study ($N = 572$) were adolescent and adult males ranging in age from 12 to 87 years, with a mean age of just over 40 years. A majority of the sample (72.4%) was Caucasian, whereas 17.3% were Black/African American, 4.1% were Hispanic, 2.7% were Asian/Pacific Islander, 1.4% was Native American, and 4.4% were of other ethnic origins (these numbers equal more than 100 because some participants reported belonging to more than one ethnic group). Most of the participants were married at the time of the study. More than half (68.1%) lived in the midwestern United States; 23.4% lived in the northeast, 3.8% lived in the southwest, 3.0% lived in the northwest, 1.4% lived in the south/ southeast, and 0.3% lived in Puerto Rico.

Undergraduate communication students at three universities participated in recruiting adolescent and adult males to take part in the study. Some male students participated themselves, whereas others asked friends, relatives, neighbors, family members, or work associates. Males who agreed to participate were given a letter from the researchers explaining the nature and purposes of the study; a short questionnaire; and an addressed, postage-paid envelope. Participants completed the questionnaire and returned it anonymously to the researchers. At the beginning of the questionnaire, participants were asked to respond to the following question:

> Think for a few minutes about being a son. What does being a "good son" mean to you? Below, please describe your thoughts on what it means to be a good son. (You might think specifically of instances in which you felt like a particularly good son, or about men you know whom you think of as good sons.) What does it mean to be a good son?

Participants were given a page of lined paper on which to write their responses. After completing their questionnaires, participants mailed them to the researchers in the envelopes provided. Participants were not asked to provide their names or any identifying information to the researchers.

The data, therefore, consisted of 572 pages of handwritten narratives. To identify the characteristics of good sonhood, we took a grounded theory approach to analyzing participants' written descriptions (Strauss & Corbin, 1990). To construct an initial coding scheme, we independently conducted open coding on approximately one-third of the written narratives. During this review, we formulated lists of categories representing participants' ideas of what it meant to be a good son. The formulation of categories followed a linear pattern whereby new categories were added when, and only when, the existing categories were insufficient to capture the ideas being offered in a narrative. After constructing coding schemes independently, we met to combine our efforts into a single coding scheme. This process involved axial coding, an approach wherein the instances of each code are compared to define the properties and characteristics of that code. Conceptually similar categories we had independently identified were combined, and categories that were identified by only one of us were discussed until consensus was reached as to their utility. Throughout this process, the categories were continually compared and contrasted and were adjusted as necessary to accommodate discrepant cases (see Creswell, 1998). The result of this iterative process was a scheme of 14 categories representing participants' ideas about good sonhood.

To establish inter-coder reliability, we then gave approximately one-third of the written narratives (a different one-third than were used for category construction) to two doctoral students who had been uninvolved in the creation of the category scheme and asked them to code the narratives using the category scheme. On the basis of this coding, we reconfigured four of the categories and did a second reliability assessment. After achieving acceptable reliability estimates for all 14 categories, the doctoral student coders then coded all of the remaining written narratives according to this coding scheme.

Results

Analyses of participants' written responses to the question of what it meant to them to be a good son produced 14 categories of responses. The top five responses are detailed below. Frequencies of use for each category appear in Table 3.1.

Honor and Respect. The most mentioned item (47.7%) was that good sons show honor and respect to their parents. As one respondent noted, "To be a good son is to be respectful of your father and mother, to be respectful of

Table 3.1   Frequencies and Inter-Coder Reliabilities for Categories of Good Sonhood

Theme	Kappa	Frequency
Affection	.65	14.8
Caregiving in old age	1.0	2.3
Friendship	.63	20.3
Help and support	.68	18.8
Honesty	.88	11.7
Honor and respect	.83	47.7
Involvement	.75	17.2
Independence	.66	25.0
Love	.76	21.6
Modeling	.75	7.0
Obedience	.88	21.9
Pride in parents	.66	1.6
Seeking counsel	.66	22.7
Teaching parents	.79	1.6

NOTE: Frequencies are reported in percentages of narratives using each theme.

their experiences, both good and bad, and to respect the sacrifices they have made to give you all that you have." Another said that "A good son is one who honors his father and mother and respects their guidance and leadership to the household." Importantly, showing honor to one's parents does not necessarily imply a loss of one's own ideas or ideals. One son wrote that "I feel like a son should respect his parents, but still hold to his own beliefs and thoughts."

Independence. The second most commonly mentioned category (25%) among respondents was the idea that a good son makes his own decisions and takes responsibility for those decisions. For example, one man wrote that being a good son involved listening to his parents' advice but "also means he [the son] has choices and the need to be independent—not a follower." Another said that a good son should "be obedient to his father yet be willing to question what his father tells him to make decisions for himself." One the topic of taking responsibility for one's actions, one respondent commented that a good son "should understand that no one is to blame for the 'short-comings' we sometimes experience in life." At issue in these and related comments was the importance of good sons making independent decisions about their own lives and then taking responsibility for those decisions, whether positive or negative.

Seeking Counsel. The third most mentioned category (22.7%) offered that a good son seeks his parents' advice—whether or not he subsequently follows that advice. That is, the comments in this category referenced the importance of asking for counsel, not necessarily following it. "A good son asks for fatherly advice," said one respondent. Another wrote that a good son "seeks for help from them [his parents] in any situation." Yet another said, "A good son takes instructions and advice from the dad."

Obedience. The fourth theme (21.9%) was that a good son obeys his parents and is loyal to them. "Being a good son is doing what is asked of you, when it is asked," said one respondent. Another said, "being a good son means to always be loyal and willing to help your father." Several respondents commented on the importance of obedience even when the son may disagree with what is being asked. Referring to his own son, one father wrote that "he obeys me even when he thinks I am wrong." Similarly, another man wrote that a good son "should be obedient to his parents yet be willing to question what they tell him." Still another said, "a good son obeys his father, even when disagreeing on a particular situation."

Love. The fifth most frequently mentioned theme (21.6%) was that good sons should *experience* love, care, and admiration (as opposed to *express* it) for their parents and their families. The distinction is illustrative, given that one can feel love without expressing it, yet can also express love without feeling it (see Erbert & Floyd, 2004). One man said that being a good son means to "love your parents as you want to be loved"; another said that a good son "likes and cares for his family." Perhaps unsurprisingly, many respondents mentioned both *feeling love* and *expressing love* as characteristics of good sonhood. For instance, one wrote that "a good son loves his parents and expresses that love to them." In a number of instances, however, respondents cited *either* feeling love *or* expressing love, but not both, as indicative of being a good son. Of course, this does not suggest that those respondents specifically thought that only feeling or expressing love—but not both—was important; in fact, many may have made no conscious distinction between the two. Given the potential for humans to separate their emotions from their expressions of them, however, we separated these behaviors as distinct categories in this typology of good sonhood and created another category (affection) to capture the idea of expressing love, care, and so on to one's parents and family.

Other Categories. The remaining categories were as follows: *friendship* ("I should behave to him [my father] as if I were his friend because he's gained my trust and friendship."); *help and support* ("A good son cares about his parents, is there for them."); *involvement* ("A good son likes and cares for his family and wants to spend time with them."); *affection* ("I tell my folks how much I love them whenever I can."); *honesty* ("Being a good son means that he (my son) is honest with me and able to talk about anything with me."); *modeling* ("My parents, and more specifically, my father, have added to who I am by the example he has been towards others in my life."); *caregiving in old age* ("Once grown, a good son should keep his parents in his life and, if necessary, be a parent to his parents once they can't perform the tasks for themselves."); *pride in parents* ("Being a good son means being proud of who my mother and father are as people and what they [have] achieved."); *teaching parents* ("Being a good son means helping my parents with advice and with teaching them how to do things, like they taught me earlier in life.").

Conclusion

In this first exploratory study into the culture of sonhood, we simply asked adolescent and adult men to respond to the question of what it means to be a good son. Our interest in the present project was to examine what it is that makes men *good sons*. This is a simple question, although it has some important and complex implications once answered. Through this inductive study, we assembled a list of referents that characterize our respondents' conceptions of a good son. In all, 14 different categories were developed to capture the wide variety in participants' responses. The categories of honor/ respect, independence, seeking counsel, obedience, and love were mentioned the most by the participants in their open-ended statements. Many of the men simply wrote a one-sentence response to the question; however, many others wrote paragraphs or filled the entire page with comments, suggestions, and insights into the culture of sonhood.

We believe that one of the main strengths of the current project is that the participants in our study did not simply respond to a predetermined list of skills or behaviors provided for them, but instead, in an open-ended fashion, were asked what they believed to be the most important factors for being a good son. Clearly, simply responding to a ready-made list of sonhood skills is not the same as asking men themselves to determine what items should be on the list of skills of sonhood issues. Thus, the current study left it open for the respondents to decide what to write, how much to write, and how many suggestions they would make. As such, we believe this data set provides a more refined and ecologically valid view of the culture of sonhood because the responses come not from simple reactions to pre-constructed lists of variables generated by others but from the sons themselves. The resulting category scheme takes us a step forward toward developing a consistent and stable list of good son characteristics that hopefully will be useful in future research efforts into the culture of sonhood.

Another advantage of the current project was the wide range of ages of the men in the study. Because men never transition out of the son role, we worked to include the perceptions of men from 12 to 87 years of age, gaining insight and perspective from across the lifespan of the son role. We also wanted to avoid the problems associated with single-source reporting bias, a common methodological concern surrounding much research on the family (Coley, 2001). Studies have found that different family members will provide different reactions to, or perceptions of, various issues surrounding family life; thus it is important to include multiple family voices in order to avoid privileging one member's perception over another. For example, a recent study found that adolescents rated perceptions of the strength of their family units significantly lower than either their mother or father. Specifically, fathers differed from their adolescent children in perceptions of commitment to the family, spending time together, and the effective handling and solving of family conflict and crisis (Greeff & Roux, 1999). Further, Kindlon and Thompson (1999) report that fathers and sons differed in their interpretation and evaluation of the same, shared experience nearly 50% of the time. Overall, adolescents have been found to be generally less positive regarding perceptions of their families than their parents (Schumm, Barnes, Bollman, Jurich, & Milliken, 1985). By using a full range of men (sons) at different stages in the life course, we hoped to avoid the problems associated with gaining responses from only one group of sons (e.g., adolescents) and instead incorporated feedback from men of all ages and stages of life regarding their perceptions of sonhood.

This project makes some important contributions to the extant research on sons and the role of the son within the family context. First, this study moves us toward not only a better understanding of the characteristics of being a good son, but also helps to establish a consistent and stable list of factors central to the concept. We are unaware of any academic scholarship that attempts to establish, through empirical scientific research practice, a participant-derived list of sonhood characteristics associated with the question of being a good son. Second, such a list becomes the topoi of a new research tool, a quantitative survey instrument that hopefully will be useful to those interested in research on the effective development of sons in all stages of life. Third, this study reports that several of the 14 variables generated as effective characteristics of being a good son could be described as being reciprocal in their nature; that is, they appear to have mutual influence on both parents and their sons (e.g., affection, friendship, help, involvement, pride, teaching). As noted above, the role of son is inherently relational and is generated as a direct result of being the son of a mother and father; thus due to the implicitly relational nature of sonhood, it should make sense that many of the characteristics of such a role would be mutually engaged and enacted by both the father/mother and the son.

Finally, many of the items described as important to the role of the good son have a much more direct connection to the relationship between a son and his father rather than a son and his mother. Over and over again, the participants in this study specifically referenced their fathers, but not their mothers, as they described characteristics of sonhood; in fact, in all of the 572 pages of open-ended, non-directed, handwritten narratives on the role of son, not a single example was offered specifically referencing the mother-son relationship. Furthermore, many of the sonhood items mentioned by the men in this study are associated with the more relational and emotional components of fatherhood (e.g., love, teaching, affection, involvement, help and support, role model) noted by Morman and Floyd (2003) in their study of the characteristics of good fathering. As such, this new set of data on the nature of sonhood provides additional support for the argument that the culture and assessment of quality fathering behaviors in the early part of the 21st century continue to evolve from the distant, provider-disciplinarian role of previous decades to the more engaged, involved, emotionally attached father of today (Morman & Floyd, 2002), mandated in part, perhaps, by demands from sons who desire more effective and positive relationships with their fathers.

Clearly, the present results are only a first step toward a more scholarly understanding of the nature of sonhood and the role of son within the family dynamic. Our intention is to build upon this first step by creating interval-level measures for each of the referents and collecting additional data to validate the scales. Interval-level data will allow us to assess the orthogonality of the categories and to determine if a simpler structure underlies them. By quantifying the concept of good sonhood, we can also address some important questions that have thus far received little direct empirical attention.

First, what factors predict how good a son a man will be? Second, what are the similarities and differences between the performance of sonhood within the father-son versus the mother-son relationship? Does each unique parent-son dyad require or emphasize a different subset of characteristics in order to be considered effective or functional? Third, how do the characteristics of sonhood change as a son grows from boy to adolescent to man? Specifically, what sonhood skills are most needed or utilized at different points in a son's development? Finally, is being a good son the same as being a good daughter, or are there qualitative and quantitative differences between the two? How much of each is unique to sons and daughters, and how much is part of a collective concept of simply being a good child, regardless of sex? These are issues that await empirical attention, and further development and refinement of our model of good sonhood will make such efforts possible.

Commentary on Part A

Anita L. Vangelisti

Although scholars vehemently argue about whether the family, as a social institution, is in decline (e.g., Amato, 2000; Walsh, 1993), few disagree that the quality of family relationships—regardless of their form or structure—has a powerful influence on people's psychological, emotional, and physical well-being. Given this, it may be surprising to some readers to learn that a number of family relationships are *understudied*. The chapters in this book in the section on family-of-origin relationships demonstrate not only that some family relationships are understudied but also that the lack of attention paid to these relationships represents a serious gap in the literature—one that has important theoretical, methodological, and practical ramifications.

The section begins with a chapter by Fisher and Miller-Day on the relationship between mothers and their adult daughters. Fisher and Miller-Day argue that understanding the mother-adult daughter relationship is central to the study of the life cycle of relationships because the mother-daughter bond is particularly intense and is one of the longest of social bonds. The authors also note that mother-daughter relationships play a vital role in maintaining the family—that mothers and daughters are *kinkeepers* and typically are more involved in the family than are other family members. According to Fisher and Miller-Day, these and other qualities of the mother-daughter relationship provide a rationale for studying the patterns of interaction that typify the association between mothers and their adult daughters.

In the body of their chapter, Fisher and Miller-Day describe the unique characteristics of the mother-daughter relationship, the dialectical forces that influence this unique association, and turning points represented in the relationship between mothers and their adult daughters. The authors contextualize their discussion of the unique strengths and challenges of the mother-adult daughter dyad by providing a brief historical overview of the ways scholars have conceptualized mother-daughter relationships. They note, for example, that in the early 1900s, clinical psychologists emphasized the importance of daughters separating from their mothers whereas scholars more recently have depicted daughters (and women in general) as inseparable from their relationships with significant others. The authors then go on to review research by Miller-Day describing the communication patterns that tie mothers and daughters together. More specifically, Miller-Day found that mother-daughter dyads were either *connected* (moderate in cohesion) or *enmeshed* (high in cohesion). These findings serve to underline the argument presented in this chapter that mother-daughter dyads are typified by strong, enduring bonds.

Another way that Fisher and Miller-Day depict the mother-adult daughter relationship is by describing the dialectical forces that influence it. Specifically, they argue that mothers and their adult daughters continually manage tensions between connection and separation, openness and closedness, and stability and change. The authors note that these dialectical forces capture some of the developmental processes that characterize mother-daughter relationships as well as the contradictions that are embedded in and punctuate those processes.

A review of Fisher's research on turningpoints offers yet another perspective on changes that occur in the mother-daughter relationship over time. In her study, Fisher interviewed 21 mother-daughter dyads about their perceptions of turning points that they believed changed the level of closeness in their relationship. She identified 10 categories of turning points for daughters and 11 categories for mothers. Fisher and Miller-Day provide insightful descriptions of many of the categories along with explanations for how the study's findings contribute to existing literature.

Fisher and Miller-Day conclude their chapter with several recommendations for future research. For example, they note that the current literature offers a very limited view of nonbiological and culturally diverse mother-daughter dyads. They also suggest that more attention be paid to change in maternal relationships and to mothers and daughters who have emotionally distant relationships.

Of course, attending to these gaps in the literature will present researchers with methodological challenges including, but not limited to, recruiting diverse samples of mother-daughter dyads, collecting longitudinal data, and accessing samples of mothers and daughters who may be less than enthusiastic about participating in research together. Scholars who take on these challenges also will need to carefully consider a number of theoretical issues. For instance, those interested in studying change in maternal relationships may need to identify factors that are likely to affect the impact of change on mother-daughter dyads. The influence of change may vary depending on its "baseline" or "starting point" (e.g., high satisfaction vs. moderate satisfaction), the rate with which it occurs (e.g., over a period of days vs. over a period of years), or the cultural context in which it takes place (e.g., one that prioritizes groups vs. one that prioritizes individuals). Similarly, those who study emotionally distant maternal relationships may find it useful to identify different manifestations of this phenomenon. Mothers and daughters who rarely interact may be emotionally distant, but so may be those who interact frequently yet feel a great deal of hostility or resentment toward each other. As scholars begin to address methodological challenges and theoretical questions such as these, it will be important for them to provide empirical evidence distinguishing mother-daughter relationships from other dyads within the family and to examine within-group differences so that the complex nature of mother-daughter relationships is not lost.

Mikkelson offers a thoughtful review of the literature on a relationship that is central to many people's lives: the adult sibling relationship. He starts his chapter by describing the unique characteristics of sibling dyads. He then goes on to note different types of sibling relationships and variables that are commonly studied in the context of sibling dyads. Mikkelson also explores the role of communication between siblings and makes a number of suggestions that researchers who are interested in siblings might address in the future.

Like Fisher and Miller-Day, Mikkelson argues that the relationship he is describing is common, involuntary, lengthy, and relatively permanent. He also suggests that sibling relationships can be the source of conflict and contradictions. However, unlike Fisher and Miller-Day, Mikkelson notes that the dyad he describes "is similar to friendships in that it is more egalitarian than other family relationships." According to Mikkelson, this peer-like characteristic not only distinguishes sibling relationships from other family relationships, but it shapes the quality of sibling interactions.

After describing the characteristics of sibling relationships, Mikkelson points out several types of sibling dyads defined in terms of such variables as common biological origin (e.g., full vs. half siblings) and legal regulations (e.g., biological vs. stepsiblings). Because, as he notes, most of the literature focuses on full biological siblings, Mikkelson limits the remainder of his review to studies of siblings who share the same mother and father. He identifies three types of biological sibling dyads (sister-sister, brother-brother, and brother-sister) and discusses characteristics that appear to be common to each type. Because, as Mikkelson notes, studies contrasting these three types of sibling relationships often yield mixed findings, it is difficult to make firm conclusions about distinctions between sibling dyads based only on the sex of the siblings.

Perhaps for this reason, researchers also have looked at siblings at different points in the life span. Mikkelson examines this literature in terms of several frequently studied variables including interaction and contact patterns, closeness, rivalry, and support. Noting the close links between these variables and communication, he then reviews studies conducted by communication scholars and makes a case for more research focusing on the interaction patterns of adult siblings. Mikkelson's critique of existing scholarship provides researchers with a blueprint for studies that need to be conducted in the future.

Although the review of literature presented by Mikkelson is thorough, it raises unanswered questions about how researchers should go about examining siblings' communication. The number of variables that might influence the interaction patterns of siblings is overwhelming. Just a few of these are the age of siblings, siblings' sex, the age difference between siblings, the number of siblings in a family, the number of siblings who reside in the same household, the degree to which siblings are biologically related, and the number of biological and nonbiological parents living with the siblings. The possible influence of these, and other, variables on siblings' communication places some serious constraints on the methodological choices available to scholars. If, for example, researchers want to look at the conflict patterns of siblings, they need to either control or account for such variables as siblings' age, their sex, the extent to which they are biologically related, and (particularly if they are not biologically related) the amount of time they spend together. Controlling or measuring these variables not only creates challenges with regard to sampling, but it also limits the generalizability of any given study. Such methodological constraints may explain why, as Mikkelson suggests, researchers still have a very limited understanding of siblings' communication.

Morman and Floyd present very interesting conceptual and empirical analyses of the characteristics of sonhood in their chapter "The Good Son." They begin the chapter by noting that "the only universal relational position that all men hold is that of son." This statement provides the basis for a compelling rationale for studying the role of son in the lives of men. At the center of this rationale is the prominence of the role that sons play in most cultures as illustrated by Biblical texts, Greek tragedies, popular Western media, and the relative value placed on sons (over daughters) in countries such as China and Japan.

After demonstrating the ubiquity of sonhood, Morman and Floyd launch into a thorough review of the literature on sons and their relationship with other family members as well as an analysis of the emotional and psychological aspects of boyhood. The review starts with a focus on the relationship between sons and their fathers. Morman and Floyd suggest that some of the first empirical studies on this relationship were provoked by an interest in the effects of father absence on children during World War II. They argue that this emphasis on father absence and father involvement is still apparent in the literature as researchers continue to investigate the association between the quality of father-son relationships and variables such as sons' academic achievement, income level, delinquency, self-esteem, cognitive development, and social competence. Morman and Floyd also note, quite astutely, that the nature of the relationship between fathers and their sons is changing. Even though many fathers are, indeed, disengaged from their families, others are spending more time with their children than they have at many other points in history.

Mothers, of course, still spend much more time with their children than do fathers. Morman and Floyd suggest that perhaps as a consequence, the nature of the mother-son relationship is quite different than that between sons and their fathers. For instance, the authors note that sons' relationship with their mother is more likely to be associated with hostility and anger than is the father-son relationship. These findings are intriguing and, along with others reported by the authors, suggest the possibility that mothers may play a pivotal role in helping sons learn to regulate their negative emotions.

Although relatively little research has been conducted examining the relationship between sons and their brothers, Morman and Floyd argue that this relationship may provide the most information about the role of son in men's lives. The authors note, more specifically, that in "doing son-hood together, the brother-brother dyad clearly provides the potential for additional insight into the sonhood experience."

The paucity of research on sons and their brothers is offset by studies of what Morman and Floyd call the *culture of boyhood*. A large body of literature focuses on the psychological and emotional well-being of pre-adolescent and adolescent boys and, as noted by Morman and Floyd, this literature offers a complex, textured view of what boyhood means. What is missing from the research, however, is description of what it means to be a son. In the remainder of their chapter, Morman and Floyd address this issue.

The remaining portion of Morman and Floyd's chapter provides a description of a very interesting study in which they address the characteristics of sonhood. They asked participants in their study to provide them with written narratives describing what being a *good son* means. Morman and Floyd then analyzed these data, generating a list of 14 different categories to capture the meaning of sonhood. They illustrate each of the categories with clear, concrete examples from their data.

As noted by Morman and Floyd, the results of their good son study raise a number of interesting questions for future research. For example, in discussing their findings, the authors ask whether being a good son differs in significant ways from being a good daughter. This question becomes particularly intriguing when considered in light of differences that research suggests exist in the behavioral patterns of adult sons and daughters. Sons, for instance, do much less caretaking of their older parents than do daughters (Allen, Blieszner, & Roberto, 2000). Yet the results of Morman and Floyd's study indicate that men believe good sonhood is characterized by *caregiving in old age*, *involvement*, and *help and support*. Does the discrepancy between what sons do and what they say they should do represent a failing on the part of sons to fulfill their role? Or is the enactment of certain aspects of the role of son only necessary under particular circumstances (e.g., when there is a crisis, when a daughter is not available)? Morman and Floyd found differences in the frequencies with which men described the various characteristics of good sonhood. Do these differences reflect distinctions in the importance of the characteristics such that, for example, showing "honor and respect" is more important than "caregiving in old age"? As suggested by Morman and Floyd, answering questions such as these would provide a clearer picture of how men enact their role as sons.

Taken together, these three chapters depict family-of-origin relationships as both fascinating and incredibly difficult to investigate. The latter of these two qualities may be one reason why, indeed, these relationships are understudied. A seemingly endless list of variables influences the quality of family relationships and, importantly, the influence of any given variable is likely to be affected by the nature of the system within which the relationships are embedded. Thus, closeness in one mother-daughter dyad may be communicated in very different ways than it is in another. Sibling rivalry may change over time in different ways in different families. Fathers and their sons may need more or less support from each other, depending on the amount and type of support they receive from other family members. The unique qualities of family-of-origin relationships and their embeddedness in family and social systems make it difficult for researchers to develop overarching theoretical frameworks to explain some of similarities that characterize these relationships—yet integrative frameworks are needed. Addressing challenges such as these will require researchers to move toward using more sophisticated theories and methods. The chapters written by these authors nudge readers in the right direction.

PART B

Extended Family Relationships

The second section of this volume groups together research centered on family relationships beyond those in the traditional nuclear family. Often overlooked and understudied, these family ties are created through the extension and expansion of the immediate family unit due to the addition of children (e.g., grandparents and aunts) or because of marriage (e.g., parents-in-law and siblings-in-law). These four extended yet distinctive family relationships also share some common characteristics. Whether the family members are connected by genetics, by law, or both, the relationship is an extended familial connection, one derived from, and because of, a previously in-act family bond (e.g., a person is connected to his or her grandparents, aunts, uncles, and cousins through the parental relationship, rather than directly as with a mother-child relationship). Similarly, an extended connection exists with parents- and siblings-in-law because of, and through, the existing relationship one has with his or her spouse, sibling, or even spouse's sibling.

Thus, all of these relationships share the characteristic of being established and maintained in and through a previously existing, usually genetic, family bond, thereby providing very little choice or voice in the acquisition or acceptance of the new family member. Furthermore, these "in-between" relationships directly affect the quality of interaction and access family members have to one another, and in many ways, mirror or mimic more immediate familiar relationships, in effect taking on a "seeming" or "sort of like" quality (e.g., my aunt is sort of like my mother or big sister; my grandfather at times seems like my dad).

In the first chapter of this part, Jordan Eli Soliz, Mei-Chen Lin, Karen Anderson, and Jake Harwood analyze and review the literature on grandparent-grandchild relationships and conclude that these intergenerational dyads are mutually beneficial to all involved, even while presenting significant theoretical and methodological challenges for communication scholars and family researchers alike. The second chapter introduces readers to the unique experience of "aunting" by providing new research on the aunt/niece/nephew relationship from family scholars Patricia J. Sotirin and Laura L. Ellingson. Their work assesses the unique communicative strengths and challenges of this relationship and provides new data on perceptions of the role of the aunt within the family. The third and fourth chapters investigate two types of in-law relationships. Mary Claire Morr Serewicz evaluates the parents-in-law relationship by considering the defining features of the relationship itself and the more relevant aspects of the communication behavior between parents, their children, and their children's spouses. Finally, the sibling-in-law relationship is investigated by Christina G. Yoshimura. Her chapter reports the results of new research addressing the nature, strength, and challenges of siblings-in-law, in particular by assessing the role and influence of envy between siblings and their spouses. An insightful commentary summarizing this section is offered by Fran C. Dickson of the University of Denver.

4

Friends and Allies

Communication in Grandparent-Grandchild Relationships

Jordan Eli Soliz, Mei-Chen Lin, Karen Anderson, and Jake Harwood

In the United States in 2000 it was estimated the population of those 65 and older was nearly 35 million, a 12% increase since 1990 (Hetzel & Smith, 2001). With the aging of the baby boomers, it is clear that this growth will continue in the forthcoming decades. One result of this population shift is an increase in intergenerational relationships within the family, the most common of which is the grandparent-grandchild relationship (Mares, 1995). In addition to its increased frequency, this relationship's duration is increasing. Uhlenberg and Kirby (1998) estimate that nearly 70% of individuals are born into families where all grandparents are alive, and this remains the case for approximately 40% at age 10. Estimates suggest that roughly 75% of all grandchildren aged 30 have at least one grandparent alive. Hence, for many, the grandparent-grandchild relationship is the first, most frequent, and most enduring source of intergenerational interaction (Williams & Giles, 1996).

In addition to the aging of the population, three emerging trends in family structure should be considered in a demographic profile of grandparents. First, as of 2000, it is estimated that there are 3.9 million multi-generational households in the United States. Often these households reflect situations in which the grandparent is serving as primary caregiver for grandchildren under the age of 18. In fact, of the approximately 5.8 million grandparents living with grandchildren, nearly half (42%) are custodial grandparents (Simmons & Dye, 2003). Second, as of 2000, nearly 8% of children are stepchildren or adopted children (Kreider, 2003). This directly increases the number of nonbiological grandparent relationships. Hence, even a basic demographic profile of the grandparent-grandchild relationship suggests diversity and complexity in this relationship. Third, Bengtson, Rosenthal, and Burton (1990) describe the ways in which families have changed, from a relatively small number of generations with many people in each to a larger number of generations populated by fewer people (as a function of increasing longevity and fewer children per family). Consequently, the family context is shifting from one that was substantially *intra*generational, to one that is substantially *inter*generational. All of these trends warrant attention with regard to their influence on family communication.

While the focus on research related to the aging of the population has primarily been on economic and health care issues, increasing consideration is now being paid to the relational aspects of this demographic trend. Recent years have seen the publication of a handbook addressing various issues pertaining to the relationship, such as grandparents as caregivers, grandparenting in different cultures, and grandparents' roles in intergenerational solidarity (Szinovacz, 1998), as well as numerous empirical articles and review chapters. However, various factors justify the inclusion of the grandparent-grandchild relationship in a book on understudied relationships. First, very little of the work on grandparenting has occurred in the communication discipline. In fact, amidst a flourishing literature on communication and aging (Nussbaum & Coupland, 2004) and intergenerational communication (Williams & Nussbaum, 2001), intergenerational *family* relationships, especially for non-adjacent generations, have received surprisingly little attention in the family communication literature (Williams & Harwood, 2004). Second, very few significant research *programs* have emerged on grandparenting. It has been the focus of scattered attention from many researchers, but it lacks the intensive focus and long-term study of a developed research program.

In this chapter, we review the current state of knowledge regarding grandparent-grandchild communication. We first elaborate on the importance and challenges evident in this relationship. Second, numerous variables will be presented as factors that *may* influence the quality or the various types of this relationship. The research findings we describe demonstrate the necessity of including grandparent-grandchild relationships in the mainstream literature on family communication. Then, we turn our attention to research focusing on communicative elements shaped by or shaping the factors introduced in the previous section. Specifically, we highlight communicative predictors of quality grandparent-grandchild relationships, as well as the communicative "negotiation" of age salience as it relates to relational satisfaction and perceptions of intergenerational communication. Finally, we outline specific areas for future research, theoretical frameworks, and methodological considerations to guide this research. Our goal is to show that this understudied relationship is worthy of more attention than it has been accorded in the past and can be promising as it connects with other lines of research beyond family communication. To begin, we outline possible reasons why the grandparent-grandchild relationship has been understudied.

The Lack of Attention to Grandparental Relationships

The lack of attention to the grandparent-grandchild relationship is in part due to a simplistic conceptualization of the relationship. Stereotypical notions of grandparents have them as warm, loving, cozy, and generally female people who bake cookies, knit, call their grandchildren "sweetie," and provide candy and generous Christmas gifts (e.g., Hummert, Garstka, Shaner, & Strahm, 1994). Such conceptions are both overly positive and overly homogeneous, suggesting a relationship involving no conflict, little intensity, only tangential involvement, and virtually no diversity. In contrast to this simplistic and fairy-tale conception, the existing literature actually demonstrates dramatic diversity in the grandparent-grandchild relationship. Scholars such as Cherlin and Furstenberg (1986) have shown that numerous types of relationships exist, from the very distant to the emotionally close, and to a grandparental style involving extensive contact and influence. Furthermore, much of the literature and research has focused on fairly young grandchildren. Explorations of relationships between grandparents and *adult* grandchildren are almost nonexistent. As with parent-child relationships, the dynamics of the grandparent relationship undoubtedly change as grandchildren move further into adulthood. Older grandchildren have the opportunity to form relationships with their grandparents that are independent of their parents, or they may share a caregiver role with their parents such as driving their grandparents to the clinic periodically. Until scholars take on board the complexity and diversity that this relationship encompasses, it is unlikely that extensive research attention will be devoted here.

Another significant contributor to the lack of research attention to grandparenting is that it is overshadowed by the parent-child relationship. Research into personal and family relationships is often troubled by the complexity of dealing with more than a single dyad. Since the parent-child relationship already offers considerable complexity (generally two parents, often multiple children), involving additional members of the extended family provides daunting methodological challenges. Add to this a general notion that the grandparent relationship simply cannot be as important as the parent-child relationship, and you have a recipe for neglect.

Finally, we suspect that certain cultural and ideological biases have crept into research in this area. Western culture tends to focus on the nuclear family. Recent trends of mobility (in jobs and retirement living) and increasing age segregation in housing have reinforced the importance of the nuclear family (Chudacoff, 1989). Western culture has also traditionally valued youth and devalued old age—who really wants to study *old* people, anyway? We suspect that researchers' preferences may have been swayed by these preconceived biases, and hence they have paid insufficient attention to grandparenting as an important relational context. In the end, the grandparent-grandchild relationship has not received the same emphasis that other family relationships have received from communication scholars. We now outline the unique opportunities and challenges that this relationship provides to researchers interested in family communication.

Communicative Opportunities and Challenges

As Kornhaber (1985) suggests, there is evidence that the grandparent-grandchild relationship may be second only to the parent-child relationship in terms of its overall impact on child development. Perhaps one of the most common perceptions of grandparents' role in the family is that they are important in transmitting family history and evoking/reinforcing family identity (Kornhaber & Woodward, 1981). Moreover, a number of studies reinforce the notion that grandparents play a symbolic role, including promulgating traditions, values, and beliefs related to family (Brussoni & Boon, 1998), cultural/ethnic identity (Wiscott & Kopera-Frye, 2000), and religious traditions and values (King, Elder, & Conger, 2000). However, minimal research has examined the actual communication practices involved in transmitting these traditions, values, and beliefs (although see Nussbaum & Bettini, 1994).

Grandparents also play an important supportive role in the lives of grandchildren (Cherlin & Furstenberg, 1986). A *supportive role* here references the ways in which grandparents are involved in their grandchildren's family lives during changes in family structure. Early discussions on the role of grandparents emphasized the supportive aspect of the relationship (e.g., Kornhaber & Woodward, 1981), and recent research has pursued this topic further, suggesting that grandparents provide emotional and financial support (Block, 2002). Emotional support is particularly crucial during family struggles such as parental separation or divorce (Cogswell & Henry, 1995). Furthermore, grandparents also emerge as key figures in assisting the family in raising grandchildren who have physical or mental disabilities (Findler, 2000). Less information is available on how the types of support and supportive interactions vary based on the age of the grandchild or grandparent as well as the physical and mental capacity of the grandparent. Hence, further research is needed to understand how support is enacted (e.g., seeking support, providing support) in this relationship, particularly with teen and adult grandchildren.

A noteworthy trend in grandparents' supportive roles is serving as caregivers (Landry, 1999). Grandparents often become caregivers or custodial parents of their grandchildren in reaction to family problems such as middle-generation substance abuse (Burton, 1992), mental/emotional illness (Jendrek, 1993), incarceration (Dressel & Barnhill, 1994), or divorce (Cherlin & Furstenberg, 1986). Although a sense of pride and joy is typically associated with raising the grandchildren, there may be some unfortunate consequences. In addition to financial strains, legal issues (Waldrop & Weber, 2001), and physical exhaustion, grandparent caregivers may experience shifts in their support networks because their friends may no longer share the role of parent (Jendrek, 1994), resulting in a sense of social isolation for many (Landry, 1999).

Such caregiver roles often reverse when grandchildren become adults. Studies suggest that caregiving is a growing challenge for *all* in that grandchildren often serve as primary caregivers to their grandparents (Giarrusso, Silverstein, & Bengston, 1996). Married grandchildren caring for their grandparents suffer strain in family relationships with their spouses and children, while single grandchildren report challenges in the development of romantic relationships. However, positive outcomes from caregiving are also found including long-lasting positive memories, generational reciprocity, and maintenance of close family relationships (Dellman-Jenkins, Blankenmeyer, & Pinkard, 2000). The caregiving component of the grandparent-grandchild relationship warrants further inquiry in terms of understanding how caregiving roles emerge and reverse and how grandparent and grandchild communicatively negotiate these changes once these roles are assumed.

In addition to the specifics of caregiving, research has also examined broader issues of relational quality in the grandparent-grandchild relationship, with a focus on the variables that have shown strong links to interpersonal solidarity in and quality of this relationship. Positive parent-grandparent relationships (past and present) are associated with parental encouragement of grandparent-grandchild contact (Cherlin & Furstenberg, 1986). The grandparent-grandchild relationship is particularly challenged if the parents are divorced, especially before grandchildren reach adulthood (Drew & Smith, 2002). When family feuds or geographic distance are added to the picture, a loss of contact between grandparents and grandchildren is particularly likely. Parental divorce has been shown to decrease the quantity of contact, especially for paternal grandparents (Cherlin & Furstenberg, 1986). However, divorce and remarriage of the parental generation generally does not affect grandparents' perceived obligations to help their grandchildren financially (Ganong & Coleman, 1998). Grandparents who foster a positive relationship with the custodial parent can overcome the challenges of parental divorce by maintaining a relationship with their grandchildren, albeit with modifications to their role. Maintaining communication through telephone, written, and face-to-face interactions may be crucial during this transitional phase (Gladstone, 1988). The marital status of grandparents also influences the level of involvement with their grandchildren (Silverstein & Marenco, 2001). King (2003) concludes that the divorce of grandparents negatively impacts this relationship, and those negative effects are stronger for grandfathers and paternal grandparents. Thus, both the parents' and the grandparents' marital status can serve as both a facilitator and a barrier to quality of grandparent-grandchild relationships.

Geographical proximity of grandparents and grandchildren functions as another key predictor of quantity of contact. Cherlin and Furstenberg (1986) suggested that geographical distance accounts for 62% of the variance in frequency of contact. However, geographical distance findings are inconsistent. While some research suggests that increased frequency of visiting and closer geographic proximity between the grandparent and grandchildren are positively associated with closeness (Harwood & Lin, 2000), additional findings indicate more satisfaction among grandchildren with long-distance relationships than relationships that are geographically proximal (Harwood, 2000a). One key area for future research might be to examine more *specific* dimensions of emotional closeness and the ways in which they change as a function of geographical distance. We suspect that geographically distant grandparents may be "idealized" to some extent, while the actual relationships remain rather superficial.

Using qualitative techniques, Holladay, Lackovich, and Lee's (1998) turning point study discovered that relationships were generally hurt by increases in distance and helped by decreased geographical proximity. Furthermore, grandparents seem fond of relationships in which the grandchild lives nearby (Falk & Falk, 2002), and the theme of distance is clearly important, as revealed by its prominence in grandparents' accounts of their relationships with their grandchildren (Harwood, 2004; Harwood & Lin, 2000).

Age is naturally a key variable in grandparent-grandchild relationships, due to both the intergenerational nature of the relationship and the changes that occur as the grandparent and grandchild age. Younger grandchildren seem to have closer relationships and more frequent interaction with their grandparents. However, some older grandchildren may have more intimate and substantial communication with their grandparents—particularly as they seek out such contact independent of parental encouragement or familial obligations (Kornhaber & Woodward, 1981). The age of the grandparent is also important. Very young ("off-time") grandparents often resist their "unexpected" role (Burton & Bengtson, 1985). They may still be working full time and have other obligations that limit their flexibility to contribute to the relationship in the same way as older grandparents. On the other end of the continuum, very old grandparents may be more likely to be suffering from health and mobility issues, and this may hinder their involvement (Barer, 2001). Grandparents who are in the "prototypical" age for grandparenting (early retirement years) tend to be most satisfied with their role, in part because they "fit" society's conceptions of that role (Harwood & Lin, 2000).

Finally, the role of grandparent sex and lineage has been noted repeatedly in the literature. While not uniformly consistent, the broad pattern of results appears to indicate that maternal grandparents and grandmothers tend to have closer relationships with their grandchildren (Williams & Nussbaum, 2001). Women appear to focus more on the emotional components of the grandparent role, whereas grandfathers often appear more focused on instru- mental features (e.g., advising about finances or careers: Downs, 1989).

The discussion above illustrates that we know a fair amount about cer- tain concepts central to grandparenting as well as structural variables that influence the quality of the relationship. Much of this research has not had a direct focus on communicative components of the relationship. Hence, the next section focuses on the findings related to grandparent-grandchild *communication*.

What Do We Know About Grandparent-Grandchild Communication?

Researchers have primarily examined two communicative features of the grandparent-grandchild relationship. First, research has examined the com- municative factors that differentiate between high and low quality grand- parenting relationships. Second, work has examined communicative aspects of age salience and the consequences of this relationship for younger people's attitudes about older adults and aging. We examine these two in turn.

Quality

Closer grandparent-grandchild relational partners are more likely to enjoy their interaction, to discuss a wide range of topics, and to interact more frequently in face-to-face settings than less close relational partners (Harwood, 2000a). In closer relationships, grandchildren were more likely to positively stereotype their grandparents (Pecchioni & Croghan, 2002). Furthermore, Anderson, Harwood, and Hummert (in press) concluded that age stereotyping, relational closeness, and reciprocal self-disclosure influence age-adapted communication behaviors (e.g., patronizing communication, under- and overaccommodation: Kemper & Harden, 1999) of young adult grandchildren with their grandparents and older adult acquaintances.

A prominent communicative act associated with older adults is storytelling (Ryan, Kwong See, Meneer, & Trovato, 1994). Nussbaum and Bettini (1994) showed that grandfathers and grandmothers have rather different storytelling styles. Grandfathers tended to discuss historical issues (e.g., the war) and health issues. Grandmothers, on the other hand, talked more about relationships and family history. However, grandchildren rarely tell stories to their grandparents. They had a difficult time doing so, perhaps revealing the broader issue of who has "license" to tell stories (those with experience) and also stereotypes of communication style (old people are good storytellers: Kemper, Kynette, Rash, O'Brien, & Sprott, 1989). More broadly, this storytelling role is probably indicative of a function that grandparents play in terms of mentoring (King & Elder, 1997) and transmitting family and cultural identity (Langellier, 2002).

Taking a communication accommodation theory perspective to examine adaptive communication behavior, Harwood (2000b) and Lin and Harwood (2003) have demonstrated that a variety of accommodative behaviors are associated with solidarity in the relationship. For instance, underaccommodation (i.e., paying insufficient attention to the other's conversational needs) and overaccommodation (i.e., overcompensating based on perceived stereotypes of aging, patronizing) are associated with lower levels of relational solidarity. Accommodating the other and feeling accommodated are both positive predictors of solidarity.

Types of communication media used in the relationship were found to affect quality of grandparent-grandchild relationship (Harwood, 2000a). Frequency of telephone communication appeared to be associated with more satisfying relationships (more so than face-to-face or written communication). Recent work by Holladay and Seipke (2003) shows that communication using e-mail is also relatively frequent in the grandparent-grandchild relationship and that it also predicts overall satisfaction and closeness in the relationship.

Age Salience

Age-related adaptive communication behavior may be a function of age salience. Age salience refers to the extent to which age-based distinctions (i.e., younger vs. older adult) pervade the interactions between the grandparent and grandchild—it is the degree to which the participants are mutually aware of, and acting in terms of, their respective age group memberships. Preliminary findings have shown that grandparent-grandchild relationships in which age is salient tend to be less positive than ones in which age is not important (Harwood, Hewstone, Paolini, & Voci, 2005). That is, when one or both parties are conscious of the age difference during their interactions, the interaction experience is less likely to be considered positive. Given that age salience has negative consequences, it is worth understanding its predictors.

Soliz (2004) found that over- and underaccommodative communication styles are both structurally linked to age salience. Under- and overaccommodative communication styles have emerged elsewhere as "intergroup" communication strategies. Hence, it is theoretically sensible that they emerge as predicting the salience of groups in a relational setting—in this case, age-group differences. Harwood, Raman, and Hewstone (2004) have taken a more exploratory approach to uncovering the communicative phenomena triggering age salience. These behaviors include talking about the past and storytelling, expressing lack of understanding of the world today, patronizing the grandchild, and dispensing wisdom. Many of these phenomena are also associated with negative evaluations of the relationship (see also Garrett & Williams, 2004), and the positive behaviors (e.g., storytelling, demonstrating wisdom) actually displayed very inconsistent relationships to age salience in Harwood et al.'s findings.

The issue of age salience takes on additional importance when considered in the context of ageism. Considerable research has examined associations between grandchildren's contact with their grandparents and ageist attitudes. As noted by Williams and Nussbaum (2001), "many of our general conceptions of growing old and of what it may be like to be old are formed with reference to our relationships with our grandparents" (p. 168). Grandparent-grandchild contact often satisfies various "facilitating conditions" that have been described in the literature on intergroup contact (e.g., contact in a long-term relationship, institutionally supported, noncompetitive: Allport, 1954). Hence, it is not surprising that some studies find positive attitudes toward aging resulting from positive grandparent contact (e.g., Soliz & Harwood, 2003). In explicitly communication-related work in this area, Tam, Hewstone, Harwood, and Voci (2004) demonstrated that self-disclosure in the grandparent-grandchild relationship may be particularly important in influencing attitudes concerning aging—grandchildren who experienced more reciprocal self-disclosure in conversations with their grandparents also tended to have more positive attitudes about aging. Negativity or unfamiliarity with the outgroup may be reduced through such experiences. However, not all research demonstrates clear associations between grandparent contact and attitudes toward aging.

Recent work suggests that age salience may moderate the association between grandparent contact and ageist attitudes. Harwood et al. (2005) and Soliz (2004) demonstrate that for grandchildren who score high on a measure of age salience in interactions with their grandparents, there is a strong association between their feelings for their grandparent and their attitudes about older adults. In contrast, for grandchildren who see age as less central to the grandparent relationship, there is very little association between feelings in the relationship and feelings about older people. In other words, the grandparent-grandchild relationship only influences attitudes concerning aging when there is a clear cognitive connection made between the grandparent and the category "older people." Interestingly, this leads to the conclusion that age salience is beneficial, whereas the research mentioned above indicated that it could be harmful. The paradoxical effects of age salience as beneficial to attitude generalization, but harmful to intimacy and satisfaction, deserve more attention. On one hand, age salience is associated with negative evaluation of the grandparent-grandchild relationship; on the other hand, age salience is a prerequisite for a connection between grandparent contact and attitudes toward aging. These findings illustrate one way in which the study of grandparenting illuminates more general theoretical concerns. The paradoxical effects of group salience have been shown in other intergroup research but never in the context of a personal relationship.

In the previous sections, we have aimed to summarize the research on grandparent-grandchild relationships with a particular emphasis on communication in this relationship. The following discussion will address additional directions for research central to broadening our understanding of this family relationship.

What's Left to Learn About the Grandparent-Grandchild Relationship?

There are three broad thematic thrusts that we see as crucial to the future development of this area: culture, technology, and identity. Given space limitations, we will briefly discuss each in the context of key theoretical frameworks and important methodological considerations. We hope to spark students' and researchers' interests in exploring these areas further.

Culture

More attention should be given to the cultural values that dictate how a person relates to his or her family members. Three areas associated with culture should be addressed in future research. First, greater attention needs to be paid to minority grandparents in the United States (Kamo, 1998). The majority of grandparent research either ignores cultural variations in grandparenting or problematically emphasizes social and family *problems* related to these variations (Szinovacz, 1998). More attention needs to be paid to how grandparenting among minorities may differ from mainstream conceptions, while at the same time accounting for variations *within* ethnic groups.

Second, we see a need for research on the influence of acculturation on the grandparent-grandchild relationship. Families of immigrants may encounter barriers as younger generations become acculturated to the mainstream culture. However, grandparents may also serve as a connection to the grandchild's cultural heritage (Pettys & Balgopal, 1998). An important communication factor related to acculturation is language and the extent to which grandparents and grandchildren are fluent in the same language. Research on Mexican American families (Silverstein & Chen, 1999) and Chinese families in New Zealand (Ng & He, 2004) suggest that language barriers can negatively influence the quality of the grandparent-grandchild relationship. In this sense, the grandparent-grandchild relationship may be especially prone to cultural gaps, which can have a negative influence on the quality of the relationship (Silverstein & Chen, 1999). Language proficiency plays a unique role in this relationship, and further research should address the ways in which family members overcome this barrier.

Finally, research should continue to examine grandparent-grandchild relationships in countries other than the United States. For instance, reciprocal responsibility and connection within families are emphasized more in collectivistic cultures than individualistic cultures (e.g., Kim, 1994). Collectivists follow different social rules and norms when interacting with family and non-family members (Gao, 1996). Xuan and Rice (2000) showed that Vietnamese grandparents expressed distinct differences regarding grandparents' roles and authority in traditional Vietnamese culture and Australian culture. In addition, in non-U.S. cultures, grandparents and grandchildren may enact different functions depending on familial lineage (e.g., Sangree, 1992). For instance, paternal grandparents may be considered as a more appropriate substitute for child caregiving than maternal grandparents as a result of strong patrilineal family structure (Chen, Short, & Entwisle, 2000). Hence, cultural variation within and outside of the United States is a notable factor to consider in further investigation of this family relationship.

Technology

Another relatively unexplored area for research is the influence of new technology on communication patterns and relationship building between grandparents and grandchildren. The Internet has shown potential for connecting friends and family by providing an opportunity for people to engage in communication across geographical boundaries and time zones (Pew, 2000). In the U.S., adults over 65 are one of the fastest-growing groups of Internet users, showing a 43% increase in usage since 1994 (Adler, 2001; Wright, 2000). Older adults' use of the Internet has begun to receive attention with regard to social relationships, well-being, and social support (Lin, Hummert, & Harwood, 2004). As well-educated and computer-literate baby boomers enter older adulthood, we anticipate a growth in older adults' use of computers to sustain relationships with their geographically distant children and grandchildren (Harwood, 2004). Furthermore, this use of technology may provide opportunities for in-depth disclosure and affection, as well as change perceptions of older people (e.g., as more "up-to-date"). Further work should examine such effects.

Identity

Social identity theorizing suggests that self-perception is, in part, a reflection of the social groups one identifies with and the evaluative and affective dimensions associated with this identification (Tajfel & Turner, 1986). Brewer (2000) points out that individuals may operate on various levels of group inclusion and exclusion, and we feel this notion is especially apt for understanding grandparenting in that there are various levels of identity for grandparents. Grandparents may identify with an older adult age group or be categorized by others as an older adult. Since ageist attitudes are present in society, there are some negative implications associated with this age group categorization, including diminished quality of relationship with younger adults (Kite & Johnson, 1988). However, unlike non-family older adults, grandparents may possess a shared family identity with grandchildren, which may ameliorate some of the negative effects of age salience, given the overall positive social representations of grandparents and grandparenting. The identity complexities here, though, are drawn out by Harwood (2004), who notes the distinctions between identifying as a grandparent in terms of role identity (a position in the family) versus social identity (a shared group membership with other grandparents). The complexities associated with communicating such varied identities, intersections of different meanings of "grandparent," and the varied evaluative and affective dimension of grandparent identities are significant areas for further research.

Theoretical Explanations

When focusing on any family relationship, it is important to consider theoretical perspectives that may guide research on the relationship *within* the family context. Obviously, any of the theoretical approaches to family communication could guide research on the grandparent-grandchild relationship. However, one unique characteristic of the grandparent-grandchild relationship is the significant age difference between the two family members in a society where old age is not highly praised. As previously discussed, this age difference may serve as a barrier to intimate and satisfying grandparent-grandchild relationships. Although age may be the most notable group distinction between the grandparent and grandchild, other group differences (e.g., cultural, religious) may influence communication in this relationship. The following discussion highlights two theoretical perspectives, Communication Accommodation Theory (CAT: Shepard, Giles, & Le Poire, 2001) and the Common Ingroup Identity Model (Gaertner & Dovidio, 2000) that are particularly well-suited to examining relationships that cross social group lines.

As discussed earlier in this chapter, preliminary examination of grandparent-grandchild relationships from a CAT perspective has revealed some positive and negative associations between specific communicative behaviors and grandparent-grandchild relational solidarity (Harwood, 2000b). Three issues can be considered for future research grounded in this approach. First, a CAT perspective draws attention to the dynamics of communication. Future work should consider not just static evaluations of communication in the relationship but also the ongoing interactive dynamics. For instance, discovering shifts in accommodative behavior associated with topics (e.g., grandchild under accommodation when issues of school achievement are raised) would provide considerably more sophisticated understanding of grandparent-grandchild communication than we currently have.

Second, examining connections between grandparents' and grandchildren's motives for various accommodation behaviors and actual behavior is important. As noted earlier, multiple identities may be salient in this relationship (age, family, role, etc.), and behaviors may be tailored to emphasize one more than another in particular contexts to achieve specific relationship goals. CAT provides a framework with which to examine fluctuations in such identities and the communicative manifestations of such changes. Third, a CAT perspective links communication to other important structural, relational, or cultural variables. For instance, the grandparenting styles identified by Cherlin and Furstenberg (1986) might well be associated with specific communication accommodation behaviors. Finally, particular CAT strategies in different cultural contexts may be evaluated differently and may be perceived as more useful or detrimental in establishing close and intimate relationships (Lin & Harwood, 2003).

Gaertner and Dovidio's (2000) Common Ingroup Identity Model (CIIM) highlights the manner in which *intergroup* interactions, typically associated with negative characteristics, can be (re)conceptualized as *intra*group by focusing on a shared identity, which often yields more positive effects in the interaction. In one sense, the grandparent and grandchild are members of separate social groups (i.e., young and older adults). However, as discussed earlier, grandparent and grandchild also share a common ingroup identity (i.e., family). Hence, the CIIM provides a framework for understanding how ingroup and outgroup distinctions may operate within this relationship. Research should investigate what communicative behaviors are associated with marking intra- versus intergroup boundaries in this relationship (and the work described earlier on age salience fulfills a part of this mandate). Although much of the research utilizing the CIIM has investigated non-family interaction, recent work has illustrated its usefulness for examining family dynamics (Soliz, 2004).

Ways of Study

When discussing this family relationship, it is important to remember that a grandchild will most likely have multiple grandparent relationships. Including stepgrandparents and great-grandparents, our recent research indicates that adults aged 18–25 have an average of 3–4 grandparents still living, and many have more. Hence, research examining only one relationship does not capture the full experience of being a grandchild. We would advocate more work examining multiple grandparent relationships simultaneously (e.g., Soliz & Harwood, 2003). In a complementary fashion, we would also encourage work that considers the entire family, not just the grandparent-grandchild dyad (e.g., Ng & He, 2004). Grandparent and grandchild roles may be modified dramatically depending upon the presence of other parties (siblings, other grandparents, the middle generation) in the conversation.

Conclusion

In close grandparent-grandchild relationships, grandparents are more likely to be socially involved, have good mental health, and to have a sense of pride in their grandchildren (Lin & Harwood, 2003). Grandchildren in such relationships are more likely to engage in activities with their grandparents, see benefits to spending time with their grandparents, be influenced by their grandparents' values and beliefs, and have positive attitudes toward their own aging. Therefore, it is important for communication scholars to understand how the challenges of intergenerational communication between grandparents and grandchildren can be overcome and positive grandparent-grandchild relationships, which are mutually beneficial to young and older adults, can be established. The relationship also offers intriguing theoretical challenges to family communication scholars and others in the field.

5

The "Other" Women in Family Life

Aunt/Niece/Nephew Communication

Patricia J. Sotirin and Laura L. Ellingson

Aunts are familiar characters in personal and popular family dramas. They may be beloved or reviled, intimately close or aloof and distant, central in family networks or rarely seen outliers, related by blood or legal ties, or unrelated except by friendship. These rich variations coupled with the gendered identity of the aunt role makes the aunt/niece/nephew relationship, or the aunting relationship as we refer to it, a rich and fascinating focus for scholarly study. Yet there has been little systematic analysis of the meanings or communicative practices that make up the aunting relationship. In this chapter, we encourage research into the aunting relationship for several reasons.

First, knowing more about aunting relationships promises to enrich our understanding of the alternative forms that familial and kinship bonds might take. As Traeder and Bennett point out in their popular tribute *Aunties: Our Older, Cooler, Wiser Friends* (1998), aunts are critical cultural resources whose contributions to childrearing, family support, self-development, relational knowledge, and kinship are both invaluable and overlooked. Second, studying aunting relationships contributes to more expansive and explicitly communicative understandings of self-with-other, family life, and community relations. Indeed, given the diverse ways in which aunting relationships are realized, the study of aunting takes up the call to understand families less as biologically, legally, or even affectively circumscribed units and more as communicatively defined and negotiated relationships, responsive to emotional, temporal, and cultural contexts (Jorgenson, 1989). Third, taking the aunt/niece/nephew relationship as a focus unsettles the dominance of parental figures in research on family and childhood communication. This may be especially important given the postmodern conditions shaping contemporary family life in which alternative family forms and nonparental relations of authority and responsibility have become, if not more prevalent, then more visible (Kirby, Golden, Medved, Jorgenson, & Buzzanell, 2003).

Finally, given that aunts are paradigmatically female, a focus on the aunting relationship also attends to processes of gendering and gendered identities and draws attention to the pernicious sexism that continues to color conceptions of familial roles and kinship relations. Taken together, these reasons warrant turning scholarly attention to the aunting relationship. In this chapter, we explore the nature of aunting and report on original research into the communication patterns of aunt/niece/nephew relationships.

The Title of "Aunt"

Seemingly, the title of aunt marks a straightforward familial or kinship relationship: an aunt is the sister of a parent or the woman married to a parent's sibling. Yet, limiting the definition of aunt to a location within a biologically or legally circumscribed network fails to acknowledge the ways this title designates cultural and affective relationships that expand the bonds of kinship beyond genealogical relations. The title "aunt" is also a cultural label that transcends the biological and legal definitions of family or kinship: my grandmother's sisters, an elderly female friend, a female mentor, a neighborhood woman, a female church member—all may be known as "aunt." In addition, bestowing the title "aunt" on a chosen person inducts that person into one's kinship network as an honorary member (Stack, 1974).

Cultures vary in the rules or standards for determining who counts as kin, in the rights and responsibilities accorded to various types of kin, and the degree to which kinship association is voluntary (Wellman, 1998). For example, the auntie in many Asian American or Hawaiian communities may be a title of respect for an elderly female regardless of kinship ties. In gay communities, referring to someone as "auntie" may indicate an intimate relationship, a mentoring relationship, or announce a familial bond among biologically unrelated men. An aunting relationship in contemporary mainstream U.S. culture affords considerable latitude for personal choice as to the rules, rights, responsibilities, and intensity of the bonds between an aunt and niece or nephew. Such latitude casts the aunt in a distinct yet ambiguous role whose only stable feature is a feminine gendered identity.

Aunting in Family Communication Research

There are no communication studies of the aunt relationship per se. Nonetheless, research in family communication suggests several potentially rich lines of inquiry into the importance of aunting relationships in family networks and the prevalence and content of communication in those relationships.

The Aunting Relationship in Family Networks

One line of research that invites research into the importance and prevalence of aunting relationships is the research on "kinkeepers" or those family members who take on the major roles for maintaining family support networks (cf. Gerstel & Gallagher, 1993). Women are the primary kinkeepers in extended families. It is women who remember birthdays, conduct holiday gatherings, and maintain communication across time and distances among relatives and friends (Dill, 1998). We find an indication that aunts may act as kinkeepers in Rosenthal's (1985) study of the kinkeeper role. She found that 52% of families reported having someone in the role of kinkeeper, and of those, 72% identified this person as a woman sibling, suggesting that these kinkeepers may be aunts as well, especially if the respondent was a parent. While the percentages in Rosenthal's study are not high, they do indicate that aunts may play a family kinkeeping role, a possibility that bears further investigation more directly focused on aunts. Similarly, in a study drawing on college students, Leach and Braithwaite (1996) found that among their respondents who indicated the presence of a family kinkeeper, 84% identified that person as a woman. Of these, 51% identified the woman as their mother, but the next largest percentage (9.8%) named an aunt. Again, this is not a large percentage, but the findings do offer direct evidence of the aunt's role as family kinkeeper. Given that one person's mother may be another's aunt, these findings, along with Rosenthal's study, invite further research into the aunt's role as a kinkeeper in extended family networks.

Two other types of kinship studies in which aunts appear are studies of kinship foster care and kinship networks among new immigrants. Studies of kinship foster care show that aunts are second only to grandmothers in numbers of kin who function voluntarily (although in increasingly regulated and, in some states, compensated roles) as foster caregivers caring for children in their extended family who have been removed from the parents' custody (Davidson, 1997). Another line of research that has identified aunting as an important caregiving relationship explores the importance of kinship networks for immigrants needing financial and social support in their new communities. For example, aunts feature prominently in the narratives of Mexican migrant women who depend on their relationships as and among aunts, or *tías,* to manage childcare and domestic responsibilities as well as locate job and housing opportunities (Bastida, 2001). Ethnographies of new immigrant families attest to the importance of aunting relationships in maintaining transnational family connections among Korean immigrant families in New York (Min, 1998) and in the routines of daily family life among the Hmong in Wisconsin (Koltyk, 1998). While aunting relationships are not the focus of these studies, the presence of the aunt in extended kinship networks is of taken-for-granted significance in the experiences of new immigrant families.

Prevalence of Communication in the Aunting Relationship

The prevalence of communication in the aunt/niece/nephew relationship varies widely. While some aunts and nieces or nephews may communicate frequently, it is not unusual for little or no regular contact to exist between an aunt and a niece or nephew. Amount of contact may be affected by the ages of the aunts and their nieces or nephews. When children are small, contact may be mediated by a parent. As children age, their contact with both family-related and honorary aunts may change. In addition to age, the amount and value of communication between an aunt and a niece or nephew varies culturally. For example, in Latino family cycles, the *tía* may be expected to interact frequently and in significant ways with a niece or nephew regardless of their ages (Sault, 2001). Hence, the prevalence of communication across aunt/niece/nephew relationships must be understood on a continuum from no communication to frequent and intense interaction.

Research on communication among adult siblings and their spouses implicitly taps communication with and by aunts when the focus is on women as sisters. Given that sibling relationships among parents affect children's perceptions of their relatives, aunts who are emotionally close to a child's parents may be perceived as more integral in the child's experiences of family life (Wellman, 1998). At the same time, Troll (1985) points out that conflicts among adult siblings obligate husbands and wives to distance themselves from their siblings, and such "family feuds" negatively impact relationships with extended family members like aunts. Sachs (1999) found that such family feuds obstruct information sharing among close kin, even of critical health-related information about genetic risks like family propensities for cancer. One woman reported that her maternal aunt was adamantly opposed to sharing the news of their genetic risk for breast cancer with children in the extended family although her brother's wife, another aunt in this family network, wanted to share the news immediately. Given her maternal aunt's reaction, this woman chose not to continue passing the information to family members.

On the other hand, adult sisters who may have gone separate ways often become closer as they begin to follow parallel paths in life (marriage, children), providing material and emotional support for each other and renewing familial bonds (Arliss, 1994). Cicirelli and Nussbaum (1989) suggest that the association of women with feminine nurturing and expressiveness leads family members to turn to their sisters for support and aid as adults. This observation implies both the likelihood that aunts will be closer to their nieces and nephews if aunts and mothers find themselves on parallel life paths and that aunts may provide emotional and material support not only for their sisters and other adult family members but for their nieces and nephews as well. While there is no scholarly research that directly supports this assumption, recent trade books on aunting strongly endorse the aunt's role in providing multiple forms of support to nieces and nephews (Sturgis, 2004).

Content of Communication in Aunting Relationships

Family communication research suggests a number of issues that characterize the content of family communication. Although none of these studies has explicitly addressed aunting relationships, we find several promising directions for research on aunting. For example, Koerner and Fitzpatrick (2002) advance a transactional theory of relational schemas for understanding how people conduct family relationships. Relational schemas contain both experience-specific knowledge and culturally prescribed ideals and scripts that are drawn on for engaging in family interactions. Koerner and Fitzpatrick argue that family relationship schema include beliefs about intimacy (trust, respect, love, and affection), individuality (including independence and equity), external factors (such as personal security or children's rights), conversation orientation, and conformity orientation (pp. 84, 88). It seems reasonable to assume that these schema also apply to aunting relationships, especially given the ambiguity and variability of the aunting relationship.

The concept of family scripts usefully complements the theory of family relationship schema. Family scripts "are mental representations that guide the role performance of family members within and across contexts" (Stack & Burton, 1998, p. 408). Stack and Burton proposed that enactments of extended kin relationships like aunting are guided by "kinscripts," which designate within a particular network who is obligated or entitled to perform types of tasks (kin-work), when such tasks should be done (kin-time), and how the process of assigning kin-work should be handled (kin-scription) (Stack & Burton, 1998).

Research on family narratives is also pertinent to communication in aunting relationships (Wilmot, 1995). Aunts often figure prominently in family stories and as family storytellers (Romberger, 1986). This may be because family culture and lore are preserved and promulgated primarily by women (Stone, 2000). Stone holds that family stories define the family, providing rules for its enactment, identities for its members, and a shared memory and view of the family and the world.

Taken together, these lines of family communication research suggest directions for research on communication in aunting relationships. Our own research draws on this work in family communication to explore communication among aunts, nieces, and nephews. We contend that aunting communication is an important aspect of family and childhood experience; subject to considerable variation; guided by cultural, familial, and autobiographical rules and traditions; and beset by issues of intimacy, obligation, circumstance, and ambiguity.

Themes and Schemas of Aunting Relationships

We have conducted original research into the themes and schemas that characterize communication in aunting relationships within contemporary U.S. families. In one study (Ellingson & Sotirin, in press), we conducted a thematic analysis of written narratives about aunts collected from 70 students in three universities. The analysis identified themes about the role of the aunt—teacher, role model, confidante, savvy peer, and second mother—and themes about practices of aunting—maintaining family connections, encouragement, and nonengagement. These themes are similar to the activities that women kinkeepers engage in, but there is clearly an affective intensity and a sense of personal connection that is missing in reports of kinkeeping. While some students reported that they had little contact with their aunts, most characterized their relationships with their aunts in highly positive and emotionally invested terms. We concluded that the aunting relationship has important personal significance beyond the role an aunt might play as a kinkeeper.

In another study, we explored cultural schemas on aunting by identifying aunt figures and aunting scripts in popular media portrayals (Sotirin & Ellingson, 2004). While media portrayals are admittedly fictional, we hold that these portrayals contribute to the cultural schemas people draw on to guide their aunting relationships. Hoover, Clark, and Alters (2004) have shown that families reflexively engage the images of kinship relationships in popular media, negotiating their own beliefs and behaviors in relation to these schemas. We found that while media portrayals often cast aunts as caregiving, they also show that aunts may deviate from conventions of maternality, domesticity, social propriety, or femininity without the social condemnation reserved for deviant mothers. Popular schemas of aunting relationships thus serve to legitimate deviations from the mother-child caregiving relationship and set up aunts as alternative female mentors and role models.

Based on our findings, we highlight two critical dimensions of aunting relationships: variability and choice. First, being an aunt is uniquely varied; there are many socially approved ways to enact aunting. Unlike motherhood, a role that is seemingly trapped in contradictory tensions too often experienced as oppressive and restrictive (Hays, 1996), the aunt has multiple options: she can breeze in for quick visits, live far away, be a nurturing "second mother," or maintain only a distant relationship with nieces and nephews without necessarily being a "good" or a "bad" aunt. In addition, variability characterizes the aunting relationship over time as both aunts and their nieces and nephews experience life changes. The aunting relationship may change dramatically as nieces and nephews become adults.

Second, aunting relationships are defined by choice in that the choice of how to enact aunting is not only acceptable but expected—even required. One must choose how to enact aunt, niece, and nephew roles because there are no singular definitions. One implication is that aunting offers family scholars, educators, and counselors working against repressive gender roles a valuable resource with which to encourage relational patterns that embrace multiplicity and variability and that affirm choice.

Descriptions and Dialectics of Aunting Relationships

The study we report here was conducted as an initial inquiry into aunting relationships. In this study, we asked participants to write brief descriptions of their relationships with aunts. Our goal was to address the aunting relationship directly to find out how people represent this relationship. Two questions guided our research:

RQ1: How do nieces and nephews describe their aunting relationships?

RQ2: How are the primary relational dialectics expressed in niece and nephew descriptions of their aunting relationships?

Method

Our data consist of responses written during 2001 to 2003 by undergraduate students enrolled in communication courses in a private university on the U.S. west coast, a public university in the northern midwest, and a public university in the southeast. The project began when Ellingson had 20 students write responses to the prompt, "Tell me about your aunt" as part of an in-class activity. Intrigued by these preliminary responses, we obtained human subject board approval to formally solicit student narratives for analysis. The informal responses were not included in our data set. However, we did read and discuss them, and hence they may have influenced our expectations when we analyzed the data.

Students in four courses were offered extra credit points to write a brief (typed) narrative in response to the statement, "Please describe communicating with one or more of your aunts." Given the exploratory nature of this study, we consciously left the parameters of the response open to participants by phrasing the prompt very broadly. Participants were also asked to provide their age, sex, and ethnic or racial group. Responses were written outside of class at participants' convenience over a one- to two-week span and returned to the course instructor.

In total, 70 responses were collected, ranging in length from slightly less than one doubled-spaced page to four pages, with an average length of about two pages, for a total of 154 pages of data. Our sample consisted of students who ranged in age from 18 to 27, with the vast majority being traditional undergraduates between 20 and 22 years of age: the median age was 21, and the mean was 21.07 years, with two students not reporting their ages. Participants reported their ethnicity as follows: 51 identified as European American or white, four as Latino/a, four as African American, seven as Asian American, and one each as Kurdish, biracial African American and white, Guyanese-East Indian, and Ecuadorian-Romanian. Our data were skewed in gender representation: 52 were female and 18 were male. The disparity in gender participation was largely due to the underrepresentation of males in the communication courses from which participants were drawn. Nonetheless, participation by women and men was roughly proportional to the number of each sex in the courses. Like-wise, European Americans are overrepresented and students of color make up 27% of our sample, such that our findings reflect predominantly European American perspectives. While we acknowledge the limitations of our sample, we also endeavored to draw examples for our analysis from as wide a range of participants as possible.

Data Analysis

We conducted an interpretive analysis of these data. As Leach and Braithwaite (1996) explained in their study on kinkeeping, "the goal of interpretive work is the identification of recurring patterns of behavior and meanings" (p. 207). To identify such patterns, Lindlof and Taylor (2002) advise adopting interpretive "tropes" or semiotic devices for deciphering the patterns or lived codes that invest experience with meaning. Following our research questions, we adopted two tropes: descriptive strategies and dialectic tensions. Using these tropes as a lens, we repeatedly read through our data to detect emergent patterns.

For the first question, "How do nieces and nephews describe their aunt-ing relationships?" we focused on the descriptive strategies students used to organize their narratives. That is, we sought to uncover patterns in *how* stories about aunts are told by their nieces and nephews. For the second question, "How are the primary relational dialectics expressed in niece/nephew descriptions of their aunting relationships?" we focused on the dialectic tensions of aunting relationships, drawing on the dialectic theory of interpersonal relationships (Baxter & Montgomery, 1996). In particular, we focused on those tensions that Wood (2000) argued are the primary dialectics in interpersonal (nuclear family or dating/marriage) relationships: autonomy/connection; openness/privacy; novelty/predictability; and stability/change. While we did not ask students directly about relational dialectics, we correctly assumed that their descriptions of their aunts would reflect common relational tensions.

How Do Nieces and Nephews Describe Their Aunting Relationships?

We noted several patterns in the manner in which nieces or nephews wrote about their aunts: use of metaphors, proliferation of adjectives, focus on self, unreflectiveness, and identification through family connections. Rather than being content themes, these patterns show us how students described their relationships with their aunts.

Metaphors and Similes. Students frequently relied on *metaphors* and *similes* that emphasized the similarities between their relationship with their aunts and another female relationship—my aunt is "like a mother," "like a grandmother," or "like a (girl)friend." As one female student put it, "What I'm trying to say is that my aunt to me is my mom, big sister, and best friend all in one. It's great." Another said, "Auntie [name] is my Godmother, and in a lot of ways, my mother." A third woman summed up, "To me an aunt is like a mom, only they don't have to enforce the rules. They just give you guidance and direction but never have to punish you, so they always stay on your good side."

Adjectives. We noted a *proliferation of adjectives* to describe the personal qualities of aunts, particularly those associated with feminine qualities such as "nice," "sweet," and infrequently, "mean." One woman recalled, "My aunt was my idol. As a young girl . . . she represented everything I thought a woman should; [sic] beauty and femininity. In my eyes she was kind, happy . . . She was perfect." The focus on feminine qualities accords with the fact that aunts are women but suggests as well an expectation of conventional femininity.

Self Focus. We were struck by the consistent *focus on self* in students' responses—aunts were referred to as possessions ("my" aunt) and descriptions centered on what "my" aunt does for me. For example, a male student observed,

> I think the characteristic that all my aunts have is that they all think highly of me . . . They all seem to have a genuine interest in me. I think that is the great thing about aunts: they make you feel good about yourself.

Another student confided, "I love talking to [my aunt] because every time we talk she just makes you feel that she is truly interested in what you are saying." We found little mention of reciprocity, of giving back to the aunt or taking the aunt's view of things. Perhaps this was an artifact of the question we asked, but it may be that "owning" one's family and the members of it contributes to a sense of identity. Students seemed to characterize communication with their aunts in terms of themselves, their childhood experiences, and their sense of who they are and want to be.

Unreflectiveness. We also noticed a quality of *unreflectiveness* in students' descriptions of their communication with their aunts. Aunts who were particularly nurturing or fun were highly valued, but their roles did not seem to bear much scrutiny or reflection. For example, one woman student told us,

> The reason why I think my aunt is the coolest, is because she is not old fashioned at all, she is out going, loves shopping, likes to be in style with the young girls and she fits in well. I also like that she has a lot of energy to keep up with me, we would often go out on Friday and Saturday night every week, and we don't get home until 5am.

Students' responses reflected stereotypical assumptions about the role of women in the family and about family relations more generally. Relatedly, we noted a striking amount of repetition across our student responses. One implication of such repetition is that students may be drawing on a cultural schema to describe their own relationships just as Koerner and Fitzpatrick (2002) have suggested.

Family Connections. Finally, we found it intriguing that virtually all aunts—whether they were aunts by blood, marriage, or held honorary aunt status—were *identified through family connections*. In their responses, students introduced their aunts initially by designating which parent's brother, sister, or friend (in the case of honorary aunts) the aunt was, the aunt's place in a sibling birth order, her age relative to the niece or nephew's parents, to whom the aunt was married, and so on. Hence, to have an aunt is to have a relationship with someone else first—usually with parents. Thus, the aunt is the mother's sister, or the father's brother's wife, rather than simply an aunt. Even those few who described honorary aunts often prefaced their descriptions with the disclaimer, "She isn't really related to me but . . ." The pervasiveness of this manner of describing their aunts suggests the importance of situating the aunt within the extended family.

How Are the Primary Relational Dialectics Expressed in Niece and Nephew Descriptions of Their Aunting Relationships?

Autonomy/Connection. The dialectic of autonomy and connection appeared in students' descriptions of their differences from their aunts and their family connections with their aunts. For example, some respondents alluded to a divide between themselves and their aunts, whether generational or in terms of their perspectives. Others described complex webs of relations connecting them to their aunts, for example, shared family events or their shared connections to a mother or grandmother or even to the aunt's children. For example, one woman reported,

> Growing up, I spent a lot of time with two of my mother's sisters. [Aunt] had a son a year older than me, and [second aunt] had a son and a daughter close to my younger brother's age. We were all very good friends and often went on extended family outings together.

A male student recalled,

> Aunt [name] has one daughter, [name], who is my cousin. I am extremely close to [name] because we see each other every summer and we are the same age . . . When I talk to Aunt [name] all she does is express her love for me.

Student responses indicated that the tensions of the autonomy/connection dialectic are often resolved incidentally due to geographical distances, time lapses between visits, generational differences, or even the way that parents' relationships with the aunt affect the aunt's relationship with her niece(s) or nephew(s). For example, a male student explained,

> Aunt [name] lives in Alameda, right out of Oakland, so unfortunately as I was growing up I did not get many opportunities to see her, as I have been born and raised in Oregon. So as a result of this distance, my relationship with Aunt [name] is not a very close one.

Yet even though the tension between autonomy and connection can be mediated by circumstances and family structure, students' descriptions showed variation in responding to this tension. For example, some students neutralized the tension between autonomy and connection with their aunts by expressing a sense that things were not in their control—geographical distances, for example, that put the emphasis on autonomy rather than connection. Another way of dealing with the dialectic was to prioritize autonomy and disconnectedness. For example, one student observed, "I have no aunts on my father's side and one aunt on my mother's side whom I've never met because my whole family hates her." In contrast, other students appeared to prioritize their connections with their aunts, seeking their aunts out and emphasizing relational closeness.

Openness/Privacy. The dialectic of openness/privacy was quite clearly evidenced in accounts of the aunt as a confidante and savvy peer and, in a contrasting way, as someone to be avoided. We asked students to focus on their communication with their aunts, so it is not surprising that this dialectic tension is evident in our data. In many of the responses, students implied that they prioritized either openness—placing value on talking with or confiding in their aunt—or privacy—whether this was enacted as talking only about superficial and "boring" topics or avoiding the aunt altogether. A woman student told us,

> I can trust her with my problems—that she'll be empathetic, loving, kind, non-judgmental, and usually positive about whatever I'm dealing with . . . not only will she be wonderful at providing wisdom . . . but she'll also call it like she sees it, whether she thinks I'll like hearing it or not. She's honest.

Another woman said, "Oh, and if I need someone to talk to about taboo issues that my mom would slip into cardiac arrest over, I call auntie [name]." But we also received comments like this one from a third woman student:

> We tend to discuss more general, "safe" topics rather than anything deeply personal. This is probably because I don't feel all that close to her and I don't particularly want her advice, as her life is not really a role model for mine.

Keeping conversational topics "safe" as a strategy for maintaining privacy contrasts with other students' emphasis on opening up conversations with their aunts to taboo issues. Overall, our analysis suggests that students and their aunts must negotiate the dialectic of openness/privacy.

Novelty/Predictability. This dialectic was less evident in our data, although students often unreflectively assumed that their aunt would enact certain relational roles. The repeated occurrence of such assumptions suggests that students expected and enacted a sense of predictability in their relationships with aunts. For example, students expected their aunts to be at family gatherings, especially during holidays. As one woman explained, "The only time I ever really see [my aunts] is during the winter holidays, and then only for short periods of time." Another aspect of predictability was the expectation that aunts would indulge their nieces and nephews and remember them on birthdays and other important events. One woman recalled, "Aunt [name] has always made an effort to honor my birthday and other holidays with gifts, homemade cards, and homemade cookies." Another woman emphasized the predictability of her aunt's indulgences:

> [Aunt] often took us out to the movies or out to dinner . . . and shopping for toys. We went to Lake Tahoe every summer together. She would cook for us every night and let us eat junk food on the beach.

Novelty seemed to take a back seat to predictability in students' descriptions as even the surprise of treats and gifts was expected.

Stability/Change. While there is a certain kind of stability to a familial relationship like an aunt relationship, change was an inherent aspect of our data given that our student respondents were in a transition period in their own lives. Many of their responses addressed the passage from childhood to adulthood and the attendant shifts in their relationships with their aunts. For example, one woman observed,

> It was only about a year ago that I went to a family gathering for my grandma's birthday. This was the first one I had gone to in a few years and it was certainly weird seeing all my relatives again. I got to talk to my aunt again and amazingly, we had a great conversation.

Many students commented on such age-related changes. Some noted that as children they had either not known or even disliked their aunt, but as they became adults, the aunting relationship had either become more comfortable and friendly or more remote and unimportant in their daily lives. For instance, one woman observed, "As I have gotten older, it seems our relationships have moved past doing activities and onto more meaningful conversations." Another woman emphasized the importance of change in her relationships with her aunts: "I am grown up now, and I realize that I have the power to change my relationship with my aunts. I do not have to wait for them to call or write me, I can contact them." Here the element of choice in an aunting relationship is experienced by the niece as empowering, a sign that her relationship with her aunts has changed from a child/adult relationship to an adult/adult relationship.

Finally, some students neutralized the stability/change dialectic by finding stability in the changing forms of their relationships with their aunts. Several students observed that their aunts had become more like friends. For example, one woman related that her aunts had taken care of her as a child,

> However, as I got older, [my aunts] become more like my peers than a mother figure, which probably stems from the fact that they no longer have to keep discipline or worry about my safety.

The assurance of affection or at least of an ongoing connection appears to mediate the changing nature of the aunting relationship.

Mediating Primary Tensions

Our student data indicate that the primary dialectics of interpersonal relationships riddle the socioemotional experience of aunting and that students and their aunts enacted a variety of strategies for mediating these tensions. In addition, we found that aunting can be a mediating agency in managing dialectical tensions in other family relationships (parental, sibling, spouse, or significant other). Baxter (1993) identified four forms of response to dialectic tensions: prioritizing, neutralizing, transcending, and reframing. An aunting relationship may enact any of these in response to the challenges of dialectic tensions felt in other relationships. For example, Wood (2002) described how being an aunt has helped balance the dialectic of seriousness/playfulness in her marriage. In playing with her nieces and nephews, she and her husband recognized that they had prioritized the serious aspects of their lives together and they began to be more playful with each other, balancing this tension rather than resolving it in favor of seriousness.

Similarly, our students' narratives credited their relationships with their aunts for mediating the tensions in their family relationships in a number of ways. For example, the dialectic of connection/autonomy becomes more critical when children leave their families to go to college, and this tension can become particularly difficult for parents and college-aged children to negotiate. The students' descriptions of their aunts implicitly mediated this tension by emphasizing family connections both because students had to locate themselves in an extended family configuration when naming their aunts and in the affection or respect students expressed for their aunts. Our student narratives also described ways in which aunts helped them to reframe the tensions of their relationships with parents. Sometimes an aunt helped a niece or nephew take a different perspective by offering sage counsel or a sympathetic ear, as when a female student admitted, "I often talk to [my aunt] about problems that I have with my parents. She listens and offers a different perspective." In a few cases, an aunt literally provided a different place from which to view their problems with parents by offering their niece or nephew a refuge or second home, as in the case of a woman student who told us,

> I lived with Aunt [name] and her two children (my cousins) for a short period in high school when I wasn't getting along with my parents. . . . This was an important time in our relationship because we both agree that a whole lot of bonding went on during that period.

In a variety of ways, some implicit and others quite dramatic, aunting relationships may enact strategies for mediating the relational tensions of family life.

Communicative Strengths and Challenges

The unique communicative strengths and challenges of the aunting relationship have not been extensively examined. But our research on aunting suggests that there are important strengths and serious issues that attend the communicative interactions of aunt/niece/nephew relationships.

One issue that is both a strength and a challenge is the flexibility and adaptability of the aunting relationship. After all, one does not have to be a blood relative to be designated an aunt, and there is tremendous variation on what makes a "good" aunt. While this means that there is considerable latitude available for negotiating rules and identities, it also means that there is considerable ambiguity. For example, kinscripts from which to pattern aunt/niece/nephew communication may be sketchy and rules of negotiation unclear. Hence, uncertainty as to how to do aunt/niece/nephew communication may be high. Further, given that this relationship may change over time as participants become older and family configurations and expectations change, the ambiguity and uncertainty characterizing aunting communication may be ongoing.

One kinscript that appears frequently in reference to aunts is the maternal kinscript, to wit, "my aunt is like my mother." Aunts are often cast as maternal substitutes, taking the place of an absent mother or serving as mentors, caretakers, and teachers. Yet there remain significant differences between mothering and aunting even when the aunt is playing a maternal role. For example, having multiple aunts simultaneously is quite commonplace and unremarkable whereas having multiple mothers simultaneously is not. Further, the aunt relationship is often engaged more intermittently, serendipitously, and in response to immediate exigencies than the mother relationship. In this sense, the aunting relationship may offer more flexibility, responsiveness, and tolerance for difference than the mothering relationship. More research is needed to unravel the relations of care and connection that distinguish aunting from mothering.

Another communicative strength and challenge arises from the fact that the aunt relationship entails choice. The amount and intensity of contact and connection are often matters of choice—one may choose to be very close or to stay distant regardless of geographical separation. Unlike a mother relationship, few eyebrows will be raised in most cultures if an aunt decides not to pursue a closer relationship with her nieces and nephews. Aunts enjoy the options of extended kin: unlike nuclear family relationships, there is more cultural tolerance for neglect, disregard, and distance as well as for care, connection, and contact. One other aspect of this issue is that when aunts and their nieces and nephews are not given a choice in whether or how to conduct their relationship, the lack of choice may conflict with expectations. For example, if an aunt is conscripted into a maternal or caretaking role, she may feel resentful because the option to stay distant and disconnected is gone. Hence, the element of choice in aunting relationships is both a strength and challenge.

Issues of family solidarity and loyalty may present both strengths and challenges as well. Sibling conflict and intergenerational loyalties can create in-group/out-group tensions and coalitions that affect the aunting relationship. For example, how one's parents relate to a particular aunt (are they friendly or antagonistic?) or one's relationship with an aunt's children (are they jealous of her attentions or open to a cousin's inclusion?) may influence whether or not and how strongly one might bond with this aunt. Taken together, these communicative strengths and challenges of the aunting relationship suggest that there are plenty of research opportunities for family communication scholars.

What Is Left to Learn About Aunting?

Given the paucity of research on aunting relationships, there is much to explore. For example, how does the voluntaristic nature of aunting affect communication processes and patterns? How do issues of role ambiguity and relational adaptability affect communication in aunting relationships? In what ways do other family relationships, for example, parents' sibling relationships or in-law relationships, affect communication in aunting relationships? What significance does the age of a niece or nephew have and how do life passages affect communication among aunts and their nieces and nephews? What are the relational outcomes of aunting?

Future research should address the aunt role itself. For example, how does the aunt role differ in different family types such as nuclear, blended, single-parent, or gay/lesbian? How do women learn to be aunts and how do nieces and nephews learn their relational roles in aunting relationships? Conceptually, we have argued that relational schemas seem to guide aunting relationships, but just what the content of such schemas may be awaits further research. How are honorary aunts designated and what are the communication patterns in such relationships? Finally, gender is clearly an important dimension for further study. For example, how does the feminine/female character of the aunt shape communication expectations and practices, and are there gendered differences in the communication of aunts and nieces versus communication of aunts and nephews?

We urge future researchers to adopt a holistic approach to aunting, including aunts and their nieces and nephews in our studies rather than depending on only one member of the relationship to give us our understanding of aunting. In addition, future research must be sensitive to age-related issues and the changes in aunting relationships over time and circumstance. Processual models of this relationship might be useful as changes over time clearly affect the nature of the relational experience and the identities of the participants, separately and together.

Conclusion

The relationship between aunts and their nieces and nephews is a rich complex of affective experiences, kinship obligations, and cultural scripts that respond to the ever-changing configurations of family life and personal experience. While aunting may not incur the intense investments, responsibilities, and proximities of parent-child relationships, the aunt nonetheless is an undeniable emotional presence in kinship and family relationships and histories. The complexities and significances of this relationship offer exciting opportunities for family communication researchers.

Despite the personal significance of aunts in lived experience and the pervasiveness of aunts in family life, there has been little direct research on aunting and there may not be much more in the future unless family scholars are willing to reconsider two pernicious preoccupations: the nuclear family and the mother. First, there has been an overwhelming concentration on the nuclear family in conventional family communication research despite considerable statistical evidence that the nuclear family model lacks "ecological validity" in the face of a proliferation of family forms in contemporary U.S. society (Koerner & Fitzpatrick, 2002). Second, mothers and mothering practices and relationships are often taken both as central to family life and essential to womanhood in popular and scholarly literatures despite historical evidence that such assumptions perpetuate institutionalized gender inequities and oppressions and disadvantage or even endanger women (Rich, 1977).

We contend that neither of these preoccupations warrants overlooking the lived significance of aunting and indeed, that they seriously inhibit an expansive understanding of family communication. As we have shown, the flexibility and variability of aunting relationships hold considerable potential for addressing the exigencies of contemporary social life. But to take the lived significance of aunting seriously, we must embrace broader conceptions of familial care and connection that move us beyond the tensions and historical baggage of nuclear families and traditional mothering.

The study of aunting relationships counters the dominance in common-sense and in scholarly models of parent/child relationships as the essence of family communication. The variety of aunting relationships that are taken to be acceptable suggests that by studying aunting, we might articulate alternative models of familial care and connection. By naming the aunt as nonnuclear and using the aunt as a reference point for recognizing and reclaiming other nonnuclear relationships as valid forms, conceptions of family may be expanded. If, as Trenholm and Jensen (2000, p. 273) observe, we are undergoing a transformation in family values, roles, and characteristics and no clear model of the "modal family" has emerged, then the aunt and aunting may well be poised to contribute to these changes and emerge as a central feature of family life in the 21st century.

6

Getting Along With the In-Laws

Relationships With Parents-in-Law

Mary Claire Morr Serewicz

In December 2004, *The Jerusalem Post* reported that musician Woody Guthrie "left behind a little-known legacy of Hannuka, Holocaust, and Jewish children's songs, and the inspiration was Yiddish poet Aliza Greenblatt, his mother-in-law" (Tugend, 2004, p. 24). The article goes on to describe the relationship between Guthrie and his in-laws. When Marjorie Mazia left her Jewish husband to marry the non-Jewish Guthrie, her father, Isidore Greenblatt, refused to acknowledge the couple until their first child was born. But Aliza Greenblatt accepted her new son-in-law right away, perhaps because of their shared interests in poetry and politics. Seeing the tension his presence in the family caused between his parents-in-law, Guthrie began to study Judaism and eventually wrote a series of songs inspired by the Jewish religion and culture. Although the Greenblatts moved to Israel in the 1950s, they returned to the United States to help care for their grandchildren when Guthrie became seriously ill. The story of Woody Guthrie and the Greenblatts illustrates the complexity of the parent-in-law/child-in-law relationship and highlights the potential the relationship holds for conflict, respect, and mutual aid.

Although parent-in-law/child-in-law relationships are very common, they have received little attention from researchers. The vast majority of individuals will have a relationship with at least one parent-in-law at some point in their lives. According to 2000 U.S. census statistics, 72% of Americans age 15 and older have been married at least once (Kreider & Simmons, 2003). Based on data for median age at first marriage (U.S. Bureau of the Census, 2003b), median age of mothers at the birth of a child (National Center for Health Statistics, 2003a), and life expectancy (National Center for Health Statistics, 2003b), couples who married at the median age at first marriage in 2002 would be likely to have living parents-in-law on both sides. Furthermore, based on these same data, a median-aged couple marrying for the first time in 2002 could expect to have parent-in-law relationships lasting at least 10 years. Evaluating the nature of parent-in-law/child-in-law relationships in Western, and particularly American, culture clarifies the reasons for the paucity of research into this very common relationship. Although most people will have parents-in-law, the importance of the parent-in-law/child-in-law relationship is downplayed in Western culture. Furthermore, this relationship is seen as being distant and negative.

The example of Woody Guthrie's relationship with his parents-in-law hints at the bigger picture of in-law relationships. In his case, a relationship that began in tension and conflict grew into an interdependent, respectful relationship that benefited all of the family members. Indeed, the existing research on in-law relationships indicates that the parent-in-law/child-in-law relationship is influential and more complex than the stereotypes suggest. Accordingly, this chapter will consider the defining features of the parent-in-law/child-in-law relationship before reviewing the aspects of the relationship that are most relevant to understanding the communication between parents-in-law and children-in-law. Finally, directions for future research will be proposed.

Defining the Relationship With Parents-in-Law

To bring up the subject of parents-in-law—and especially mothers-in-law—in casual conversation often invites an onslaught of jokes, negative stereotypes, and horror stories. The Web site www.motherinlawstories.com (B A Squared, Inc., 2004) catalogs contributors' mother-in-law stories and mother-in-law jokes. Some children-in-law who post their stories on the site have established their own "Frequent Fry-Her" pages to update readers on their ongoing mother-in-law strife. For instance, a woman posted her complaints about her mother-in-law's habit of playing favorites with her children, and now her grandchildren. The woman has two daughters, and her mother-in-law has always ignored the older girl but now dotes on the younger child. The woman's husband, who is his mother's acknowledged favorite among her own children, doesn't see the problem (B A Squared, Inc., 2004).

Stories and jokes in American culture tend to depict parent-in-law/ child-in-law relationships as distant, negative relationships that are over-shadowed in importance by marital and parent-child relationships. Given these characteristics, it is not surprising that in-law relationships are under-studied. If parents-in-law are relatively unimportant and distant, how significant can they be as subjects of research? Actually, what little research exists shows that in-law relationships do affect the in-laws and their extended families in significant (though not always negative) ways. Though in-law relationships are likely to be regarded as less important than marital and parent-child relationships, their effects on those more central relationships should not be underestimated. Furthermore, the relationships of parents- and children-in-law are much more complex than these dismissive depictions would have us believe. Before moving on to consider the complexity of parent-in-law relationships, it seems appropriate to spend some time considering the research evidence related to the popular characterization of relationships with parents-in-law as distant and negative.

The distant nature of in-law relationships is understandable in Western cultures, in which couples are expected to be relatively independent of their family (e.g., Altman, Brown, Staples, & Werner, 1992) and spouses are expected to remain closer with their own family of origin than with their in-laws (Datta, Poortinga, & Marcoen, 2003). For instance, Altman et al. (1992) presented case studies of courtship, weddings, and placemaking (i.e., establishing a home for the newlyweds) in different cultures, including the practices used in one Western culture. This detailed description of 1960s Welsh culture included couples who dated, got to know each other, and became engaged with little involvement of the family. Their wedding festivities involved the parents in some respects (with the bride's parents often paying for the wedding and her father "giving her away"), and they set up their home apart from either spouse's family. The general picture of the Welsh wedding holds true in many respects for couples in the United States That is, family involvement in courtship and selection of a spouse is often limited, the couple is very much involved in planning (and, more often today, contributing payment for) their wedding, and the spouses usually have a residence separate from their parents. The independence of the couple from parental involvement sets the stage for relationships with in-laws that are not particularly close.

Furthermore, when married couples are involved with their extended families, it is generally expected that they will be closer with their own family of origin than with their in-laws. Datta et al. (2003) conducted a study cross-cultural study of women's in-law and parent-child relationships. In the Western culture they studied, modern-day Belgium, women were likely to see their own mothers more frequently than their mothers-in-law, feel more attachment and responsibility for providing care to their own mothers than to their mothers-in-law, and live closer to their mothers than to their mothers-in-law. Judging from the research on parents-in-law in Western cultures, distance is built into cultural expectations for in-law relationships. But distance also can result from the other feature prevalent in popular impressions of parents-in-law: negativity.

There seems to be some empirical basis for the stereotypes of in-law relationships as negative. In her investigation of in-law relationships, Duvall (1954) asked 1,337 individuals to nominate the in-law with whom they had the most difficult relationship. Of the individuals who participated, 74% were able to name a troublesome in-law. Tension in the parent-in-law/child-in-law relationship was common among this group, with 59% of those with at least one difficult in-law naming a parent-in-law or a child-in-law as the most problematic. And the mother-in-law was the most common focus of discontent: the 59% was distributed unevenly among family members, with 49% naming the mother-in-law, 5% naming the father-in-law, 4% naming the daughter-in-law, and 1% naming the son-in-law as most difficult.

In-law relationships, therefore, are known to often involve trouble or negativity. Furthermore, in-laws are involved in a nonvoluntary relationship; though in Western cultures a person typically chooses his or her spouse, that person does not have a choice about the relatives who come with that spouse. Recent research on nonvoluntary relationships with disliked partners indicates that distancing is a common method for handling maintenance of such relationships (Hess, 2000). Not surprisingly, Duvall (1954) found that a common theme among responses from participants in a national radio competition who complained about their mothers-in-law was the use of distance to manage the relationship. Cross-cultural research comparing attitudes in the United States, Kuwait, Egypt, and Sudan has found that even across cultures, mothers-in-law are generally perceived to be interpersonally distant for participants, and the authors of that study argue that interpersonal distance is a result of negative relationships (Adler, Denmark, & Ahmed, 1989). Perhaps the independence of Western couples from their extended family allows them to use distancing behaviors, such as geographical distance and reducing frequency of contact, to manage the negativity of their obligatory in-law relationships.

In general, research on adults' relationships tends to focus on their relationships with their romantic partners or spouses and with their children, with little emphasis on other types of relationships. For example, in their analysis of research on conflict in adult friendships, Canary, Cupach, and Messman (1995) argue that research on adult friendships is lacking in part because friendships are thought to be less salient for adults than are relationships with romantic partners and with their family of procreation. Similarly, research on relationships with parents-in-law likely suffers from a belief that these relationships are much less important than the romantic or marital relationship and relationships between parents and young children. Moreover, the independence of Western marital couples from the extended family and the common negative perception of in-laws contribute to a characterization of in-law relationships as distant. It is not surprising that a relationship thought to be distant, negative, and relatively inconsequential should be understudied.

But none of this discussion gets at the root of the difficulties with parent-in-law relationships. Questioning the source of these problems, challenges, and stereotypes can help to explain why parents-in-law are the way they are—and why some fit the stereotype and others don't.

The Nonvoluntary, Triadic Structure of the Parent-in-Law/Child-in-Law Relationship

In the film *About Schmidt*, Warren Schmidt's daughter, Jeannie, is about to marry Randall, a water bed salesman with a bad haircut who tries to interest Warren in a business opportunity that he insists is *not* a pyramid scheme. Warren can't stand his future son-in-law because he thinks Randall isn't good enough for his "little girl." Warren begs Jeannie to call off the wedding, but she marries Randall anyway. At the wedding reception, tension builds as Warren approaches the microphone to give a toast, but he proceeds to compliment Randall and his entire family, even though his personal feelings toward Randall haven't changed at all.

Although the film is fictional, Warren's actions ring true. The story works because it illustrates the key elements that make in-law relationships challenging: parents- and children-in-law are bound together in a triadic, nonvoluntary relationship. Based on Thibaut and Kelley's (1959) social exchange perspective, Serewicz (in press) argues that the nature of the parent-in-law/child-in-law relationship as triadic and nonvoluntary makes the relationship difficult to maintain and negotiate.

First of all, these relationships are triadic in that the connection between the parent-in-law and child-in-law exists through their mutual connection to a third party: the child/spouse. And the in-laws are likely to value their relationships with the child/spouse more highly than they value their relationship with each other. Some parent-in-law/child-in-law relationships are good examples of Thibaut and Kelley's (1959) description of a common tension in triadic relationships (Serewicz, in press). This tension is played out when one member of the triad (A) would rather have a dyadic relationship with another member (B) than have a triadic relationship between all three members (A, B, and C). However, member B doesn't reciprocate A's preference.

In the example of Warren Schmidt, Warren would much prefer his father-daughter relationship with Jeannie over the triad that includes Randall, but Jeannie clearly rejects Warren's preference. Thus, in order to maintain the desired relationship with the child/spouse, the in-laws must maintain a relationship with each other, whether they like it or not. Because triad members' actions affect the triad as a whole, Warren engages in positive behavior toward Randall so that he can keep his relationship with his daughter. Warren realizes that since he, Jeannie, and Randall are in a triadic relationship, his actions toward Randall (toward whom he feels no great affection) also affect Jeannie (toward whom he *does* feel great affection).

A second aspect of the relationship between parents- and children-in-law that contributes to the difficulties is the nature of in-law relationships as nonvoluntary. The key aspect of Thibaut and Kelley's (1959) definition of involuntary relationships is that the costs of dissolving the relationship would be so great that members are forced to remain in the relationship. In the case of the triadic in-law relationship involving a couple and a parent-in-law, the triad could be dissolved if any link in the triad is broken: the parent-in-law and child-in-law could refuse contact with one another, the spouses could divorce, or the parent and child could disown each other. Usually, the costs inherent in dissolving any of these links would be great enough to keep the members in the triad (Serewicz, in press). For instance, Warren Schmidt failed to dissolve the triad through his pleas that his daughter call off her wedding. At that point, his choices would be to maintain the triadic relationship or end his relationship with his daughter. Disowning his daughter would cause such pain that he doesn't even consider the option.

The combination of the triadic and the nonvoluntary aspects of the parent-in-law relationship helps to explain the potential negativity between parents- and children-in-law. The uniqueness of the in-law relationship lies in this combination of features, distinguishing it from other relationships that are nonvoluntary but not triadic or triadic but not nonvoluntary. In Thibaut and Kelley's (1959) discussion of nonvoluntary relationships, they explain that the stronger the forces holding a person in the relationship, the more negative outcomes the person can be forced to endure. Forces keeping children-in-law in the triad include factors like love for the spouse or financial dependence on parents-in-law. Forces keeping parents-in-law in the triad include similar factors, such as love for the child or dependence on the child and child-in-law for care. The stronger these forces become, the greater the possibility that a person would endure a miserable in-law situation. But variations in the strength of the forces holding the parent- and child-in-law in the relationship, as well as differences in the ability of the parent- and child-in-law to affect each other's outcomes directly, will lead to different results (Serewicz, in press).

If in-laws are roughly equal in their power to influence each other's outcomes and both experience strong forces keeping them in the relationship, they are less likely to engage in negative behavior toward each other. Equality of power, combined with the mutual influence of triad members, would reduce negativity for two main reasons, from a social exchange perspective: the potential for retaliation, and the possibility to maximize one's own outcomes by maximizing the outcomes of the triad (Serewicz, in press).

To go back once more to the *About Schmidt* example, Warren is tied in to the triadic relationship by forces including his love for his daughter and his loneliness following his retirement and the death of his wife. He recognizes that Randall is also tied to the triad by the strong force of his love for Jeannie. Given that Jeannie refuses to leave Randall and actually has little contact with Warren, who lives in the next state, Warren's ability to influence Randall's outcomes is relatively low. By giving a nice toast at the wedding, Warren uses the small opportunity he does have to influence the outcome of the whole triad for the better.

If, however, the situation were different, with an in-law who is not so strongly bound to the triad and who has great power to influence the other in-law's outcomes, the potential for negativity is great. For example, if a mother has a conflictual relationship with her daughter, is financially independent, and has other close relationships in her life, she may be tied to the triad with her daughter and son-in-law only weakly. If, on top of this, the son-in-law is tied into the triad strongly and is dependent on the parents-in-law financially, the mother-in-law would be in a position to make his outcomes quite negative if she so chose. An imbalance between in-laws in terms of power and ties to the triad can be a fertile ground for negativity.

The qualities of parent-in-law/child-in-law relationships as triadic and nonvoluntary can help to explain the negativity possible between in-laws. But whether the in-law relationship is negative or not, these characteristics make the relationship complex and difficult to manage. Even when in-law relationships are positive, the interdependence of the in-law relationship with the marital and parent-child relationship raises the stakes of interaction between two people who didn't choose each other and can't leave their relationship. Although *About Schmidt* provides a useful illustration of some of these theoretical concepts, the real support for these ideas comes from the research investigating interaction between parents- and children-in-law.

Interaction Between Parents-in-Law and Children-in-Law

Research into the relationships of parents- and children-in-law illustrates the ways that the triadic, nonvoluntary relationship affects the lives of the in-laws, the child/spouse, and their extended families. First, the mutual assistance exchanged by parents and adult children/children-in-law emphasizes the ways that triad members' actions affect the whole triad—in this case, for the better. Second, interdependence and nonvoluntariness of the relationship are shown in the ways that interaction between two members of the triad involve and affect relationships with the third member. Finally, researchers have investigated ways that the triad is embedded in the extended family.

Patterns of Mutual Aid

> Whenever I need help—and the mother of four lively youngsters ages 14 months to 5 years often needs help—she [mother-in-law] never hesitates—just says, "All right, what's to be done?"—and does it. When I had the last baby she came and took over the other three and my housework for the week I was in the hospital . . . She stayed on, doing most of the work, for almost three weeks after my homecoming (Mrs. C., Wisconsin). (Duvall, 1954, p. 145)

The story told by "Mrs. C." might be a bit dated (how often do mothers and newborns stay in the hospital for a week these days?), but help given by parents (-in-law) to their children (-in-law) has followed a consistent pattern over the years. The reciprocal nature of the help and support given and received ensures the good of the whole family. So, assistance given and received within the triad exemplifies the influence of triad members upon each other and the ways that triad members can often maximize their own benefits in the relationship by providing benefits to others.

The help and support given by parents (-in-law) and children (-in-law) tend to peak according to major life events. Times of particular significance for giving and receiving support occur in early years of marriage, preschool years of children/grandchildren, and when aging parents need assistance

(Goetting, 1990). The types of help and support vary according to the needs of the support receiver and the resources of the support giver. For instance, in the early years of marriage, parents/parents-in-law give lots of support—especially financial support—to children/children-in-law (Goetting, 1990). Of course, financial support is dependent upon the parents' (-in-law) circumstances: parents in lower socioeconomic classes are less able to give their children (-in-law) financial support, and give more support in the form of services instead (Sussman & Burchinal, 1962). In general, support given in early marriage focuses on launching the young couple by supplying them with money, a home, and furnishings.

Not surprisingly, at the point of early parenthood/grandparenthood, the types of support given and received shift. In Mrs. C.'s story, she and her husband didn't need financial help or help setting up a home anymore—they needed help taking care of the children and the house. Support in the form of services (like childcare) peaks when the young couple has been married three to nine years, commonly the time when children/grandchildren are in their preschool years (Goetting, 1990). Of course, new mothers need more help from their own mothers and their mothers-in-law after their first child is born than they did before (Fischer, 1983b). Both the mother and the mother-in-law of the new mother are likely to help by babysitting and giving needed money and gifts. However, mothers are somewhat more likely to babysit and perform other needed tasks, whereas mothers-in-law are more likely to give gifts. It comes as little surprise that new mothers are also much more likely to ask their mother than their mother-in-law for advice about childrearing (Fischer, 1983b).

Finally, the pattern of aid shifts in the parents' later years as they come to need more help from their children and children-in-law. Bengtson (1993) explains that a "set of shared expectations and obligations" (p. 4) between generations includes the expectation of family caregiving when the older generation needs help from the younger generation. Kivett's (1985) research on help older, working class adults received from family members indicates that older adults receive assistance from many family members, but children and children-in-law gave the most aid and the most varied types of aid. As Goetting (1990) points out, even when children-in-law are not direct caregivers, they may provide indirect support to parents-in-law because their spouse is a caregiver. In most cases, a daughter gives the most care to her parents, and the son-in-law might contribute indirectly by giving up shared time with his wife and family. However, other research found that husbands of caregiving daughters also contributed a significant amount of help to their widowed mothers-in-law (for a review, see Goetting, 1990). The most help is probably given in the situation where an aging parent moves in with an adult child, and this relationship most often involves aging mothers living with a daughter and son-in-law (Goetting, 1990).

This brief description shows the significance of the support exchanged between children-in-law and parents-in-law. Besides demonstrating the ways that triad members can contribute to the good of the triad as a whole, this research contradicts the idea that in-law relationships are insignificant. It's interesting to note that the type of aid given and received is affected by a wide range of factors. As mentioned, gender of the parent (-in-law) and child (-in-law) plays a role in caregiving relationships, and socioeconomic class affects the kinds of support given. Furthermore, proximity of the parents-in-law influences the type of assistance given to children and children-in-law. For example, geographically distant parents-in-law are able to send money and gifts more than they are able to provide childcare or other services. In fact, proximity influences the amount of help received by older adults across all types of kin (Kivett, 1985). As will be discussed later, qualities of the marriage between the child and child-in-law also influence the type and amount of aid exchanged. Despite the considerable variation these factors introduce, the existence of these commitments to provide instrumental aid to one another shows the significance of the parent-in-law/child-in-law relationship for the well-being of the family.

Effects of In-Law Interactions on Relationships with the Child/Spouse

> When at last it was decided that I should tell the folks of our engagement the mother quietly said to me that she thought it proper that I not see my intended for one year. There was no protest. It was an ultimatum not to be ignored and for a whole year to the day I was banished as completely as though I had been sent to Siberia. (Duvall, 1954, p. 56)

This unnamed participant in Duvall's study had an unusually dramatic story to tell about how his interaction with his mother-in-law affected his relationship with his wife. Most in-law relationships exert a more subtle influence on the marital and parent-child relationships within the triad.

Because of the links between members of the triad, interactions between the parent-in-law and child-in-law have the potential to influence the marital relationship. The therapeutic literature indicates that problems with in-laws are likely to develop (Silverstein, 1990), especially around major changes in the family structure, including marriage, birth of a child, divorce, or death of a family member (Meyerstein, 1996). Not surprisingly, existing research supports the argument that problems with in-laws are relatively common in unhappy marriages (Terman, Buttenweiser, Ferguson, Johnson, & Wilson, cited in Gottman, 1982). Specifically, discord with in-laws is negatively related to both spouses' marital quality over time (Bryant, Conger, & Meehan, 2001).

Proximity also appears to have some interesting effects on in-law conflict. Bryant et al. (2001) found that the wife's conflict with her in-laws had greater influence on the marriage than did the husband's conflict with in-laws. Interestingly, in this rural sample, men tended to farm with their fathers, so the couple likely had more frequent contact with the husband's family (Bryant et al., 2001), in contrast to the more typical pattern in which married couples have greater contact with the wife's family (Sussman & Burchinal, 1962). Marotz-Baden and Cowan (1987), on the other hand, found that daughters-in-law's stress increased with distance from their mothers-in-law. The sample for this study consisted of mothers- and daughters-in-law in two-generation farming or ranching families. The authors suggested that the sons and daughters-in-law may have chosen to live as close to the parents (-in-law) as they could tolerate—so the daughters-in-law who were most stressed chose to live furthest from their mothers-in-law (Marotz-Baden & Cowan, 1987).

Of course, research also documents positive effects of in-law relationships on marriage. Timmer and Veroff (2000), in a study of black and white married couples, found that closeness to one's spouse's family was positively related to marital happiness and that low levels of conflict with one's in-laws was related to greater marital happiness. Moreover, a wife's closeness to her husband's family predicted increasing marital quality over time (Timmer & Veroff, 2000). Similarly, Serewicz (2004) found that satisfaction with one's in-laws was positively related to satisfaction with one's marriage. On the other hand, Meyerstein (1996) points out potential benefits that in-law conflict may have on marriage. For instance, conflict between a child-in-law and a parent-in-law may work out latent parent-child conflicts while allowing the child to avoid confronting the parent directly. Furthermore, the in-law conflict can distract from marital tensions for both the parents (-in-law) and the child and child-in-law as the spouses show loyalty to each other in the face of the parent-in-law/child-in-law conflict.

Although the influence of in-law relationships on marriage has received more research attention than the influence of in-law relationships on the parent-child relationship, some evidence exists to show an influence on the parent-child connection. Golish (2000) found that acceptance of a child's spouse was a turning point in relationships between parents and their adult children. From the child's perspective, acceptance of the spouse tended to increase closeness between the parent and child, whereas rejection of the spouse decreased parent-child closeness (Golish, 2000). Similarly, Fischer's (1983a) research found conflict between sons and mothers increased with the birth of a grandchild, and Fischer explained this finding by arguing that the tension between the daughter-in-law and mother-in-law causes the increase in mother-son conflict. From the parent's perspective, approval or disapproval of the child's marriage influences the likelihood of the parent providing aid to the child and child-in-law (Sussman & Burchinal, 1962). In these ways, the quality of the in-law relationship can affect the quality of the relationship between parent and child.

Furthermore, research on post-divorce relationships shows the complex influence of the marital relationship on in-law relationships. The triadic relationship dissolves when the child and child-in-law divorce. Therefore, the connection between former parent-in-law and former child-in-law is no longer involuntary in the way it was when the couple was married. Rather, the relationship between ex-in-laws can become more complicated after divorce. Former in-laws are no longer obligated to each other because of their family connection (Coleman & Ganong, 1998); however, they may continue their interaction depending on the quality of the relationship they developed with one another during the marriage (Duran-Aydintug, 1993). Although people expect former in-laws to interact with each other only by choice, depending on the quality of their interpersonal relationship with one another, they perceive obligations of grandparents to their grand-children (Coleman & Ganong, 1998) and expect that the custodial parent will strive to maintain his or her children's relationship with his or her former parents-in-law (Duran-Ayduntig, 1993).

Many divorced individuals report that they receive support from their former in-laws. In Duran-Ayduntig's (1993) study, participants who inter-acted frequently with their former in-laws cited the quality of the relation-ship with their ex-in-laws as the reason for their continued interaction. Those participants who interacted with their ex-in-laws rarely or never indicated that their reasons for the lack of interaction were either poor rela-tionship quality with in-laws during the marriage or negative treatment by in-laws during the process of the divorce. Similarly, Serovich, Price, and Chapman (1991) found that considering a former parent-in-law to be a relative predicted the amount of support participants received from the former parent-in-law, as did the former parent-in-law's approval of the divorce. When the defining factor of the in-law relationship, the marriage of the family member and the in-law, ceases to exist, the relationship between parents-in-law and children-in-law must be redefined.

That many divorced individuals continue to maintain relationships and support each other attests to the complexity of the relationship between parents- and children-in-law that forms over time. The research literature again refutes the notion that in-law relationships are relatively insignificant by showing that in-law relationships influence other, more intimate relationships.

The Triad and the Larger Family System

I love my mother-in-law because we share the love of her son—my husband. She makes me feel as welcome as her own daughters. She doesn't play any favorites and all of her daughters and sons-in-law love her (Mrs. E., Tennessee). (Duvall, 1954, p. 120)

The testimonial from "Mrs. E" hints at the broader context of the in-law triad. The triad of Mrs. E., her husband, and her mother-in-law does not exist independent from the larger family context. By acknowledging their embeddedness in the family system and comparing their in-law triad with the triads involving the mother-in-law and her other children and children-in-law, Mrs. E. can see that she's loved and valued equally with other members of the family. Research indicates that parents- and children-in-law often perceive and evaluate their relationships by placing them in the context of other relationships within the family.

One area that illustrates the way the in-law triad is situated within the larger family is in the way children-in-law address their parents-in-law. In her investigation of the terms used to address parents-in-law, Jorgenson (1994) found that sons- and daughters-in-law referred to considerations involving extended family on both sides. That is, in deciding whether to call one's parents-in-law "Mom and Dad," individuals considered claims of other family members to those titles. Not only were they concerned about the implications of calling the in-laws "Mom and Dad" for their loyalty to their own mother and father, they were also wary of offending their siblings-in-law by using an address term to which their spouse and siblings-in-law might claim exclusive rights (Jorgenson, 1994).

Comparisons with "true" parents and children give parents-in-law and children-in-law a framework to evaluate their relationship with each other. However, expecting duplication of a parent-child relationship might be detrimental for the in-law relationship. For example, some of Pfeifer's (1989) participants had difficulty in the mother-in-law/daughter-in-law relationship because the daughters-in-law "expected that their mothers-in-law would grant them the same code of behavior and/or share the same type of information as other 'in blood' family members" (p. 206), whereas others had difficulty because the mothers-in-law wanted to have a closer relationship than did the daughters-in-law. Daughters-in-law did seem to use comparison with extended family members in evaluating the quality of their relationships with their mothers-in-law, comparing the mother-in-law's contact with them to her contact with her other children and children-in-law (Pfeifer, 1989). Interestingly, daughters-in-law who described their relationships with their mothers-in-law as a parent-child relationship tended to be happy with that relationship, while also recognizing a respectful distance in their relationships with their mothers-in-law that did not exist in their relationships with their own mothers.

A crucial factor in the development of the parent-in-law/child-in-law relationship involves granting of family member status to the in-law. Of course, when a marriage takes place, in-laws become members of the same family by definition. But although family membership status of an in-law may be a matter of legal fact, the communication of family members does not necessarily reflect family members' recognition and acceptance of the new member. In fact, Jorgenson's (1989) research, which asked newlyweds to identify their family members and explain their criteria for inclusion, found that people were considered to be family members according to criteria like time spent together and participation in important family events. In other words, membership in the family is not established simply by a person's position in the family's structure, but by the person's interpersonal behavior with family members. This argument lines up with Petronio's (2002) assertions in her Communication Privacy Management theory. Petronio explains that membership in a group is conferred, at least in part, when existing members share the group's private information with the new member. Although a person might be made a member of a group or family in a legal or structural way, true interactional membership is established in a negotiated process of communication. By their shared time, participation in events, and exchange of information, new and existing family members come to see each other as family.

The complexity of the process of gaining and granting family membership status poses challenges for the family. Difficulty in identifying appropriate roles for and drawing boundaries around family members can result in problems for the family, whereas clearly defined roles and boundaries seem to affect families positively (Madden-Derdich, Leonard, & Christopher, 1999). Disappointing family relationships are sometimes connected with unrealistic or unfulfilled expectations about the roles in-laws should play, as in Pfeifer's (1989) finding that some mothers-in-law wanted closer relationships than did their daughters-in-law and that some daughters-in-law were unhappy with their mothers-in-law because they expected to be treated the same as "blood" members of the family. Similarly, Jackson and

Berg-Cross (1988) found that a woman's desire for inclusion (that is, for others to take the initiative to begin interaction and to invite her to participate in activities) was negatively related to her adjustment to her mother-in-law, perhaps because the high desire for inclusion resulted in unrealistic expectations for her mother-in-law to seek out her company. Thus, difficulty in establishing whether an in-law is a family member, along with incongruous role expectations among in-laws, likely poses problems for the family.

Difficult though the process may be, successful negotiation of membership for the new in-law is tied to positive relationships in the family. In research on ex-in-law relationships, considering one's former parents-in-law to be "relatives" is a factor closely related to the quality and continuation of the relationship (Serovich et al., 1991). Furthermore, research has identified acceptance as a key component in a good in-law relationship (Duvall, 1954; Pfeifer, 1989). In recent research on the communication between newlyweds and their in-laws, a focus group investigation supported the notion that disclosure of private information belonging to the family was significant for the new family member (Morr, 2003). A second study, surveying newlyweds about their marital and family relationships, found that disclosure from in-laws about the family's private information was positively related to the newlywed's satisfaction with the family and feelings of acceptance as a family member (Serewicz, 2004). In turn, family satisfaction and acceptance together were strong predictors of marital satisfaction (Serewicz, 2004).

As complex as the triadic relationship of the parent-in-law, child-in-law, and child/spouse may seem, the relationship becomes even more complicated when the triad's ties to the larger family system are considered. In-laws often gather information about their relationships with each other by comparing them with other family relationships. As the relationship between in-laws develops over time, the status of the in-law as a member of the family is negotiated, and this complex process has the potential to affect the family positively or negatively.

Conclusion

Although there are some productive lines of research directly addressing or indirectly relevant to the parent-in-law/child-in-law relationship, future research is needed to explain the complexities of this important relationship. Although many possibilities exist, a few areas demand particular attention. First, more research attention should be focused on communication between parents- and children-in-law. For instance, further investigation along the lines of Jorgenson's (1994) study of names children-in-law use to address their parents-in-law would provide important insights into the actual communication that constitutes the relationship. In addition, research on the ways that interaction and specific messages in the parent-in-law /child-in-law relationship affect the outcomes of all triad members would be useful.

Next, research needs to expand the scope of in-law relationships to include multiple members. Much of the existing research focuses on relationships between mothers-in-law and daughters-in-law, with little research on other relationships between parents- and children-in-law. The perspective of the parent-in-law is rarely investigated, with most research focusing on the perspective of the child-in-law. More research considering the perspectives of both parent- and child-in-law is needed. Furthermore, although the in-law relationship is triadic in nature, very little research has been conducted with all members of the triad. Finally, although the research becomes more theoretically complex and pragmatically difficult as more family members are added, investigating the influence of extended family relationships on relationships with parents-in-law is also needed.

Finally, research on family membership status of in-laws deserves further attention, and research should be extended to investigate changes in membership status over time. Similarly, research tends to focus on significant turning points in the lives of family members, including marriage, divorce, childbirth, and health crises. Although this research is important and should be continued, more research into the relationships of in-laws at less critical moments should be undertaken to understand the full range of experience of the relationship with one's parents-in-law. In general, much research on in-law relationships is cross-sectional, with longitudinal research involving in-law relationships often focusing primarily on the marriage of the child and child-in-law and including a small number of variables related to the in-law relationship. More longitudinal research studying a wide range of variables relevant to the parent-in-law/child-in-law relationship is needed.

The common perspective on in-law relationships in American culture is that they are negative and distant. Existing research paints a much more complex picture of the in-law relationship. Because in-law relationships are triadic and nonvoluntary, they can be difficult to manage. But research shows that relationships with parents-in-law can be sources of support, can affect marriage and parent-child relationships in both positive and negative ways, and play an important role in defining family membership. Future research will fill in the details yet to be discovered about this often-overlooked relationship.

7

Getting Along With the In-Laws

Relationships With Siblings-in-Law

Christina G. Yoshimura

When we announce our matrimonial plans to our siblings, we are likely to assume that they will feel much of the joyful anticipation that we do about creating a new family bond. After all, we've gone out into the world and found a new audience member for all the old family stories; we've drawn in a new source of support, humor, and free labor for the entire family to appreciate. Yes, we think, certainly our siblings must be just as excited as we are about this new person being brought into the family fold.

Yet, an odd thing happens when the situation reverses and a sibling comes to tell us about his or her own plans to marry. Yes, we are likely to feel the excitement and anticipation of gaining a new family member. But there are also endless questions. Who *is* this person our sibling is pressing on us? How will he or she react to our family rituals and quirks? Will this person expect to take our sibling away on the holidays, or have appalling family names to foist on their future progeny—our future nieces or nephews? It becomes especially apparent when we are not the ones initiating this new family addition that the extension of family through marriage means the introduction of quite a bit of uncertainty and change into the family system.

In 1990, Goetting remarked that in-law relationships were virtually absent from textbooks or studies of family interaction; a decade later, we find our situation much the same. A handful of researchers have chosen to investigate the parent-in-law relationship (e.g., Fischer, 1983b), yet sibling-in-law relationships have not only been understudied, they have remained virtually unstudied. This chapter examines the nature of the sibling-in-law relationship, poses some possibilities regarding communicative strengths and challenges within this relationship, and reports the results of some introductory empirical work that has directly addressed this unique family connection.

What Is a Sibling-in-Law?

In-law relationships result from the expansion of a family system through marriage. Siblings-in-law, specifically, result either from a personal choice to marry an individual with a sibling or from a sibling's choice to marry. In neither of these routes to becoming siblings-in-law do we have much choice regarding who this new family member will be. This stands in distinct contrast to the nature of marital relationships in much of the world.

Marital relationships overall tend to be initiated as primary relationships voluntarily chosen and enacted for the purpose of relating with a specific person. These relationships may be chosen due to liking, mutuality, and attraction on a number of bases. As such, they are *social* relationships; the individuals in these relationships interact because they *like* to or perceive some social benefit from doing so. Yet marriage entails not only social benefits and obligations but legal benefits and obligations as well. Depending upon local stipulations, marital partners may be held accountable for one another's financial decisions and well-being or may have the responsibility to decide what type of medical care a partner will or will not receive in life-threatening situations.

In contrast to the primacy of marital relationships, sibling-in-law relationships tend to develop as secondary relationships. Outside of rare cases, we do not go out and tap a person we find likable, similar, and rewarding to become our sibling-in-law. Instead, we generally initiate a sibling-in-law relationship with whomever our sibling brings home, or whomever our chosen marital partner happens to have for siblings. Yet, like a marital relationship, some of the obligations in a sibling-in-law relationship can also be quite binding. For instance, the sibling-in-law relationship is considered an obligatory family responsibility in the family and medical leave policies of many states, universities, and corporate organizations (although, notably, not in the federal

Family and Medical Leave Act passed in 1993). These policies may grant leave and even financial compensation if an employee must care for a sick brother- or sister-in-law. Thus, although this is a secondary and involuntary relationship that we engage in out of duty to the more primary relationships of siblinghood or marriage, the sibling-in-law relationship may still become a binding and enduring part of our family systems.

The fact that an obligatory rather than social relationship is usually the basis of the sibling-in-law relationship does not preclude the possibility that a strong social relationship might develop. In fact, Serovich et al. (1991) found that 25–40% of people who were no longer related through legal ties (due to divorce) still considered a parent- or sibling-in-law to be a family relative. It is likely, then, that some individuals voluntarily choose to befriend a sibling-in-law and establish a social relationship over and above (or regardless of) legal and obligatory responsibilities.

What Is Known About Communication Among Siblings-in-Law

Sibling-in-law relationships have remained obscure in studies of family interaction, but this is not for a lack of prevalence. The U.S. Bureau of the Census (2002) indicates that 75.6% of people 18 years of age or older have been married at one time, and the 1998 General Social Survey indicates that 96.6% of Americans have at least one sibling (National Opinion Research Center, 1998). This means that *most* people will experience a sibling-in-law relationship at some point in their lives.

Rather, the lack of focus on siblings-in-law in research is likely a result of the presumed low intensity of the sibling-in-law relationship. When a family system is expanded through marriage, research has often focused on the marital relationship or the parent-in-law relationship as salient foci for examining the new family. These relationships are presumed to involve more negotiation of power and behavioral control than do peer-based, secondary relationships with siblings-in-law, and thus, investigation of these relationships has overshadowed the study of sibling-in-law relationships. However, the sibling-in-law relationship differs in several ways from other relationships, such that it may have a unique role to play in the dynamic of a family system.

First, as previously noted, the sibling-in-law relationship differs from the marital relationship because it is an involuntary and secondary relationship. Another notable difference between these relationships, however, is the number of such associations one is expected to manage. An individual must manage only one marital relationship at a time (in a monogamous society). Yet this same individual may manage any number of separate sibling-in-law relationships. For example, my husband has one sibling and I have six siblings. This presents the possibility of having six sibling-in-law relationships for each of us to eventually initiate and manage. This, of course, does not even take into account the number of relationships that may develop if any one of us decided to remarry. Although a similar role is being negotiated in each of these relationships, different individual characteristics mean that multiple sibling-in-law relationships will not be identical; new, individual relationships may be created with each new sibling-in-law.

The sibling-in-law relationship differs from the parent-in-law relationship in a similar way. When an individual marries, he or she acquires one mother-in-law and one father-in-law (and possibly a stepmother-in-law and stepfather-in-law). However, the number of siblings-in-law that one acquires through marriage can range dramatically, as already mentioned. The focus on creating and maintaining a relationship with one set of parents-in-law has overshadowed studies of the management of a number of sibling-in-law relationships.

Even though they are often overshadowed by other relationships, sibling-in-law relationships have potentially unique characteristics or dilemmas to add to the family system. Although the distinctive nature of the sibling-in-law relationship could easily be obscured if previous research were simply applied to it indiscriminately, research in several areas of study can be used to point us in potentially fruitful directions for studying siblings-in-law. Specifically, research that has previously been conducted on friends and family members in the areas of disclosure and privacy, jealousy and envy, affection, and relational maintenance might be put to good use to begin writing upon the blank slate of communication among siblings-in-law.

Disclosure and Privacy

One of the unique tensions present in the relationship between siblings-in-law is that of conflicting loyalties regarding shared information. In many countries, there are both social and legal expectations that marital partners have the privilege of being able to share information with one another without penalty or intrusion from others. Yet all family members do not share this convention of openness in regard to information. In fact, Petronio's (1991) communication privacy management theory identified mechanisms by which individuals construct a system of rules and boundaries to control privacy and access to information. This has been used to evaluate management of information between marital couples (Petronio, 1991) as well as parents and children (Afifi & Guerrero, 2000).

A salient issue that may arise when siblings-in-law are introduced into the family system is how boundary management and boundary coordination (the process of reinforcing or renegotiating an existing boundary around information, according to Petronio, 2000) are carried out. For instance, a pair of siblings may have an intrafamily secret that only they share access to. If one of these siblings marries, does this mean that the boundary surrounding this secret remains with these two siblings, or does the boundary extend to encompass the new marital partner? If it extends, which would be consistent with the previously mentioned norm regarding information sharing in marital relationships, how does this happen? Does it transpire automatically, without discussion with one's sibling, or is this a process of boundary coordination that is openly communicated between siblings?

We might additionally consider what happens to privacy and information boundaries if siblings-in-law initiate a genuine friendship, instead of merely an obligatory role relationship. If the conditions are acceptable, friends may share family secrets with one another in order to gain an outside perspective or to receive support (Vangelisti, Caughlin, & Timmerman, 2001). If a sibling-in-law is a friend, what communication boundaries are considered when discussing family secrets? What are the repercussions on the variety of relationships involved if the information being discussed between siblings-in-law is about a third family member who is the marital partner to one and a sibling to the other? The process of managing boundaries through both concealment and disclosure has been suggested to promote family bonding, liking, and social support (Caughlin & Petronio, 2004); the complexities regarding how this occurs when siblings-in-law enter into a family system have yet to be specifically evaluated.

Jealousy and Envy

While social prescriptions may prohibit jealousy and envy from occurring in a family system as frequently as they may occur with strangers, these emotions are nonetheless experienced and communicated with some regularity among family members, especially siblings (Aune & Comstock, 2001). Research has shown that siblings often want something another sibling has that they themselves do not have (envy) or fear that something they already have will be taken from them (jealousy) (e.g., White & Mullen, 1989). This is logical, given that siblings are in competition with one another from an early age for resources from the same source—parents. Fitness and Duffield (2004) indicated that jealousy and envy are especially prevalent among siblings in contemporary society because older siblings have less of a caregiving role and more of a peer-based role with younger siblings than they had historically. Even though parental resources aren't stretched as thin as they were in previous centuries, these resources are still re-allocated with the birth of each child (Fitness & Duffield, 2004). Even as siblings age, jealousy and envy continue to occur and can introduce uncertainty into the sibling relationship (Aune & Comstock, 2001).

So, how might jealousy or envy between siblings-*in-law* be experienced differently than between siblings? First, siblings-in-law do not share the same source of parental aid as one another. Thus, they may experience less *jealousy* over parental aid than siblings, as they do not have to worry that parental aid will be taken away from them as directly due to the actions or needs of a sibling-in-law. However, siblings-in-law may actually encounter more *envy* over resources than siblings, given that siblings-in-law will have received resources from different parental sources. For instance, we may feel resentful that a sibling-in-law was granted a college education or money for a down payment on a home, when our own parents were not able to furnish these resources.

Envy and jealousy between siblings-in-law may spring from other sources as well. For instance, I might feel jealous of my brother-in-law when he spends time with my husband without me, and wish that I could spend that time with my husband instead. Or, I might feel envious of my sister-in-law's relationship with her daughter as a stay-at-home mother, dissatisfied that she has an opportunity to parent in a way that I do not. Since sibling-in-law relationships are largely secondary, involuntary, and lacking in social proscriptions for behavior, it is impossible to assume how jealousy and envy transpire or are communicated in these relationships. Previous research (Aune & Comstock, 2001) has indicated that siblings express jealous emotions through open communication—is this the case with siblings-in-law as well? As the study of jealousy and envy within families expands, it should do so with the inclusion of a variety of family relationships to be studied, including sibling-in-law relationships.

Affection

Floyd and Morman have engaged in an extensive research program to investigate the function of the communication of affection in relationships (Floyd & Morman, 1997, 2000, 2002). Although their affection exchange theory (AET) has been used to show that affection can increase survival chances and reproductive opportunities in potential mate relationships, it has also been used to show that affectionate communication between parents and children can provide children with models of affection that will benefit them when they reach the age of procreation (Floyd & Morman,

2003). Affection is also important in a variety of family relationships because it communicates value and is positively related to relational satisfaction (Floyd & Morman, 1997; Floyd & Morr, 2003).

Affection within sibling-in-law relationships may entail unique communicative challenges when compared with other family relationships, for a number of reasons. First, affection may be an effective way to begin moving from an obligatory role relationship between siblings-in-law to a more social relationship. Signs of affection may even serve to strengthen the primary sibling or marital relationship, as affection signals value for a sibling or marital partner's social network. However, sibling-in-law relationships generally occur between sexually mature adults who do not have a history of shared familial interactions. Thus, the incest taboo that is present in other familial relationships that may help regulate perceptions of appropriate/inappropriate communication of affection may not be present.

Further, Floyd and Morman (1997) reported that affectionate communication is viewed as more appropriate among siblings than friends. Where siblings-in-law fall into the mix is unclear. As neither fully voluntary friends nor true siblings, it is difficult to ascertain how family members perceive affectionate communication between siblings-in-law. It is possible, for instance, that certain forms of affectionate communication become perceived as more or less appropriate over the course of the sibling-in-law relationship. Specifically, doing favors for a sibling-in-law is probably a less direct expression of affection than nonverbal expressions like hugging would be, which in turn is still less direct than verbal expressions, such as "I love you." All forms of affectionate expression may not be perceived as equally appropriate in all stages of the sibling-in-law relationship.

In a study of nonromantic relationships, Floyd and Morman (1997) found that affectionate expression was seen as significantly more problematic between opposite-sex dyads than for either male-male or female-female dyads; this may mean that mixed-sex siblings-in-law may have a more difficult time negotiating appropriate means of communicating affection than their same-sex counterparts. In research on mixed-sex friends, Cupach and Metts (1991) report that friends may use sexual banter or teasing to manage underlying sexual attraction. Is this tactic used between siblings-in-law in a manner similar to that of friends? If so, how is this received by other family members, especially marital partners?

Relational Maintenance

Finally, relational maintenance may prove to be an area of study for siblings-in-law that encompasses many of these previously mentioned research topics. Relational maintenance researchers have identified a number of objectives for utilizing maintenance behaviors, the most unanimously agreed-upon being to sustain a relationship at a desired state (Canary & Stafford, 1992). Maintenance behaviors may be enacted strategically (Canary, Stafford, Hause, & Wallace, 1993) or routinely (Gilbertson, Dindia, & Allen, 1998) and include behaviors such as positivity; sharing tasks; engaging in social networks; openness; assurances; joint activities; avoidance behaviors; antisocial behaviors; humor; and use of cards, letters, and calls (Canary et al., 1993).

Research shows maintenance behaviors are enacted differentially based on relationship type and longevity (Canary et al., 1993). In a study focused specifically on relational maintenance behaviors enacted between siblings, Myers & Members of COM 200 (2001) found that sharing tasks is the most frequently enacted maintenance behavior, while openness is used the least. Although it is useful in a practical sense to discover which behaviors make each type of personal relationship "work," what is more interesting is the subsequent identification of the goals being served by these behaviors. Understanding what communicative behaviors maintain a relationship with siblings-in-law may help to illuminate the specific benefits that are being received and needs that are being met by these relationships. For example, the fact that self-disclosure is an important maintenance behavior for romantic relationships but is used very infrequently in sibling relationships may indicate an important difference in the nature of these relationships. Openness aids growth and stimulation in romantic relationships, to keep partners invested in one another. According to Myers and Members of COM 200 (2001), this is not a goal that needs close attending to in involuntary sibling relationships, where a constant degree of baseline investment is presumed.

Additionally, maintaining a relationship with a sibling-in-law may be a paradoxical situation. We may choose to engage in maintenance behaviors with siblings-in-law as a form of social networking, aimed at maintaining our primary sibling or spousal relationship. However, behaviors such as sharing information with or showing affection to a sibling-in-law may unwittingly interfere with a primary sibling or spousal relationship. For instance, I may believe I will improve my relationship with my sister if I am kind to her husband, since I will be showing her that I value her social network. However, if she perceives my behaviors as patronizing or flirtatious, my behaviors may actually make our sibling relationship less satisfactory. Thus, further exploration is warranted to determine motivations for engaging in maintenance behaviors with siblings-in-law, as well as the behaviors that are perceived as most appropriate and effective to maintain satisfactory sibling-in-law relations.

Contemporary Research on Siblings-in-Law

The research reviewed to this point can be used to form questions regarding the sibling-in-law relationship, but because the relationships focused upon in these studies were other family relationships or friendships, they give us no empirical evidence that the sibling-in-law relationship employs distinct communicative behaviors. As most of this chapter has been spent generating questions, let us review two studies that *do* examine sibling-in-law communication patterns specifically in order to identify that which *has* been answered regarding siblings-in-law.

First, Floyd and Morr (2003) examined siblings-in-law directly as a part of a larger study on affectionate communication within the family. Due to the embedded, secondary nature of the sibling-in-law relationship within the family system, this dyad was studied together with sibling and spousal relationships. Triads (a pair of married spouses and a sibling of one of the spouses) from 109 families were recruited and asked to complete scales describing the ways in which they shared affection with one another, the level of relational closeness they felt, and the amount of relational satisfaction they experienced.

As a result of this study, Floyd and Morr (2003) were able to identify several important ways in which the sibling-in-law relationship fits within the family system. First, although this relationship is secondary rather than primary, the sibling-in-law relationship varied consistently with the more primary relationships of spouses and siblings within each triad in the use of direct verbal expressions of affection (e.g., saying "I love you"), direct non-verbal gestures of affection (e.g., shaking hands or kissing), and affectionate social support (e.g., doing a favor for the other person). In other words, a positive relationship exists between the affection shown to one's sibling or spouse and the affection shown to one's sibling-in-law. This indicates that although the amount of affection shown to siblings-in-law is often less than that shown to siblings or spouses, the three types of relationships share interdependence and vary together.

Second, Floyd and Morr (2003) found that affection within the sibling-in-law relationship was significantly and directly related to relational closeness and satisfaction. That is, a satisfying and close relationship with a sibling-in-law tended to be characterized by a greater degree of affectionate communication than did less close or satisfying relationships. Although Floyd and Morr (2003) avoid causal inferences, the fact emerges that in general, individuals do not seek a distant or detached relationship with siblings-in-law. Despite the involuntary nature of these relationships, people derive satisfaction and closeness from verbal, nonverbal, and social support expressions of affection in the sibling-in-law relationship, just as they do in their sibling or spousal relationships.

Floyd and Morr's (2003) study illuminated the light side of the sibling-in-law relationship. However, just as in other family relationships, a dark side exists in the relationship that siblings-in-law share. As an extension of the Floyd and Morr (2003) study, Yoshimura (2005) also utilized triads of family members, consisting of a pair of married spouses and the sibling of one of the spouses. Given different socioevolutionary mandates, it was predicted that siblings-in-law, siblings, and spouses would not only experience significantly different degrees of envy within their relationships, but that they might also have different "triggers" for envy and different preferences for communicating envious emotions.

Yoshimura (2005) found that consistent with previous research on sibling rivalry, siblings experienced the highest frequency of envious emotions out of all three relationship types—significantly higher than both marital and sibling-in-law relationships. Interestingly, siblings-in-law did not differ significantly from marital relationships in regards to the frequency of envious emotions. However, it is possible that envious emotions are reported similarly in marital and sibling-in-law relationships for quite different reasons. Societal prescriptions for altruism and shared resources may account for the lack of envy in marital relationships, while a lack of closeness or regular interactions from which to generate comparisons may account for the lack of envy in sibling-in-law relationships. Further motivations and communication patterns between siblings-in-law must be revealed before a full explanation of this finding is available.

Yoshimura (2005) also found that all three familial relationships experience envy in response to some common triggers—such as envying another's free time, finances, and fun—as well as envying the ease with which another person succeeds, either on his or her own or through parental aid. However, the overall rankings of triggers did significantly vary from relationship to relationship, indicating that spouses, siblings, and siblings-in-law may compare themselves with others differentially, depending upon the relationship in which the comparison takes place. Specifically, siblings-in-law reported envying one another's success because of parental support more than did either spouses or siblings and also reported envying a sibling-in-law's romantic relationship more than siblings envied one another's.

Finally, communication regarding the envy experienced in these three relationships was quite telling. Even though siblings experienced significantly more envy than spouses or siblings-in-law, it was spouses who communicated the most about their envy with one another. Perhaps the social prohibitions against spousal envy leads to attempts to remediate this emotion through communication more so than in relationships where envy is expected, such as the sibling relationship. Importantly, siblings-in-law were *least* likely to communicate their envy for one another, even though the level of envy experienced in this relationship was statistically no different from that experienced in spousal relationships, where the *most* communication of envy occurred. Again, this may indicate that infrequent or impersonal communication is a general characteristic of sibling-in-law communication, or it may indicate that negative emotions are withheld in efforts to maintain other familial relationships.

Further exploration will be needed to fully explain the findings of these two initial studies on sibling-in-law communication patterns. However, these studies clearly indicate that the sibling-in-law relationship is bound to primary family relationships and that it shares in the interdependent nature of the overall family system. It is also clear that the characteristics and the communication patterns of this relationship are distinctive in many ways from other types of family connections. Thus, as a functional yet unique relationship type within the family, it deserves to be understood to the degree that we have come to comprehend the quality and influence of other family ties.

Conclusion

Several avenues for future research on siblings-in-law have been presented here. The first studies of the communication behavior of sibling-in-law relationships have identified some intriguing details regarding affection and envy, but there are still many more questions to be answered about how both affection and envy are managed in sibling-in-law relationships. Further, investigations of information management and privacy boundaries within and around sibling-in-law relationships may elucidate the nature of the sibling-in-law relationship as well as potentially extend communication privacy management theory. Finally, further focus upon the patterns of relational maintenance and the implications of those maintenance behaviors among siblings-in-law will help us to understand the complicated and interconnected practice not only of maintaining sibling-in-law relationships but of maintaining relationships across the family system.

In the end, although research into the sibling-in-law relationship will benefit the study of family communication overall, such research is ultimately warranted in order to understand the sibling-in-law relationship as a distinctive relationship. We should not remain content to rely upon the results of other dyadic studies within the family to understand, evaluate, and predict communicative behaviors in the sibling-in-law relationship.

Commentary on Part B

Fran C. Dickson

This section of the book focuses on extended family relationships that are typically understudied and misunderstood. Two chapters discuss the in-law relationship, specifically the parent-in-law and the sibling-in-law. The in-law relationships discussed are viewed as involuntary, obligatory in nature, and typically distant. These relationships are often characterized by infrequent, forced, and negative interaction. Another chapter discusses the understudied aunting relationship. This is the only extended family relationship discussed in this section that appears to be established and maintained through voluntary interaction. While the aunting relationship has an obligatory nature to it, it is really maintained through voluntary interaction. Finally, the grandparent-grandchild relationship is explored in detail. Each chapter offers a different and provocative view on extended family relationships.

Within this section of the book, traditional definitions of family are being tossed aside, while the extended family relationship is privileged. This section represents how other extended family relationships can become primary, problematic, or joyful for family members. These chapters remind us of the need to move away from traditional models of family research in order to have a more accurate representation and understanding of communicative experiences in families today.

The chapter on grandparental relationships by Soliz, Lin, Anderson, and Harwood explores the complex relationship of the grandparent and grandchild. This chapter highlights how the changing definition of family has an impact on the dynamics of the grandparent-grandchild relationship. It reviews the present research on the grandparent-grandchild relationship with an emphasis on the identifying factors that influence this relationship and the way family identity and successful aging relates to the quality, attributes, and opportunities that this relationship provides for family members, specifically the grandchildren. Communication opportunities for the grandparent-grandchild relationship, predictors of closeness and solidarity, and important communication findings and directions for future research are also discussed.

This chapter gives us a new perspective on the grandparent-grandchild relationship by emphasizing that we do not know "how" this family relationship is enacted. We know that the grandparent can play a supportive role for the grandchild or function as a caregiver, but we do not know how these roles play out in everyday interaction within the family system. This chapter takes the position that researchers need to change their research focus from describing the roles that grandparents serve to exploring the everyday interaction.

The chapter by Morr Serewicz on relationships with parents-in-law discusses the family relationship that is the target of many family jokes and negative associations. In many ways, this chapter discusses the dark side of involuntary family relationships. It discusses how the parent-in-law relationship is typically viewed as a distant, obligatory relationship. Morr Serewicz highlights how the parent-in-law relationship is typically viewed with negative filters and is a source of conflict for the married couple. It is clear that Western culture has demonized the mother-in-law relationship, which creates expectations and barriers to a healthy, satisfying in-law relationship.

This chapter focuses on how to enhance the parent-in-law relationship, which is identified as one of the major problem areas for young couples (Gottman, 1999). Interestingly, Morr Serewicz points out that problems with parents-in-law are most common in distressed marital relationships. This finding implies that problematic in-law relationships may be an indicator of marital dysfunction, not necessarily a cause for marital distress, as many couples report. This finding can lead one to question whether or not in-laws are in fact a real problem for couples, or whether the problem resides in the ways in which couples discuss and manage conflict about in-laws.

This chapter offers an interesting picture of a typically negative relationship associated with family interaction. A fascinating dynamic that Morr Serewicz discusses is how, once the in-law relationship has been established (legally, through the marriage of a child), the new in-law is recognized and accepted as a new family member. This transition from non-family member to family member is an interesting transformation process that needs further research. Morr Serewicz also presents a unique discussion on the dynamics associated with the in-law relationship when it is no longer an obligatory relationship, when it exists beyond the divorce of the marital relationship that initially created the in-law relationship.

Finally, instead of exploring the characteristics of in-law relationships, family communication researchers need to move toward exploring the processes and challenges associated with the new relationship definition. As in the previous chapter, this chapter also highlights the need to explore how communication processes occur within this family relationship. In reality, the "butt of jokes" among comedians really needs to be rethought of as a complex family relationship that has implications for the grandparent-grandchild relationship and harmony in the family.

According to Yoshimura's chapter, one of the most understudied and misunderstood relationships is the sibling-in-law relationship. Most family communication scholars study mainstream family relationships such as the parent-child relationship, sibling relationships, and marital relationships. However, this articles touches on a family relationship type that is virtually never studied. This article advocates a systems approach as well as socio-evolutionary theory to exploring sibling and sibling-in-law relationships. Previous research indicates that the sibling and sibling-in-law relationship is satisfying, positive, and affectionate.

This chapter presents a study that examines the relationships between envy, relationship satisfaction, and relationship closeness between siblings, their spouses, and siblings-in-law. Not surprisingly, these findings indicated that siblings were most envious of each other and that spouses were least envious of each other. This study also found that spouses were most likely to communicate with each other about their feelings of envy while siblings-in-law were least likely to discuss their envious feelings. This finding is not surprising in that spouses most likely have the opportunity to discuss this matter and they are most likely highly invested in the marital relationship, while siblings-in-law typically do not interact with each other as frequently as spouses and their relational investment may be significantly lower than that of spouses.

Again, as in other chapters in this section, Yoshimura highlights the involuntary, obligatory nature of this relationship type. As this chapter discusses, low levels of affection, infrequent interaction, and even envy can typify the sibling-in-law relationship. Yoshimura opens up the door to exploring envy and the interconnectedness among siblings, their spouses, and siblings-in-law. This opening can lead to interesting and provocative questions on family dynamics. For example, what are the communication antecedents of envy among siblings-in-law in a family? What does it looks like, how is it experienced, and what are the communicative outcomes associated with it? This research on sibling-in-law relationships leads to other questions about envy in families in general. For example, is envy in a family a relational outcome or an intrapersonal process? We really do not know much about envy in families; exploring this process in more detail can enrich our understanding of sibling relationships in general, as well as specifically the sibling-in-law relationship.

The chapter by Sotirin and Ellingson on aunt/niece/nephew communication also explores a family relationship type that is typically ignored in the family communication literature. In this article, it is interesting how a noun, "the aunt," becomes a verb, "aunting," which implies the need for action. The exploration of the aunting relationship provides an interesting opportunity to examine an alternative form of family bonding. While this relationship type is involuntary in nature, it differs from the other relationships discussed in this section in that the establishment and maintenance of this relationship may challenge traditional family roles and rules. For example, Sotirin and Ellingson note that exploration of this relationship can be unsettling since it appears to undermine the authority of the parental figure in the family structure. This article defies traditional notions that the parental figures need to have the authority over the children. It presents the possibility that the aunt could undermine or usurp the parental authority.

This chapter highlights that the aunting relationship offers more relational options for the niece or nephew than the mother relationship. This chapter emphasizes that aunts have the freedom to play various and diverse roles for their nieces and nephews. An aunt can be a confidante, peer, role model, teacher, and even a second mother. The question is, does the aunting relationship undermine the mother's relationship with the child? Is it a relationship type in which the mother and aunt compete for the child's affection?

The chapter discusses the unique communicative strengths and weaknesses associated with the aunting relationship while stressing the flexibility and adaptability associated with this relationship type. It also emphasizes that the aunting relationship is a voluntary relationship. While it is technically defined as a familial relationship, the frequency of contact and the depth of the relationship are typically formed outside the traditional familial structures, and it is a relationship of choice, not bound by family lines. This is a unique pattern that exists in very few traditional family relationships. There is freedom to define the relationship, and there are very few family expectations and norms to follow in this unique and understudied relationship type.

This chapter presents data in which nieces and nephews describe their aunting relationship and the dialectic tensions that appear in this relationship. This chapter presents a number of suggestions for future research; however, I would like to suggest other areas of interest not mentioned. For example, is the quality of the aunting relationship dependent on the quality of the parent's relationship with his or her sibling (the aunt)? What factors contribute to a close or distant relationship with an aunt? How does frequency of interaction relate to the quality of the aunting relationship? Does the quality of the aunting relationship change if the aunt is also a mother? How does the grandmother role relate to the role of the aunt in the family system? How does the cousin relationship impact the aunting relationship? Again, this is a family relationship type that should be viewed from a systems perspective. It is meaningless to explore this relationship type without conceptualizing the relationship within the larger family system.

A synthesis of these four chapters brings to light the complexity associated with family relations. These chapters not only discuss the intricacy of these family relationships, they also speak to the issue of family membership. The family relationships examined in this section utilize structural family terminology that defines membership in a family. Traditionally, these roles are "mother," "father," "sister," "brother," and so on. Structural theory (Parsons & Bales, 1955) defines family in and through these assigned roles. A communication perspective on defining family (Whitchurch & Dickson, 1999) emphasizes that a definition of family needs to embed in the interaction that occurs within the family. In other words, the roles assigned to family members are assigned as a result of the attributes and qualities of the interactions.

All four of these articles examine family roles through the eyes of the study participants. While the roles contain "labels" associated with familial relationships, it is clear that these family relationships are only meaningful when the interaction is perceived and experienced as meaningful. For example, Morr Serewicz discusses how once the in-law relationship has been formally and legally formed, the new family member still feels excluded from membership in the family. While the in-law has the assigned role of daughter- or son-in-law, they reported that it did not always feel like they were a family member. They were not treated as if they were a member of a new family.

In the rare examinations of the aunt or sibling-in-law relationships, it was evident that the aunt was experienced as important when the interaction was characterized by closeness or support. In addition, jealousy was experienced with siblings-in-law because they were perceived as not having a "right" to family rewards, since they technically were not a family member. Finally, the discussion of the grandparenting relationship offers insight into the intergenerational component. Families can expand and extend the definition of family membership, with the caveat that the interaction experienced needs to be rewarding.

While all these chapters explore understudied family relationships, they also extend our perspective of what it means to be included in the select group of a family. As a whole, these chapters advocate the position that family is defined in and through interaction and the meanings assigned to those interactions. Notions of family membership need to move away from traditional family roles and move toward examining the importance of extended family members in the nuclear family circle.

PART C

Relationships Created Through Divorce, Remarriage, or Adoption

The chapters in this final section of the book are united by one primary variable: all of these family relationships are established as a result of some type of definitive legal action concerning the membership and structure of the family unit. Family relationships created through adoption serve as one type, while family relationships terminated through divorce represent another. A third type of family dynamic created through legal action is the stepfamily, a new familiar structure resulting from the remarriage of one, or both, parents. Historically, adoption and divorce were secret and hidden aspects of family life within American culture, often carrying with them the stigma of shame or guilt in the eyes of the community or within the larger family of origin. Fortunately, most of the socially negative associations these types of family relationships harbored have long since been replaced by more positive, helpful, and supportive attitudes, perspectives generated in part by the explosion of divorce, adoption, and remarriage within our culture and the subsequent acknowledgement, openness, and acceptance such a huge demographic shift of family structure has brought with it. Additionally, the family has been forced to renegotiate not only the structure of family life but the familiar roles within that structure as two people, for example, transition from a spousal relationship to something else, or as a newly adopted child must renegotiate his or her role with a new set of parents.

The first chapter of this section, by Kathleen M. Galvin, provides a rich review of the literature on adoption and adoptive family relationships in the United States. She explores the unique communication issues and challenges of the adoptive family and details methods used by adoptive families to more deliberately manage their identities. In the second chapter, Dawn O. Braithwaite, Paul Schrodt, and Leslie A. Baxter assess the state of the literature concerning stepfamily relationships, reviewing research focused on stepfamily development, types, boundaries, and communication behaviors within this challenging family structure. Finally, the third chapter in this section explores the challenges of privacy dilemmas within post-divorce families. Tamara D. Afifi and Tara McManus discuss the difficulty faced by many post-divorce families as they deal with redefining privacy boundaries between former spouses and between parents and their children. The final thought-provoking commentary for this section is presented by Beth Le Poire of the University of California at Santa Barbara.

8

Joined by Hearts and Words

Adoptive Family Relationships

Kathleen M. Galvin

Adoption, previously perceived as a secret permutation of a biologically formed family, emerges today as one way to create a family with multiple enactment possibilities. Recent definitions of adoption include "the legal act whereby an adult person takes a minor into the relation of a child" and "the receiving into a clan or tribe of one from the outside and treating him as one of the same blood" (Funk & Wagnall's, 2001, p. 20). Although most adoptive families are formed through legal processes, the members' ongoing communicative interactions create the family identity, an identity that the family manages discursively over time. As family life is increasingly formed and lived along the boundaries of kinship ties, adoption provides a fertile site for examining communication processes such as disclosure, privacy management, dialectical tension management, narration, and socialization.

Compared to adoption in earlier times, adoption today is more *complex* as the process becomes more open. It is more *flexible* as older persons, biological parents, single individuals, stepparents, and same-sex partners are able to adopt, while sibling sets, older children, or children with disabilities or special needs are finding new family ties. Finally, adoption is more *visible*, as numerous families are formed through international or transracial adoption, frequently rendering the family-building process transparent.

Such changes impact the communicative complexities of all family members' lives as multiple parties negotiate and renegotiate their familial identity across their lifetimes.

Whereas adoption is a longstanding and accepted means of building families through law and language, political and social changes have transformed adoption practices and associated communication practices. Therefore, the following pages will address the current demographics of U.S. adoption, historical and current adoption trends that impact communication practices, key communication issues, and future research directions.

How Common Is Adoption?

Approximately two to four percent of children in the United States are adopted, slightly more than half by relatives or stepparents (Brodzinsky, Smith, & Brodzinsky, 1998). The 2000 Census, which included "adopted son/daughter" for the first time, revealed that 2.5% of children under 18 were adopted (Kreider, 2003). At the turn of the 21st century, 12.6% of adopted children under 18, or almost 200,000 children, were foreign born; today approximately 18,000 children arrive each year (Kreider, 2003). In 1997, the Evan B. Donaldson Adoption Institute released comprehensive data indicating that approximately 60% of Americans had a "personal experience" with adoption—they knew someone who was adopted, adopted a child themselves, or relinquished a child for adoption. Currently there are five to six million adoptees in the United States and, when the other persons (adoptive parents, birth parents, siblings) directly connected to this practice are factored in, the number of persons affected by adoption soars into the tens of millions (Pertman, 2000). Thus, the adoption of one child impacts not only the adoptive parent(s) and extended family but also the birth parents and the adoptee's future children.

Background of Adoption Practices

Adoption represents a centuries-old practice evident in "ancient Greece, Egypt, Rome, the Middle East, Asia, and the tribal societies of Africa and Oceania" (Carp, 1998, p. 3). Today, adoption practices vary greatly worldwide (Patton, 2000); the meanings of adoption and kinship vary across cultures (Wegar, 1998). Adoption practices in the United States reflect a Western European orientation, emphasizing the primacy of the biological family. Adoption practices evolved with the development of the nation, each phase creating new sensitivity to communication practices. In the Colonial era, children born out of wedlock, orphaned, abandoned, or neglected were apprenticed to masters who maintained them in exchange for labor. The 1800s witnessed the necessary rise of orphanages as increased urbanization and economic stress forced humanitarian and religious child welfare reformers to place children in institutional care. Massachusetts passed the first modern adoption law in 1851, emphasizing children's needs and the contractual and egalitarian nature of adults' guardianship (Carp, 1998). Orphan trains traveled from the east coast westward to Kansas leaving groups of children in new communities in the mid 1850s. During these periods families addressed adoption openly.

The last half of the 19th century witnessed the rise of movements to maintain children's ties to their biological families, whenever possible, as well as the emergence of organizations, such as the nationwide Children's Home Society, designed to place needy children into adoptive homes. As a result of child advocates' commitments to avoid severing the biological bonds, the number of dependent children in institutions nearly doubled during the first three decades of the 20th century. Low adoption rates also reflected the growing eugenics movement that linked illegitimacy with lower mental capacities.

By the second quarter of the 20th century, the U.S. Children's Bureau and the Child Welfare League of America reformed adoption laws, trained professional adoption workers, and educated the American public on the topic (Carp, 1998). Illegitimacy rates soared during wartime, accompanied by an increase in the number of infants available for adoption. The first small wave of international adoption began at the end of World War II through the efforts of American veterans returning from Europe and Asia. Until recently, this practice primarily involved Asian children who were adopted into Caucasian families, creating families formed through international and transracial adoption (Simon & Alstein, 2000).

The post–World War II period fostered a pro-family climate, creating pressure on couples to become parents. Adoption agencies and private lawyers increasingly provided healthy Caucasian infants, or "blue-ribbon babies" (Patton, 2000), to infertile couples through a process of physical and intellectual matching designed to protect the parents from a stigma of infertility. The goal was to render the family formation process invisible to outsiders; children were selected to resemble their adoptive parents. Secrecy emerged as the key communication dynamic. Until the 1980s, agencies attempted to match adoptive parents and their child on physical characteristics, intellectual potential, and talents (Reitz & Watson, 1992). Birth parents disappeared from the picture through legal means—secret or closed records. Infertile couples' demands for children escalated as increasing abortion and single motherhood reduced the number of available infants. During the past 30 years, due to the difficulty in adopting Caucasian infants, prospective parents increasingly turned to transracial adoption, international adoption, and open adoption, challenging the agency practices of matching and serving only infertile couples. These movements rendered secrecy meaningless.

Contemporary Adoption Practices

Today, adoption involves creating a family "that is connected to another family, the birth family, and often to different cultures and to different racial, ethnic, and national groups as well" (Bartholet, 1993, p. 186), creating unique communication challenges for those involved. It "does not signal the absolute end of one family and the beginning of another; nor does it sever the psychological tie to an earlier family. Rather, it expands the family boundaries of all those who are involved" (Reitz & Watson, 1992, p. 11). The adoption process involves the adoption triangle—the adoptee, the birth parent(s), and the adoptive parent(s)—with variable contact among members. Points of the adoption triangle eventually may involve multiple individuals because the birth mother or birth father may have partners or spouses and other children and the adoptive parent(s) may have other children (Elmhorst, 2003). Triangle members are repeatedly engaged, sometimes with each other, in the emotional arenas of loss and grief, bonding and attachment, denial and shame, and integration and self-esteem (Silverstein & Demick, 1994). Some members may interact over the adoptee's life span; others may never meet due to specific legal agreements or adoption circumstances. In some cases, the birth father may be excluded from these processes, unaware that he fathered a child.

In recent decades, adoption practice shifted from matching physical and intellectual characteristics of unrelated persons to creating an open system of connections, crossing religious, racial, and national lines. Today's adoptive families appear in multiple forms, each of which may involve different levels of privacy ranging from secret to fully open. As the number of available infants declined, prospective parents faced the challenge of marketing themselves to birth parents. Because the demand for infants affords birth parents some control over the placement process, they may participate in the choice of the adoptive parents and stipulate access conditions as part of open adoption placements. Currently, the open adoption movement may account for a slight rise in the availability of healthy infants for adoption (Hwang, 2004).

Open adoption creates an active and interconnected adoption triangle. Full disclosure allows adoptive parents, and often the adopted child, to interact directly with birth parents (National Adoption Information Clearinghouse, 2004). Birth parents have access to information about the adoptive parents and, frequently, some level of contact, ranging from letters and pictures to visits, with the adoptive family.

Infertility no longer drives adoption practice. Families with biological children add members through international adoption because birth country officials seldom restrict placement to infertile couples. Children in these families are referred to as "mixed siblings" if they represent different cultural or racial heritages. Current international adoption data reflect a shift in countries of origin. In 2003 children were adopted primarily from the People's Republic of China (6,859), Russia (5,209), Guatemala (2,328), and South Korea (1,790) ("Immigrant visas," 2004), with smaller numbers arriving from countries such as India, Vietnam, Kazakhstan, and Colombia. International adoption may not always involve racial differences between parents and children, while domestic adoption may involve crossing racial lines. When racial differences among members occur, this is referred to as a family formed through visible adoption. In addition, families with biological children may adopt hard-to-place children including those in sibling sets, with disabilities, or with special health needs. Foster parents, with or without biological children, frequently choose to adopt a child in their care who becomes available.

Other variations occur. Stepparents may adopt their stepchildren; this usually occurs if the biological parent dies or relinquishes parental rights. Not much is known about these adoptions, possibly because the child already is living within the family. Single individuals are finding adoption possibilities, frequently through international opportunities or domestic transracial adoption; frequently they are expected to demonstrate the willingness of extended family and friends to create a supportive community for the adoptive family.

In certain states gay males and lesbians may adopt, but the practice remains controversial (Brodzinsky, Patterson, & Vazizi, 2002). In their comparison of lesbian and heterosexual adoption experiences, Shelley-Sireci and Ciano-Boyce (2002) found general similarities, although lesbians were more likely to adopt a female child, perceive discrimination due to sexual orientation, and omit information in the home study. In some states, second partner adoption is available, permitting the partner of a biological or adoptive parent to become a legal parent.

Although most adoptive relationships are formalized through legal ties, informal adoption still occurs as extended family members or caring community members serve as surrogate parents, providing children with emotional and economic resources. These ties may be formalized at a later date. Informal adoption occurs more often within African American or Hispanic communities, reflecting their collectivistic orientations.

Why Is Adoption Historically Understudied?

In contrast to other family-building processes, adoption has been shrouded in silence. Communication practices have been intertwined with issues of history, morality, psychology, and politics. During the era when matching adoptive parents and children served as the norm, the goal was to make the adoption invisible; this goal, coupled with secrecy, created access problems for researchers in all fields.

Until recently, mental health professionals paid limited attention to adoption. Adoption research eventually blossomed in the 1960s due to the efforts of researcher Marshall Schechter, who recognized that adoptees used a far higher percentage of mental health services than did biological children, and David Kirk, whose 1964 publication *Shared Fate* addressed the tasks, challenges, and dilemmas faced by adoptive family members (Brodzinsky & Schechter, 1990). Their leadership stimulated wide-ranging studies of such issues as identity formation, long-range placement outcomes, the meaning of the search process, and the birth mother experience. The practices of international, transracial, and open adoption have transformed adoption practices, making them visible, discussable, and more accessible to researchers.

Currently the academic visibility of adoption remains limited. Fisher's (2003) study of the adoption portrayal in 21 college textbooks and family readers reveals that in textbooks published from 1998 to 2001, 1 out of every 200 pages (barely .48% of the space) was devoted to adoption. Almost one-fifth made no mention of the subject. Within the 16 edited collections, adoption was mentioned mainly in passing. Fisher criticizes the overall dearth of adoption coverage; these findings reflect the continuing ambivalence surrounding adoption.

Historically, communication-oriented writings on adoption tended to be prescriptive, frequently directed at adoptive parents in need of guidance as to how to discuss the topic with their children. Family communication, an area of academic study for approximately 40 years, initially focused on marital or parent-child interaction. The secrecy surrounding adoption, coupled with the relatively small number of adoptees, renders it a specialized area; adoption appeared only recently in the family communication field's scholarly conversations as more specialized topics gained prominence.

Communication Challenges of the Adoptive Family

Today, more U.S. families are formed and maintained, in part, by discursive processes as individuals create families outside of the traditional biological and adult legal ties. Members of families formed outside of full biological and adult legal ties need to engage in lifelong processes of identity maintenance including positioning, explaining, legitimating, and defending familial identity across external family boundaries as well as naming, discussing, narrating, and enacting rituals within the family boundaries. Essentially, these families become discourse-dependent (Galvin, in press). Families formed through adoption, especially visible adoption, depend on discourse processes to establish and maintain their bonding, providing members with an internal sense of identity as well as a public identity. Adoptive families' communicative identity maintenance depends, in part, on the degree to which the family structure presents intrinsic reminders that the child's biological roots are different (Kaye & Warren, 1988) and the openness of family communication (Powell & Afifi, 2005).

Although all families engage in some level of discourse-driven family identity building, less traditionally formed families engage more frequently in recurring discursive processes aimed at maintaining and managing their familial identity. In adoptive families, these needs surface as members revisit their familial identity at different developmental stages or face outsiders' questions and challenges regarding the veracity of their relatedness claims. Thus, the greater the ambiguity, the more elaborated the communication patterns.

The limited research on adoptive family communication patterns focuses on secrecy versus disclosure, language choice, narratives, discussion of physical differences, cultural socialization processes, as well as the role of artifacts and rituals. The following section details the development of communication concerns within adoptive families as silence has given way to deliberative management of identity.

Secrecy Versus Disclosure

Secrecy and disclosure in U.S. adoption has a complex history. Great debates raged about the impact of learning negative information about one's parentage, breaking the promise of anonymity given to birth parents, and having one's infertility implied or revealed. Historically, some adoptees never learned the truth; in other cases, there was a private parent-child "big talk" of revelation, sometimes the only discussion of the subject (Reitz & Watson, 1992). The prescribed versions of the "big talk" had a predictable focus—the joy of parents in gaining a child, specifically a "chosen child," an expression taken from the title of a 1939 children's book. Parents said little or nothing about why a child was available for adoption; they withheld painful or ugly information for the child's benefit. Over the past two decades, however, adoptive parents have been encouraged to engage their children in an ongoing dialogue rather than just the "big talk" because information professionals insisted that children need the story retold as they develop and encounter new questions (Brodzinsky, Singer, & Braff, 1984). Today adoptive parents are advised to mention adoption before a child is old enough to comprehend the concept in order make it a safe topic for discussions.

Openness is rapidly becoming a common practice that "affirms that communication or contact is not only manageable but—despite its complexity—might even enhance the quality of adoptive family life" (Silverstein & Demick, 1994, p. 119). Adoptive parents report that having birth family information positively affected their perceptions of the birth parents (Hollenstein, Leve, Scaramella, Milfort, & Neiderhiser, 2003). Birth mothers who maintain some contact with the adoptive family appear to handle the adoption experience more positively (Cushman, Kalmuss, & Namerow, 1997). Fully disclosed open adoptions work well if both the adoptive parents and birth parents are engaged, but "success depends on ongoing management of boundaries and commitment to the relationship" (Grotevant, 2000, p. 51).

In light of recent adoption practices, entire families find themselves involved in multiple, complicated conversations across life stages, including discussions about the reason a child became available for adoption. Although important, such conversations are seldom easy. The key parental issue remains—how to make adoptees feel they are irresistible when they were not kept by the people most likely to find them wonderful (Melina, 1998). Parents of transracial and international adoptees must prepare to face challenges from strangers presenting a variation of the question, "Are those kids yours?" (Register, 1991). Because of members' physical dissimilarity, mixed siblings encounter challenges to their familial ties, necessitating linguistic explanations or defenses of their connections. Members of mixed sibling pairs report handling such questions by enacting communication strategies ranging from straightforward explanations about adoption to sarcastic responses. For example, a Caucasian-Asian pair of teenage sisters report, "When we got the question, 'How can you two be sisters?' we would respond, 'The Mailman' and walk away" (Galvin & Fonner, 2003. p. 1).

As children age, or older children are adopted, the question arises, "Whose information is it?" Families involved in open adoption also need to manage a privacy-disclosure dialectic.

Although contemporary practice emphasizes the need for disclosure, adoptive families differ on the extent to which they engage in high or low "distinguishing" between their own experiences or feelings about being adoptive families and those of biological families, or ongoing acknowledgement of differences versus no acknowledgment of differences. In their study of intact families with teenagers adopted as babies, Kaye and Warren (1988) found that acknowledgments of differences were outnumbered by assurances about non-differences. Within this group, low acknowledgment of adoption was not necessarily denial whereas high acknowledgment may be a coping mechanism for adoptees experiencing difficult development. In their study of 54 adult adoptees, Powell and Afifi (2005) found that those who experienced high levels of uncertainty and ambiguous loss "also experienced closed family communication or avoidance" (p. 146). The secrecy-disclosure dialectical tension underpins most adoptive relationships.

Language

The language of adoption, socially constructed and frequently emotionally charged, carries communicative power. In past eras, children of unmarried mothers were referred to as "bastards," "illegitimate," or "born out of wed-lock," or as "abandoned by real parents." Adoptive parents are faced with discussing the linguistic implications of expressions such as "relinquished," "placed," or "made an adoption plan." Parental guidance is available for today's parents regarding problematic as well as "adoption-friendly" termi-nology; the latter includes terms such as *birth parents* to describe the man and woman who conceived and gave birth to the child or *adoption plan* to acknowledge careful birth parent decision making (Lambe, 2004).

Open adoption provides a unique set of linguistic challenges, given the lack of common terminology for any extended family members in the adop-tion triangle. The following birth mother's comment, as she prepares to introduce her younger birth children to the older daughter she placed for adoption, captures the linguistic complications of her arrangement:

> I said, "She would be, if I had kept her, she would be your older sister . . . It's hard to explain how I feel when I see her as to why it doesn't bother me that she calls me [first name] rather than, you know, her mom. Because I'm not. I can't put it into words. (Fravel, McRoy, & Grotevant, 2000, p. 429)

Naming a child, especially an older child or a child adopted internation-ally and transracially, presents linguistic challenges because children arrive with names reflecting their birth family and birth culture. The decision to maintain a name or rename a child carries meaning. Names carry identity for adoptees; "That was really all I had when I came to this country: that name. And my parents overlooked it and chose another one" (Kroll, 2000, p. 18). Parents are torn between desiring to symbolize family and, possibly, cultural inclusion with an American name and indicating respect for their child's identity as expressed in his or her birth name.

Narratives

Creation or entrance stories, including how adult partners met and birth or adoption narratives, answer the question, "How did this family come to be?" (Galvin, Bylund, & Brommel, 2004). The way the story is told or retold can impact the child's adjustment and well-being (Friedlander, 1999). Krusiewicz and Wood (2001) identified the following five themes that resonated across adoptive parents' entrance stories: destiny, compelling connection, rescue, legitimacy, and dialectical tensions. The first tension reflected both the birth parent's misfortune and the adoptive parent's fortune to adopt the child; the second reflected the adoptive parents' experience of having their desires for parenthood met through another's rejection of parenthood. In cases of open adoption, a birth parent may participate in the narrative's construction, helping the adoptive parent understand the decision. An adoptive parent who can understand a birth parent's underlying feelings and beliefs is more likely to help their child understand his or her early history (Neil, 2003). Such narratives create meaningful links across boundaries and, in cases of ongoing contact with birth family members, elaborated narratives may evolve over time. Many international adoptions present challenges due to missing narratives or pieces of the narrative. Depending on the country of origin, existing narratives may not refer to a child's specific biological birth mother or birth father because frequently such information is unavailable (Johnson, Banghan, & Liyao, 1999).

The lack of personal stories about the birth family contributes to an adopted child's sense of loss (Stone, 1988), leaving him or her with only adoptive creation stories. This loss may be exacerbated when siblings hear detailed birth stories. Conversely, open adoption raises the possibilities of competing versions of an adoptee's creation story. Although most narratives focus on the child, adoptive parents report five narrative themes reflecting their transition to parenthood: turning point story, legitimizing story, normalizing and familiarizing story, receiving story, and "baby" stories (Manning, 2000).

Addressing Physical Differences

Families with visually dissimilar members regularly confront the need for elaborated communication patterns. In the past decade, adoption researchers have focused on identity development of transracial adoptees raised by

Caucasian parents. Patton (2000) suggests they construct their identities through the social narratives and cultural meaning systems in which they find themselves. Frequently parents overlook the need for the entire family system to discursively construct an identity for itself, not just the adopted individual(s). Because extended family members may resist or reject a child from another country, potential adoptive parents need to address racial and national issues directly with family members (Deacon, 1997).

Physical differences, usually signaling racial differences, become part of ongoing family conversations, which may be carried out in reluctant acknowledgment or with continuous, open dialogue. Transracially adopted children begin to question the physical differences between themselves and other family members at an early age; 39% of adult adoptees from Asia remember when they first realized they looked different from their parents (Simon & Alstein, 2000). Such moments represent turning points in the adoptive process. Siblings may point out differences playfully or in anger. This awareness intensifies as children enter school and peers bring the topic up in conversation or teasing; some children may resist acknowledging their racial heritage for a period of time as they try to avoid appearing different (Wilkinson, 1985). Korean college-age adoptees report race was the most difficult topic to discuss with their families (Fujimoto, 2001).

Cultural Socialization Practices

Defining self and defining family involve discursive struggles as members of families formed through international or transracial adoption address their identity issues. In their attempt to describe American families who have adopted children from China, Tessler, Gamache, and Liu (1999) chose to call them "American and Chinese" families, distinguishing them from "Chinese-American" families in which ancestors emigrated from China and "Chinese and American" families formed through ethnic intermarriage. Many families describe themselves as "American" while a few develop a self-identity such as "Irish-Polish-Vietnamese American."

Families may actively seek contact with their child's birth culture, either for the family as a whole or for the child. Summer culture camps and cultural schools provide opportunities for adoptees to experience their birth culture. Denver's Joyous Chinese Cultural School, designed for children ages two to six years old, provides opportunities for adopted children to experience culture, language, history, and celebrations as well as to interact with other mixed-race families and with native Chinese participants (Manning, 2001).

Birth culture biases impact certain adoptees. Families who adopt from certain nations often face a gender paradox. Parents of girls adopted from

China confront the challenge of positively socializing their female children to their birth culture while also explaining why almost all the children available for adoption in China are female due to the higher birth culture value placed on boys and practices related to China's one-child-policy (Galvin, 2000). Caucasian parents involved in domestic transracial adoption confront society's biases and face the issues of socializing an African American child. "Black children adopted transracially often do not develop the coping mechanisms necessary to function in a society that is inherently racist against African Americans" (Simon & Alstein, 2000, p. 39) because their parents have not prepared them for such encounters. When transracially adopted African American young adults were asked for the advice they would give to Caucasian parents adopting someone like themselves, over 91% essentially said, "Do it, but be sensitive to racial issues" (Simon & Alstein, 2000, p. 125).

Artifacts and Rituals

Artifacts play a role in family formation as well as in identity development. Potential adoptive parents frequently present themselves discursively, visually, and verbally, in portfolios, scrapbooks, or Web sites where they are compared to others seeking to be selected as "the one" by birth parents. Mittino (2004) identifies the following generalizations characterizing prospective parents' self-presentations on adoption Web sites: Participants are primarily Caucasian, heterosexual couples who extol each other's positive characteristics and tell "how we met" stories. They discuss the importance of marriage, family, education, and religion. Self-presentations include careers and educational background, hobbies, and significant friends and family who are depicted as adoption supporters. Towns, neighborhoods, and houses are shown. Similar self-representations may be found in scrapbooks or portfolios. Currently the increase in Internet, newspaper, and brochure self-promotion by adoption agencies, birth parents, and prospective parents represents a significant shift in adoption artifacts.

Objects facilitate family conversation as memories, present experiences, and future dreams are inextricably linked to the objects within a family environment (Csikszentmihalyi & Rochberg-Halton, 1981). Many families create life books as a way to honor a child's history; some display cultural artifacts, such as Russian dolls, and personal mementoes, such as adoption documents (Evans, 2000). Others avoid such practices. What is revealed by, and who controls access to, such artifacts impacts family interaction within and across boundaries.

Rituals serve to reinforce family identity. Many adoptive families celebrate the arrival or "gotcha" day(s) of family members in addition to birthdays. Some families celebrate days culturally significant to a child, such as Chinese New Year. In cases of open adoption, members of the birth family may participate in rituals such as a child's confirmation, a practice that contributes to all members' family identity development.

What We Need to Learn About Adoption

Ongoing research on adoptive families is important for two reasons: (1) it contributes to an understanding of the communication dynamics within a range of adoptive systems, and (2) adoptive family research can inform investigations into the communication patterns of other types of discourse-dependent families. As an understudied area, adoption presents communication researchers with multiple questions involving the following family processes: family identity development, boundary management, uncertainty management, socialization, and developmental processes. Many of the issues discussed in the last section on communication issues and challenges serve as future research directions. The following topics represent key issues that have been understudied or are emerging due to advances in technology.

The Secrecy-Disclosure Continuum

Ongoing research should investigate the implications of high acknowledgment versus low acknowledgment of differences across types of adoptive families, particularly the emerging forms that deemphasize secrecy and matching. There is a need for greater understanding of the information management processes of older adoptees who may have been socialized into rules regarding collective boundaries by their birth families that run counter to the adoptive families' rules, and issues of co-owned information, such as the child's birth parent information or reason for placement (Elmhorst, 2003). Although research on open adoption is a fertile area for communication scholars, few have addressed it. Communication privacy management theory (Petronio, 2002) provides one valuable lens for examining many of these issues. The following questions merit attention: "How do members of adoption triangles define their roles and manage their interactions across developmental stages?" "What linguistic codes develop as members interact within their boundaries and across boundaries?"

Discourse Strategies for Boundary Management

The identity of less traditionally formed families is more dependent on the discourse processes of its members due, in part, to issues of boundary ambiguity that exist any time members' physical and psychological presence are incongruent (Boss, 1999). Thus physical dissimilarity among members, continued connections to a birth mother, members' lack of shared early childhood experiences, or visits by birth family relatives (grandfather, aunt) to the adoptive family create ambiguity and an inevitable need to actively manage familial identity within and across family boundaries.

Adoptive families rely more heavily on social interaction to create their identities than do families formed fully through biological and adult legal ties. Discourse-dependent families are dependent on key strategies to construct and maintain identity within and across family boundaries. Key questions emerge: "What specific discourse practices do adoptive family members enact to construct and manage their internal identity as well as their external identity?" "To what extent do these strategies differ across types of adoptive families?"

Discursive Family Representations

Open adoption renders potential adoptive parents and birth parents visible to each other. Persuasive messages, usually presented verbally and visually on Web sites, represent attempts by couples or individuals to discursively construct their lives in hopes of achieving parenthood. Although the practice is less common, some birth parents represent themselves on Web sites in order to attract prospective adoptive parents. Adoption agencies maintain Web sites with information and pictures of children who are considered hard to place. An examination of Web sites, scrapbooks, life books, and their target audiences—the child, other family members, outsiders—would extend the current work on social influence. Related questions include "What verbal or visual persuasive strategies are most effective in attracting birth parent interest or for attracting potential parents for hard-to-place children?"

Adoptive family members increasingly turn to the Internet for information and social support. International adoptees maintain their own elaborately networked cultural communities. Web sites offer chat rooms and information about heritage tours, culture camps, and resources for finding biological relatives (Melosh, 2002). Professional adoption Web sites are sources of information on developmental and psychological processes of adoptees, as well as communication advice designed for adoptive parents (*Adoption Learning Partners*, 2004).

General Complexities

Emerging adoption practices create numerous challenges. Some children experience multiple identity issues that necessitate explanation; some adoptive triangles involve many highly active participants. Few studies address the experiences of children who need to make meaning of both their experiences as a transnationally adopted child and a child of a lesbian or gay couple (Grotevant, Dunbar, Kohler, & Esau, 2000). In addition, birth fathers and siblings remain the "missing pieces" in most studies as well as in adoption practice (Wegar, 1997).

Transracial adoption provides an important site for communication research focusing on the relationship between language, interaction, and culture and the process of bi-cultural identity development (Manning, 2001). Transracial adoptees do not deny their racial identification, nor do their parents or siblings (Silverman & Feigelman, 1990), but little is known about how parents prepare their adoptive or biological children to encounter racial derogation (Galvin, 2003). As adoption of older children or those with special needs increases, the generally low number of adoption disruptions is rising. Estimates vary greatly, but 10–15% of adoptions of children over three years of age result in disruptions associated with characteristics of the child, the parents, and the family (Hollingsworth, 2003).

Adoption's future is intertwined with new technologies and medical breakthroughs. Many individuals are achieving parenthood through assisted reproductive technology, thus lowering the number of potential adoptive parents. A residual issue arising from these technologies is how to think about the 100,000 spare embryos that remain in a frozen state and, according to some, are potentially available for adoption (Freundlich, 2002). This concern raises investigation possibilities for scholars interested in decision making and the intersection of the public and private spheres.

Communication research stands to contribute to these increasingly complex adoption practices because "successful relationships in such complex family situations hinge on participants' flexibility, communication skills, and commitment to the relationships" (Grotevant, Perry, & McRoy, in press). These trends call for answers to questions such as "How do members of complex adoptive families communicate their identity?" "How can Caucasian parents prepare adopted children of different ethnic heritages to respond to racism?" "What are the communication patterns that accompany the dissolution of an adoptive relationship?" "How do prospective adoptive parents engage in decision making when considering an embryo adoption?"

Conclusion

Adoption continues to provide one viable and meaningful way to construct families. Adoption research blossomed in the last half century as the adoption process became more open, but few scholars have addressed the communication processes inherent in this family form. Due to ongoing developments in adoption practice, studies of adoptive families can serve as a valuable laboratory for studying discursive processes that will impact all family members' lives throughout the 21st century.

9

Understudied and Misunderstood

Communication in Stepfamily Relationships

Dawn O. Braithwaite,
Paul Schrodt, and Leslie A. Baxter

A research team brought college-aged stepchildren together in focus group interviews to talk about communication in their stepfamilies. At the end of the discussion, we asked the groups to give advice to parents and stepparents concerning stepfamily communication, and they took on this task with great enthusiasm (Braithwaite, Toller, Daas, Durham, & Jones, 2004). Many of the focus groups chose to draw pictures to illustrate their advice. One group drew a picture of a scared-looking young child whose hands and feet were being stretched to the four corners of the paper, representing being caught in the middle between parents and stepparents. Another group drew a very different picture of a little girl standing between two sets of parents, their hands joined to hers by hearts. This group told the researchers that the hearts represented communication, explaining that strong and happy stepfamilies can exist when the members communicate well (Braithwaite et al., 2004). As we prepared to write this chapter on stepfamily communication, these two portraits represent the extremes of stepfamily functioning and highlight the importance of studying communication in the stepfamily context.

In this chapter, we reflect on the current state of research on communication in stepfamilies, an understudied family form. Ganong and Coleman (1994) define a stepfamily as a family in which "at least one of the adults has a child or children from a previous relationship" (p. 8). Stepfamilies involve a wide range of personal relationships that vary considerably in form, structure, and complexity. The three authors of this chapter have been involved in stepfamily research for a number of years. To begin, four observations about communication in stepfamilies shaped our thinking about this chapter. First, the stepfamily is an important and expanding family form that scholars need to be studying. In the late 1980s, 32% of the population and at least one of every four to five children were estimated to live in stepfamilies (Marsiglio, 1992). As of 1996, 17% of all children living in the United States (or 11.8 million) lived in stepfamilies (including the presence of a stepparent, stepsibling, or half-sibling), of which 42% (or 4.9 million) lived with at least one residential stepparent (Fields, 2001).

Second, stepfamilies are one context in which researchers and practitioners from a variety of disciplines can come together to make a difference. Stepfamilies have been studied from a wide variety of academic and clinical specialties, for example, family studies, sociology, psychology, law, social work, anthropology, and communication. Ganong and Coleman (2004) pointed out that clinicians were writing about stepfamilies well before researchers (e.g., Visher & Visher, 1979). Ganong and Coleman (2004) described these early days: "researchers and clinicians, like the proverbial blind man and the elephant, were discovering truth separately about stepfamilies with little evidence of communication between them" (p. 189). In the past 10 years, researchers and clinicians have done a better job of attending to each other's work.

Third, we believe that a focus on communication in stepfamilies is important to both clinical practitioners and researchers. As we take the perspective that personal and family relationships are constituted in communication (Baxter, 2004, in press), we believe communication scholars have much to bring to the study of stepfamilies. Beginning with Cissna, Cox, and Bochner's initial study in 1990, communication scholars are in relatively early stages of research programs on stepfamily interaction. We believe that communication researchers are uniquely positioned to highlight the central role of communication in the development and enactment of stepfamily relationships.

Finally, and perhaps most importantly, we want to help shift the focus away from looking at only problems with stepfamilies. While the amount of published research on stepfamilies tripled during the 1990s (Coleman, Ganong, & Fine, 2000), most of the research took what Ganong and Coleman (1994) labeled a "deficit-comparison approach." There was a bias toward a traditional, nuclear family ideology where the conventional, "nuclear" family was the conceptual framework against which the step-family was compared and found to be different, and thus, deficient (Baxter, Braithwaite, & Nicholson, 1999). While scholars have warned against viewing stepfamilies as inherently problematic and inferior to nuclear families (Baxter et al., 1999), few researchers have yet to adopt this focus. We agree with Golish (2003), who called for a focus on stepfamily strengths rather than only on problems, as we believe that stepfamilies will benefit from good models as well as from suggestions for how to improve their interaction.

Our goal in this chapter is to explore the state of stepfamily communication research. We talk about where we believe stepfamilies are understudied, and we provide directions for researchers to follow. We begin by suggesting that you read the chapter on post-divorce communication by Afifi and McManus (Chapter 10). There are certainly going to be some similar issues raised in both chapters because, after all, stepfamilies are post-divorce families. In our chapter, we will stress research findings that are focused on the stepfamily stage of life.

Stepfamily Development and Types

Scholars studying stepfamilies have focused on two broad areas: (a) step-family development and types, and (b) stepfamily boundaries, both internal and external. We discuss each of these issues and suggest places we believe stepfamilies are understudied.

Stepfamily Development

Researchers have worked to identify the stages of stepfamily development as well as different types of stepfamilies. One important question for understanding communication in stepfamily development is "When does the stepfamily begin?" Coleman, Ganong, and Fine (2004) indicated that answering this question is like "beginning a novel in the middle of the book" (p. 216). Many researchers identify marriage as the starting point for the stepfamily, yet, as Ganong and Coleman (1994) pointed out, members often perceive that their stepfamily began prior to the marriage of the parents (if they marry at all). Baxter et al. (1999) tested this assertion by asking stepfamily members to indicate the date their stepfamily started feeling like a family. Most respondents chose a date well before marriage. Therefore, if we begin our studies at the point of marriage, we are missing important interaction in the lives of stepfamilies.

It is important to understand how the members of the stepfamily-to-be interact and communicatively construct their family. Coleman et al. (2004) indicated that one of the big challenges during the formative period is that stepfamily members have relationships at very different stages of development. While the dating couple presumably knows each another well, children may not. In fact, we have found in our own studies that some stepsiblings do not meet one another until cohabitation, the wedding, or even later. Complicating matters, Coleman et al. stressed that different members of the developing stepfamily also have varied levels of motivation to communicate and to help the new family to develop.

Papernow's (1993) model of stepfamily development has been well regarded, especially in clinical circles. He proposed a seven-stage model that includes (a) a fantasy stage characterized by unrealistic and idealized expectations of the stepfamily, (b) an immersion stage in which challenges of stepfamily life confront expectations, (c) an awareness stage in which members attempt to make sense of their confusion, (d) a mobilization stage with attempts to manage difficulties, (e) an action stage where new agreements create a base on which to build, (f) a contact stage in which positive emotional bonds form, and (g) a resolution stage where a more solid stepfamily unit emerges. Papernow argued that problematic stepfamilies typically do not advance beyond the fourth stage.

Despite the popularity of Papernow's (1993) model, some scholars have criticized stage models of relational development (e.g., Baxter & Montgomery, 1996), as these models do not emphasize the possibility of multiple developmental trajectories, and they oversimplify relational development as a linear process. In particular, Baxter et al. (1999) extended these criticisms to Papernow's (1993) model, noting the inability of his model to capture the variety of ways stepfamilies develop.

To address these criticisms, stepfamily communication scholars have focused on the turning points, developmental processes, and stepfamily types that differentiate among different stepfamilies. For example, Baxter et al. (1999) identified stepfamily turning points during the first four years of stepfamily life, as previous scholars have highlighted the first four years of development as the "make or break" period for stepfamilies (e.g., Papernow,

1993, Visher & Visher, 1979). In the interviews, members of stepfamilies identified their stepfamily turning points and indicated changes in the level of "feeling like a family" for each turning point identified. From 566 turning points identified by stepfamily members, the researchers categorized 15 turning point types, which are events that represented a positive or negative change in feeling like a family. These included changes in household configuration, holiday/special events, conflict episodes, and family crises. The researchers then identified five developmental pathways found in the first four years of stepfamily development: (a) accelerated pathways (i.e., a pattern of quick movement toward 100% feeling like a family), (b) prolonged pathways (i.e., stepfamilies that progressed to higher levels of feeling like a family, although not as quickly as accelerated pathways), (c) stagnant pathways (i.e., stepfamilies that "never took off"), (d) declining pathways (i.e., stepfamilies that began with a high level of feeling like a family, then declined to zero), and (e) high-amplitude turbulent pathways (i.e., stepfamilies who experienced dramatic up and down shifts in feeling like a family).

Extending this study, Braithwaite, Olson, Golish, Soukup, and Turman (2001) examined how stepfamily members in the five trajectories interact and adapt during the process of becoming a family. They focused on issues related to boundaries, solidarity, and adaptation, discovering that members of families in each of the trajectories experienced different processes of interacting and forming appropriate roles. Their findings provided further evidence to suggest that a diverse number of stepfamily experiences can be differentiated based on an analysis of interaction.

Other researchers have focused more specifically on the communication strategies and activities that facilitate stepfamily development. For example, Golish (2003) examined stepfamily development using systems theory to identify the communication strengths and weaknesses that differentiated strong from struggling stepfamilies. She found strong stepfamilies were more likely to spend quality time together; to establish a sense of unity through enacting family rituals; and to resolve conflicts through family meetings, open communication, and compromise. Likewise, using a dialectical perspective, Braithwaite, Baxter, and Harper (1998) discovered that the most productive ritual enactments in stepfamilies enabled family members to embrace their new family while valuing what was important from their old family.

Stepfamily Types

In addition to considering the communication and relationship processes that characterize stepfamily development, scholars have also studied the cognitive and behavioral outcomes associated with different types of established stepfamilies. Coleman et al. (2004) divided stepfamilies into four broad types: (a) "Brady Bunch" families that mimic first-marriage families, with stepparents taking on a traditional parenting role; (b) stepfamilies with a detached stepparent and engaged parent; (c) couple-focused stepfamilies where the marriage and adult needs are put first; and (d) progressive step-families that develop ways to effectively problem solve and communicate. Progressive stepfamilies do not try to act like first-marriage families but find ways to meet the needs of different stepfamily members by enacting roles and structural qualities that best fit family members' needs.

In a somewhat different vein, Schrodt (2003, in press) recently adopted schema theory to examine the different types of organized knowledge struc-tures, or schemata, that emerge in stepchildren as they manage the challenges and relational complexities associated with stepfamily life. He developed two new measures useful for synthesizing and assessing the ways in which stepchildren "think about" their stepfamilies, and he identified five types of stepfamilies that differ in terms of how stepchildren think about stepfamily life as well as their relationships with their primary stepparent.

First, bonded stepfamilies were characterized by low levels of dissension and avoidance and relatively high levels of stepfamily involvement, flexibil-ity, and expressiveness. Second, functional stepfamilies were characterized by moderately high levels of stepfamily involvement, flexibility, and expres-siveness, as well as moderately low levels of stepfamily dissension and avoidance. These stepchildren tended to think of their stepparents as friends rather than parents. Third, indifferent stepfamilies were characterized by slightly above-average levels of stepfamily dissension and avoidance and slightly below-average levels of stepfamily involvement, flexibility, and expressiveness. They demonstrated general ambivalence toward their step-family. Fourth, avoidant stepfamilies were characterized by moderately high levels of dissension and avoidance and moderately low levels of step-family involvement, flexibility, and expressiveness. Avoidant stepfamilies appeared to function less well than bonded, functional, and indifferent stepfamilies, due primarily to a lack of open communication within the stepparent-stepchild relationship and in the stepfamily as a whole. Last, conflictual stepfamilies were characterized by somewhat higher levels of expressiveness than avoidant stepfamilies, as well as the highest levels of stepfamily dissension and avoidance and the lowest levels of stepfamily involvement and flexibility among the five types.

With his typology, Schrodt (2003, in press) has extended recent efforts to identify the cognitions and communication constructs that distinguish strong stepfamilies from stepfamilies having difficulty (cf. Golish, 2003), claiming that the five types of stepfamily schemata represent, to some extent, cognitive communication outcomes that developed in stepchildren as a result of different developmental pathways (cf. Baxter et al., 1999; Braithwaite et al., 2001).

Understudied Aspects of Stepfamily Development and Types

While we are making advances in understanding the development of stepfamilies and different stepfamily types, how stepfamilies interact and become functional families is still understudied. Research is needed to be able to link different developmental trajectories with different established stepfamily forms. Scholars are helping shed light on multiple stepfamily types, which is an important move forward in the way stepfamilies are understood and viewed. At this point, scholars need to focus on communication at different points in the developmental process and within different stepfamily types. For example, researchers might consider comparing the interaction patterns that characterize stepfamilies formed after divorce with those that characterize stepfamilies formed after the death of a parent (e.g., Bryant, 2003), as well as with the patterns that characterize stepfamilies formed after the dissolution of a non-marital relationship. Likewise, scholars need to examine the messages that constitute and reflect different developmental pathways in problematic stepfamilies and in strong, functional stepfamilies (cf. Golish, 2003; Schrodt, 2003).

Another issue that is understudied is how stepfamily members interact and come to develop a sense of family identity, as well as feelings for other members of the stepfamily. How, if at all, do members of stepfamilies come to love one another? Our reading of the stepfamily literature is that the dominant view of love in stepfamilies is often conceived of as companionate love based on affinity (Hendrick & Hendrick, 1992). Stepparents are advised not to try and duplicate the children's parents but rather to develop a modified friendship with them. As one extension of this research, we offer Bakhtin's (1990) notion of aesthetic love as a way to understand love in stepfamilies. With aesthetic love, one has a commitment to listen to the other, to give him or her respect, and to recognize and legitimate the other's worldview. Aesthetic love is built on an appreciation of difference (Baxter & Braithwaite, 2004) and may help us understand love in the complexity of stepfamily interaction and relationships. This is just one potential approach to the larger task of understanding how stepfamilies develop and communicatively constitute family.

Communication and Stepfamily Boundaries

Boundary issues have been a second main focus of stepfamily research (as well as with post-divorce scholarship in general; see Afifi & McManus, Chapter 10). The term boundaries serves as a useful metaphor, as it highlights the borders that mark ownership lines so issues of informational and relational control are clearly understood (Petronio, 2002). The types of boundaries negotiated in stepfamilies often include physical boundaries (i.e., changes in household structure) (e.g., Baxter et al., 1999), emotional boundaries (i.e., issues of closeness and family membership) (e.g., Afifi, 2003; Golish, 2003), relational boundaries (e.g., Fine & Kurdek, 1995), and informational boundaries (i.e., topic avoidance and privacy) (e.g., Golish & Caughlin, 2002), to name a few. Boundary issues also involve membership in the stepfamily (i.e., in-group vs. out-group) as well as issues pertaining to the permeability of stepfamily boundaries. As Coleman et al. (2000) noted, boundaries among subsystems in stepfamilies may be differentially permeable (i.e., flexible or rigid) for different stepfamily members.

To date, stepfamily researchers have focused primarily on various dyads and subsystems within the stepfamily home, most often the marital couple and the stepparent-stepchild dyad. Researchers have begun to argue for moving the focus on stepfamilies beyond the boundaries of a single household, accounting for the larger webs of individuals who live in different residences and comprise the stepfamily system (Braithwaite, McBride, & Schrodt, 2003; Coleman et al., 2000). Consequently, we have divided stepfamily boundary scholarship into two areas by focusing on issues related to communication within the internal boundary of the stepfamily home and then on communication outside of, or external to, the stepfamily home.

Communication Within the
Internal Stepfamily Boundary

Researchers have examined a number of communication issues that occur within subsystems in the stepfamily home. To follow, we highlight research focusing primarily on the remarried couple, the stepparent-stepchild, stepsiblings, and communication triads of residential parent, stepparent, and children.

The Remarried Couple. Cissna, Cox, and Bochner (1990) investigated the dialectical tensions associated with the marital couple, focusing on the challenges of managing contradictions associated with remarriage and stepparenting. They found that the more effort remarried couples invested in their marriage, the less available they were to invest in parenting; thus marital and stepparent relationships were oppositional. Couples often took actions to privilege the solidarity of their marriage, believing that the stepfamily stood little chance of success if the adult marriage failed. The adults in the Cissna et al. study reported that they then used their relationship security as a platform upon which to support and validate stepparent authority. Consequently, Cissna and his colleagues highlighted the importance of remarried couples establishing the credibility of the stepparent in the eyes of the children, most notably by communicating a "unified front" between the parent and his or her new spouse.

The Stepparent-Stepchild Relationship. The stepparent-stepchild relationship has received by far the most attention, in part because this relationship is considered by many to be the most challenging and stressful relationship within the stepfamily (Ganong & Coleman, 1994). Ganong, Coleman, Fine, and Martin (1999) explored the strategies that stepparents reported using to develop and maintain affinity with their stepchildren, noting three patterns of affinity-seeking and affinity-maintaining strategies among stepparents: nonseeking stepparents, early affinity-seeking stepparents, and continuous affinity-seeking stepparents. Not surprisingly, continuous affinity-seeking stepparents, who were genuinely interested in establishing and maintaining close relationships with the stepchildren and who continued their efforts well beyond the formation of the stepfamily, were more likely to have stepchildren who returned their affinity-seeking efforts and developed closer stepparent-stepchild relationships (Ganong et al., 1999).

In terms of stepchildren communicating with stepparents, further research is needed to explore the message behaviors that characterize this relationship, though a few have provided some insight. Earlier reports suggested that adolescent problems with stepfathers focused primarily on issues of authority and discipline (Giles-Sims & Crosbie-Burnett, 1989), while stepchildren in general experience more problematic interactions in the family than children from first-marriage families (Grinwald, 1995). At the same time, Fine, Coleman, and Ganong (1998) found that stepchildren had clearer perceptions of the stepparent role than stepparents. Consistent with these earlier trends, Golish and Caughlin (2002) found that adolescents and young adults engaged in the most topic avoidance with their stepparents, followed by their fathers and then their mothers. In a similar vein, Afifi and Schrodt (2003b) compared uncertainty and avoidance processes in stepfamilies, post-divorce single-parent families, and first-marriage families, and found that children avoided discussing the state of their family most with their stepparents, less with their fathers, and least with their mothers.

Although this research provided general comparisons of avoidance and uncertainty levels among step-relationships and other types of parental relationships, Baxter, Braithwaite, Bryant, and Wagner (2004) focused more broadly on stepparent-stepchild interaction. Framed in relational dialectics theory, Baxter et al. identified three underlying contradictions that animated communication in the stepparent-stepchild relationship. First, stepchildren expressed a desire for both emotional closeness and distance with their stepparent. They wanted to have a relationship with the stepparent and at the same time often rejected closeness with them out of loyalty to their nonresidential parent. Second, stepchildren expressed a desire for open communication with the stepparent, yet resisted such openness, a finding consistent with previous research on stepchildren's topic avoidance (e.g., Afifi & Schrodt, 2003b; Golish & Caughlin, 2002). Stepchildren wanted their stepparent to be open with them but found openness difficult; for example, they didn't want to hear expressions of affection or input on their behavior. Finally, and perhaps most intriguingly, the stepchildren experienced a dialectical tension between a desire for family authority to reside solely in their residential parent and a desire for both the residential parent and the stepparent to share authority. Collectively, then, scholars have shown increasing interest in the communication processes that facilitate and inhibit the stepparent-stepchild relationship, and thus, this relationship is a critical area of continued research for communication scholars.

Stepsiblings. The stepsibling relationship is the most understudied dyadic relationship within the stepfamily home (Coleman et al., 2004), and with a few notable exceptions (e.g., Ganong & Coleman, 1993; Hetherington, 1999b), much less is known about the interaction patterns of stepsiblings and half-siblings in stepfamily systems. Not only are children's interactions with half-siblings and siblings slightly more positive than with stepsiblings (Ganong & Coleman, 1993), but Hetherington's research suggests that unrelated stepsiblings are more likely to be disengaged emotionally than are full-siblings or half-siblings in stepfamilies. One possible explanation for these trends may be that many stepsiblings move into the stepfamily situation involuntarily, living with people who may be relative strangers to them. As such, Walsh (1992) argued for the importance of studying stepsiblings as they have the potential to be one of the most conflict-ridden relationships in the stepfamily (Rosenberg & Hajal, 1985).

In more recent research, Lambe (2004) studied the communication patterns of stepsiblings and found that in the early stages of the stepfamily, stepsibling communication is often characterized by the desire to separate, maintain rigid informational and physical privacy boundaries, and disassociate from one another. She found that as time wore on, stepsiblings began to pursue integrated boundaries, either on their own or with the intervention of one or more parents. Lambe concluded that increased boundary integration helped stepsiblings feel more positive about their stepsiblings and the stepfamily as a whole. Clearly, stepsibling interaction is very important and in further need of systematic investigation.

Communication Triads Within the Stepfamily System. Despite the value of examining specific dyads within the stepfamily home, another way to conceptualize interaction patterns within the stepfamily home is to look at the communication of different combinations of members of the stepfamily household. For example, Coleman, Fine, Ganong, Downs, and Pauk (2001) examined different types and sources of conflict within the stepfamily. They found that the majority of conflicts revolved around resources (possessions, space, time, attention, privacy, money), loyalty divides, parents favoring their "own" children, and conflicts with extended family. Coleman and her colleagues concluded that each of these conflicts, and the strategies used to manage them, were inherently tied to the ways in which stepfamilies negotiated boundaries within and outside the stepfamily.

In a different vein, Baxter, Braithwaite, and Bryant (2004) recently focused on the residential parent-stepparent-stepchild system, identifying four triadic communication structures. First, in the linked triad, stepchildren wanted their residential parent to function as a linchpin between themselves and the stepparent, acting as an advocate for them. Second, in the outsider triad, stepchildren perceived a limited need to communicate with the stepparent, focusing most interaction on their residential parent. Third, in the adult-coalition triad, stepchildren perceived a compromised relationship with their parents because of their parents' loyalty to their new spouses. Finally, in the complete triad, stepchildren reported functional communication throughout the triad, family solidarity, and open communication with the parent and stepparent. Although they studied triadic structures from the perspective of stepchildren only, Baxter and her colleagues argued for the potential of this triadic approach to understanding communication of all stepfamily members.

Other researchers have investigated the notion of triangulation in stepfamilies as well (e.g., Afifi, 2003; Afifi & Schrodt, 2003c; Golish, 2003), noting the challenges that stepfamily members face as they manage the uncertainty (e.g., Afifi & Schrodt, 2003b), ambiguity (e.g., Braithwaite et al., 2001), and conflict (e.g., Coleman et al., 2001) associated with stepfamily relationships. In particular, Afifi (2003) and Afifi and Schrodt (2003a) examined the communication patterns that foster and ameliorate triangulation in stepfamilies (and see Afifi & McManus, Chapter 10). Stepchildren, as well as other members of the stepfamily, often experience enmeshed communication boundaries that contribute to feelings of being caught between other members of the stepfamily system. As Afifi (2003) concluded, these feelings of being caught are inherently tied to the dialectical tensions of loyalty-disloyalty and revealment-concealment, contradictions that often produce turbulence in the family's previously established communication rules.

Understudied Aspects of Communication and the Internal Stepfamily Boundary

While researchers have made strides studying communication within the stepfamily home, limitations to this work abound. For example, with a few notable exceptions, scholars have focused largely on dyads in the stepfamily without focusing on the interaction patterns that emerge from within the larger stepfamily household. Reasons for this abound, not the least of which is the sheer complexity of stepfamily types and structures, the logistics of collecting data from a whole family, and the need for sensitivity to what is often a fragile peace, if one exists, especially in the early years of the stepfamily. We see great promise in future work examining a variety of interaction patterns among multiple members of the stepfamily household.

Collectively, then, scholars have begun to examine communication issues that both facilitate and hinder stepfamily relationships within the home. At the same time, researchers have stressed the need to focus beyond the walls of a single stepfamily household.

Communication and the External Stepfamily Boundary

Scholars have begun to examine several stepfamily relationships that extend beyond the walls of a single household, including communication with nonresidential parents, co-parenting relationships across households, relationships that foster feelings of being caught in the middle of parental and nonresidential parent households, and the influence of deceased family members on stepfamily interaction.

Nonresidential Parenting. Once parents have separated and entered into the stepfamily phase of life, the nonresidential parent often remains a key and influential member of the larger stepfamily system. A "nonresidential parent" is defined as a parent who does not live with his or her child(ren) all or most of the time (Braithwaite & Baxter, in press). The large majority of nonresidential parents are fathers, and most of the research on nonresidential parenting concerns fathers (Ganong & Coleman, 1994).

The nonresidential parent is understudied to date (Coleman et al., 2000), especially with regard to his or her interactions with the children. Most children experience a marked decrease in interaction with their parent who moves out, and for some children, contact ceases. The most recent data available indicated that only about a fourth of the nonresidential fathers see their children at least once a week, while up to a third see their children only a few times a year, if at all (Emery & Dillon, 1994). Researchers have studied the influence of the nonresidential parent on children, and their findings are mixed. Despite disagreements over the implications of children's interaction with non-residential parents, in general, researchers do agree that this relationship is in need of further investigation.

Children in stepfamilies are often challenged with trying to negotiate and maintain a relationship with their nonresidential parent at the same time they are part of a stepfamily. Afifi and Keith (2004) called for scholars to pay attention to how to reduce the ambiguous loss that children in post-divorce families experience, especially in their relationship with nonresidential fathers. To further address these issues, Braithwaite and Baxter (in press) studied nonresidential parenting from the perspective of children. Using relational dialectics theory, they found that stepchildren's perceptions of communication with their nonresidential parent were animated by interwoven contradictions of parenting/nonparenting and openness/closedness. Stepchildren's discourse reflected tremendous ambivalence over parenting attempts of nonresidential parents. They wanted their nonresidential parent to be involved and parenting them and, at the same time, they resisted it. Stepchildren wanted open and intimate communication with their nonresidential parents, yet, at the same time, they found openness to be problematic. In general, the nonresidential parent relationship provides an additional site in which communication scholars can contribute to a better understanding of the stepfamily as a system that extends beyond the walls of a single household.

Co-Parenting Relationships. The challenge of communicatively navigating the waters of nonresidential parenting has led researchers to focus on communication and co-parenting relationships in stepfamilies (Cherlin &

Furstenberg, 1994). Scholars have stressed the importance of studying co-parenting relationships in stepfamilies as they exist across households (Braithwaite et al., 2003).

Upon divorcing, co-parents must renegotiate the boundaries of intimacy, access, and power (Emery & Dillon, 1994), as well as children's schedules, visitations, discipline, and finances. Braithwaite et al. (2003) argued that the enactment of these boundaries affects the experiences of both children and adults. To date, there have been few studies that examine messages and interaction of co-parents. One exception involves Braithwaite and her colleagues' (2003) recent study of everyday interactions among "parent teams" in stepfamilies. As reflected in diary entries, adult interactions averaged about three times per week, were brief and informal (e.g., quick exchanges when dropping off children), and involved mundane issues surrounding the children (e.g., schedules and activities). The researchers were surprised at the lack of conflict between the adults, given the pervasiveness of conflict in the stepfamily literature. They noted that the mean length of the stepfamilies in the study was 6.5 years and speculated that perhaps they were seeing established co-parenting communication patterns in successful stepfamily systems. This, in turn, led Braithwaite et al. (2003) to call for future research on the process co-parents go through as they negotiate co-parenting throughout the development of the stepfamily.

In one effort to address this call, Schrodt, Baxter, McBride, Braithwaite, and Fine (2004) adopted structuration theory (Giddens, 1984) to examine the various ways in which co-parent communication structures the divorce decree as a meaningful basis for action in co-parenting relationships. They identified two structures of signification with respect to the divorce decree that enabled and constrained co-parenting interactions. The first signification structure was one in which the divorce decree was framed as a legal document dictating the rights and responsibilities of parenting, especially with respect to child access and financial issues. The second signification structure was one in which the decree was viewed as a negotiating guide or backdrop for more informal co-parental decision-making processes. These two signification structures, in turn, were patterned in three ways among co-parenting systems, creating systems that enacted legal contract–only structuration processes, guide-only structuration processes, or a process of mixed structuration, in which both processes were enacted in an alternating pattern. Collectively, then, communication scholars have begun to examine the various messages and message behaviors that constitute co-parenting across stepfamily households, though much more research is needed.

Caught in the Middle Between Parents. One area of growing interest for communication scholars involves a metaphor of how different family members feel "caught in the middle" in the stepfamily (e.g., Afifi, 2003). This is an important issue in the post-divorce stage (see Afifi & McManus, Chapter 10) that continues on into the stepfamily stage and often well into the adult years for stepchildren. Children in stepfamilies are particularly susceptible to being caught in the middle between their parents and between parents and stepparents (Afifi, 2003). In particular, family scholars have focused primarily on the ways in which these feelings of being caught are heightened by triangulation, or the coalitions forming among family members (Baxter, Braithwaite, & Bryant, 2004). While children seek to maintain equitable relationships with each of their parents, many endure stress and guilt in the process (Afifi, 2003; Braithwaite et al., 2004).

As part of this area of research, Afifi (2003) studied how parents, stepparents, and children managed feelings of being caught in the middle due to enmeshed communication boundaries. She analyzed interaction boundaries in terms of how family members managed dialectical tensions of loyalty-disloyalty and revealment-concealment, highlighting the boundary turbulence (cf. Petronio, 2002) often associated with feeling caught. Although feelings of being caught in the middle are not unique to stepfamilies (cf. Afifi & Schrodt, 2003a), in general, children of divorce (including stepchildren) do report greater feelings of being caught than children from first-marriage families (Afifi & Schrodt, 2003a).

To extend this research, Braithwaite et al. (2004) brought adult stepchildren together in focus groups with the goal of understanding what being caught in the middle means to children. These researchers sought to understand how stepchildren communicatively negotiate this center ground with their parents. If stepchildren do not want to be caught in the middle, metaphorically, where do they want to reside in stepfamilies? Braithwaite and her colleagues adopted a dialectical perspective and argued that for children, "not caught in the middle" is to feel they are centered in the family. They found that a stepchild's desire to be centered in the family is animated by a contradiction of freedom-constraint, which is informed by a contradiction of openness-closedness.

Deceased Parents. One assumption of stepfamily research that often goes unnoticed, and therefore largely ignored, is that most stepfamilies form through divorce and remarriage. Although this may be true, Bryant (2003) took the external focus on stepfamily interaction in a somewhat different direction, studying interaction in stepfamilies that form after the death of a parent. Adopting a dialectical perspective, she identified three contradictions that characterized children's communication in stepfamilies that form post-bereavement: stability-change, openness-closedness, and presence-absence. In particular, the presence-absence contradiction turned on how much the stepfamily brought the deceased parent into the new stepfamily, for example, via discussion (e.g., whether the stepfamily talked about the deceased parent), rituals (e.g., remembering the deceased parent on holidays), and artifacts (e.g., whether pictures of the deceased parent appeared in the stepfamily home). The enactments of these contradictions led Bryant to develop a typology of three types of stepfamilies forming post-bereavement, ranging from integrating the deceased parent into the stepfamily (e.g., talking about him or her) to denial of the deceased parent's presence (e.g., having no pictures or artifacts of the deceased parent in the stepfamily home).

As we examine internal stepfamily boundaries, it is important to note that stepfamilies may form in even more complex ways than from a single divorce or death of a parent. A stepfamily may form through multiple marriages of parents, through non-marital cohabitation, or through a divorce that is coupled with the death of a parent. As we have worked with stepfamily members, we are continually amazed at the complexity of many of these families. For example, one woman we interviewed talked about her various stepfamilies as her parents had both been married three times. Even answering questions as simple as "how many brothers and sisters do you have?" is difficult for stepchildren who have been members of multiple stepfamilies. Clearly, researchers need to keep the structural complexity of stepfamilies front and center and to study the interaction needed to manage different stepfamily developmental pathways and types.

Understudied Aspects of Interaction and the External Stepfamily Boundary

In just the past several years, researchers have begun to make progress in moving their focus past the physical borders of the stepfamily household. There has been limited research on nonresidential parenting and co-parenting, but there has been little focus on interaction with the extended family. This is important, as Coleman et al. (2001) found extended family to be one of the main topics of conflict in stepfamilies. Extended family members have the potential to provide support and stability in times of stress and change, yet there is little research on communication with grandparents and other extended family members, how the interaction changes over time, and what role these family members play in the stepfamily.

Conclusion

Although family communication scholars have made significant strides in recent years to understand communication processes and messages in stepfamilies, there is much work to do, and we believe this research is important to help stepfamilies develop and interact the best they can. We believe researchers need to continue their studies on stepfamily development and maintenance, and they need a diversity of perspectives and approaches to study stepfamily communication. Family communication scholars have used a variety of theories that both inform and challenge our current understanding of stepfamily dynamics, including relational dialectics (Baxter & Montgomery, 1996), communication privacy management (Petronio, 2002), and structuration theory (Giddens, 1984), to name a few. Braithwaite and Baxter (2005) stressed that we need a variety of theoretical approaches to understand family communication, and we believe this is especially important to understand the challenges facing stepfamilies. Another strength of stepfamily communication research is that scholars have used a wide variety of research methods representing multiple paradigms to begin to capture the rich complexity associated with stepfamily life, including survey methods, diaries, in-depth interviews, and focus groups. We encourage stepfamily researchers to continue to be open to a variety of approaches. While we see a number of strengths in a communication focus on stepfamily relating, worth noting are challenges that provide directions for future research.

First and foremost, we believe that it is important to bring a stronger focus on the specific messages and message behaviors that create, sustain, and alter stepfamily relationships. Although we have advanced our understanding of some of the cognitions and perceptions that characterize stepfamily development, as well as perceptions of stepfamily membership in general, there is much to do to gain a clearer picture of the verbal and nonverbal messages that encourage stepfamily development and lead to strong stepfamily relationships. Second, we see great promise in looking at stepfamily interaction from a wider variety of theoretical lenses (see Braithwaite & Baxter, 2005). For example, we suggest using symbolic convergence theory to examine rhetorical visions concerning what it means for a stepfamily to be a family (Braithwaite, Schrodt, & Koenig Kellas, in press). Likewise, a life-span perspective on communication in stepfamily development (Afifi & Nussbaum, in press) will help us understand how stepfamilies change over time.

We also see a need to better understand the various relationships that occur beyond the walls of the stepfamily household (e.g., grandparents and other extended family members, friends) and comprise the larger web of relationships within the stepfamily system. In addition, we believe it is important to understand how members of "former families" communicate. We have worked with stepchildren whose parents have married three or four times. How, if at all, do stepfamily members interact with those who are no longer legally a member of their family?

Finally, and perhaps most importantly, we need to keep working to understand how communication processes in stepfamilies are both similar to, and unique from, communication processes in other family forms (cf. Afifi & Schrodt, 2003a, 2003b, 2003c). There are those who believe that stepfamily communication processes are not qualitatively different from other family types, or perhaps should not be. We contend, however, that this belief is, in fact, misinformed. We need to keep expanding our understanding of the messages and relationships that comprise the stepfamily. With tremendous promise, we encourage family communication scholars to further our understanding of how stepfamilies are distinct from other family forms, as well as how stepfamilies can reach their greatest potential.

10

Investigating Privacy Boundaries

Communication in Post-Divorce Families

Tamara D. Afifi and Tara McManus

Dear Abby: My parents have been divorced for six years. I am 11, and I have a sister who is 15. Since our parents divorced, my sister and I fight a lot more, but I still look up to her for every-thing. I love my parents, but I hate it when each of them asks questions about the other instead of enjoying our company. It's just not fair. What do you think?

—Sick and Tired of Fighting, Greenville, TX

D ivorce is never a painless process. As this Dear Abby letter illustrates, even if children do not directly witness their parents' conflict, they can become indirectly and subtly enmeshed in it through the parents' inappropri-ate disclosures and requests for information. On the surface, one would think that it would be relatively easy for parents to recognize that their children feel caught between them and to change their communication. Yet, it is often much more difficult than it seems. As anyone who has experienced divorce, or who has had a close friend or family member who has experienced divorce, knows, it is a very complex and emotion-filled process. Even spouses who have the very best intentions and who have an amicable divorce can have difficulty redefining their relationship and determining what information is appropriate to share with their children about the divorce. Regardless of the circumstances of the divorce, however, one thing remains constant: communication is often at the heart of a family's ability to adapt to it.

This eleven-year-old girl is also certainly not alone in her feelings about her parents' divorce. Divorce is all around us and has become commonplace in U.S. culture. As Amato (2000) contends, one of the most profound changes to the American family during the 20th century was the rise in the divorce rate. Even though the divorce rate has remained relatively stable since the 1980s, it rose steadily after 1940 and increased at an exponential rate during the Women's Movement in the 1970s (Teachman, Tedrow, & Crowder, 2000). Today, it is estimated that approximately half of all first marriages end in divorce (Teachman et al., 2000). Most people, however, still want to be married, and the majority of people who divorce will eventually remarry at some point (U.S. Bureau of the Census, 1998). Because of these changes in family structure, the "traditional" nuclear family is no longer the most common family form, representing only about one-quarter of all family households (U.S. Bureau of the Census, 2000).

The increase in the divorce rate has prompted a great deal of attention from scholars, practitioners, policy makers, and the lay public over the past few decades. Post-divorce relationships, *in general*, are by no means an understudied area. One only has to surf the Internet to find hundreds of advice columns, support groups, and Web-based diaries designed to help people cope with divorce. Because of the rising divorce rate, researchers also began to examine the impact of divorce on family functioning (Coleman et al., 2000). More specifically, they have focused quite extensively on the consequences of divorce for children's physical and mental well-being (e.g., Booth & Amato, 2001), children's own marriages later in life (e.g., Amato, 1996), parent-child relationships (e.g., Booth & Amato, 1994), and former spouses' relationships (e.g., Madden-Derdich et al., 1999).

What is often *missing* from this body of literature, however, is the *role of communication* in post-divorce family life. One reason communication processes in post-divorce families have been understudied is communication is typically only one variable among many that are being investigated. When communication processes are explored, they are often examined from more of a "macro" approach. For example, researchers have examined interparental conflict and its influence on children's well-being after divorce (e.g., Booth & Amato, 1994), but it is often the sheer amount of conflict that is investigated and not the specific aspects of the conflict that impact children. Not all conflict is likely to have the same influence on family functioning. For example, some scholars (e.g., Emery, 1994) suggest that demand-withdraw patterns are characteristic of divorced couples and that the tugs and pulls associated with this type of conflict can be especially harmful to children. Others contend that it is former spouses' negative disclosures and conflict about the other parent that are especially detrimental to children (e.g., Buchanan, Maccoby, & Dornbush, 1991). Even the amount of conflict is likely to be more complex than what was once assumed. Recent research has shown that too much interparental conflict is detrimental to children's well-being, but never witnessing one's parents argue also tends to produce difficulty adjusting to a divorce, perhaps because the divorce is unexpected (Amato & DeBoer, 2001). This issue will be discussed in greater detail later in the chapter.

Because communication is often a way in which families structure and maintain themselves (Whitchurch & Dickson, 1999), further investigation into the communication processes involved in post-divorce family life could help explain why some post-divorce families are more resilient than others. Communication in post-divorce families could also lend insight into why there is such variation in how individuals respond to similar post-divorce circumstances (Afifi & Hamrick, in press). Finally, additional exploration into specific communication patterns in post-divorce relationships could help parents, spouses, and children, like our Dear Abby writer, improve their communication with one another and better adapt to the divorce process.

Communication scholars have begun to contribute significantly to this aim in recent years. In particular, they have examined communication patterns that help and hinder family functioning. Researchers have explored how rituals and family-making practices help families regain a sense of identity following divorce and remarriage (e.g., Afifi, Hutchinson, & Krouse, 2005a, 2005b). For example, Braithwaite, Baxter, and colleagues (e.g., see Chapter 9) found that stepfamilies experienced numerous developmental trajectories toward feeling like a family and that these trajectories were often managed communicatively through openness and rituals. Communication scholars have also identified specific communication strategies that families use to manage the stressors of divorce and remarriage (Afifi & Keith, 2004). For instance, research has found that strong families report using more communal coping strategies, such as actively confronting their stressors together through family problem solving, communicating resolve, and directly confronting their stressors as a group, than families experiencing greater difficulty (see Afifi et al., 2005a).

Communication researchers have also delineated the patterns of uncertainty, information regulation, parenting, and affection that characterize divorced families and the relationships in them (e.g., Afifi & Schrodt, 2003b; Caughlin et al., 2000; Floyd & Morman, 2003). For instance, numerous studies (e.g., Braithwaite et al., 2001; Golish & Caughlin, 2002) have found that divorced family members often experience heightened uncertainty and avoidance in their relationships because of the transitions in their roles, family structure, and routines. This uncertainty, however, may subside over time as children become accustomed to their parents' divorce and their new family configurations (Afifi & Schrodt, 2003c). This process often involves families renegotiating their communication boundaries.

Research has also examined former spouses' communication with one another and parents' communication with their children before and after divorce. For instance, Graham (1997) used turning point analysis to investigate changes in commitment between former spouses. Her work illustrates the complexity and wide variety of trajectories that former spouses follow in the renegotiation of their relationship over time. Graham (2003) also analyzed the dialectical contradictions that characterize the "postmarital" relationship. As she notes, the balance of autonomy and connection in postmarital relationships is especially delicate because divorce symbolizes a new beginning and the desire for autonomy. Yet, many former spouses also want or need to remain connected because their lives are so enmeshed. Their connection to their former partner is also often a testament to their binuclear family. Other research has examined the divorce decree and the structuration of co-parental relationships (Schrodt et al., 2004) and communication skills that foster effective co-parenting (Braithwaite et al., 2003; see Chapter 9). Finally, several studies have also looked at children's feelings of being caught between their parents' conflict (e.g., Afifi & Schrodt, 2003b; Amato & Afifi, 2005; also see Chapter 9). In general, these studies have investigated the communication patterns that strengthen and deter family members' ability to adapt to their new relationships and family forms.

Scholars in other disciplines (e.g., sociology, psychology, family studies) have also made great strides toward understanding communication processes in post-divorce families. In particular, this work has focused on conflict and interpersonal skill deficiencies (e.g., Gottman, 1994), stress and coping (e.g., Sandler, Tein, Mehta, Wolchik, & Ayers, 2000), and emotional and interpersonal boundaries (e.g., Madden-Derdich et al., 1999). At a fundamental level, some individuals may simply lack the communication skills necessary to sustain a healthy marriage and family environment. These skill deficiencies may be learned from one's environment or be a part of one's genetic composition.

Most of these studies focus on interpersonal deficiencies that predict marital dissolution rather than on how individual or family communication skill deficiencies affect families. For example, numerous studies have found that inadequate interpersonal communication skills, such as stonewalling, aggressiveness, negativity, demand-withdraw patterns, and a lack of impulse control, are risk factors for divorce (e.g., Amato, 1996).

Another primary area of research on divorced families that is communicative in nature is the work on stress and coping. The majority of the research on coping in divorced families, like the larger body of work on coping, has focused on the cognitive capacities of the individual to manage divorce-related stressors (e.g., Richmond & Christensen, 2000). Research on social support in divorced families (e.g., Holloway & Machida, 1991) has provided a better understanding of the interactive nature of coping. This research, however, still tends to view social support as simply a resource or as one person merely helping another (Lyons, Mickelson, Sullivan, & Coyne, 1998). Communication scholars have furthered this area of research by examining communal coping, or the interactive and synergistic efforts of multiple family members coping with similar stressors, in post-divorce families (e.g., Afifi et al., 2005b).

One of the most common ways that communication scholars have contributed, and can continue to contribute, to the study of post-divorce families is with the examination of boundaries. The study of "boundaries" in post-divorce families is an area where scholars from a wide variety of disciplines, including communication, intersect. The purpose of the rest of this chapter is to take an in-depth look at how scholars from different disciplines analyze communication boundaries in post-divorce families. More specifically, we examine boundaries from a communication perspective by detailing how inappropriate privacy boundaries, and their interdependence with other types of boundaries, foster privacy dilemmas in former spouses' and parent-child relationships. As the following sections demonstrate, family relationships change after divorce, sometimes getting closer and sometimes growing further apart, and people's privacy boundaries also change. As the Dear Abby writer also alluded to, people are often unaware of how their disclosures and inability to regulate their privacy boundaries affect other family members. Parents, for instance, may not know how much information to reveal to their children about the divorce. Through research, we are better able to determine what information is appropriate to reveal and conceal. In the process, we can help raise family members' awareness about their regulation of private information. These issues, among others, are explored below.

The Role of Privacy Boundaries in Post-Divorce Family Relationships

Boundaries often assume multiple forms in the divorce literature and are distinct, but not mutually exclusive, constructs (see Chapter 9). From a systems theory framework (Minuchin, 1974), boundaries are often conceptualized in three ways. They can refer to physical boundaries from one system or subsystem to another, such as children having access to, or a permeable physical boundary between, different households. A second conceptualization consists of intimacy or emotional boundaries (e.g., re-establishing an appropriate intimacy boundary with one's former spouse). A closely related type of boundary is that of a role or relational boundary. This boundary typically refers to rules and norms for appropriate behavior in a family (e.g., not engaging in role reversals with one's child). A fourth type of boundary is what Petronio (1991, 2000, 2002) labels a privacy boundary in her communication privacy management theory (CPM).

CPM theory provides an important lens through which scholars and practitioners can begin to understand disclosure and privacy issues in post-divorce family relationships. At its essence, CPM theory is grounded in the dialectical tension of openness and closedness. That is, individuals often struggle with how much, and what type of, information they should reveal to and conceal from others. Because revealing information can present certain risks to one's self or one's relationships (e.g., exposure of self, hurting a relationship), people erect metaphorical boundaries around themselves in order to protect against those risks. These boundaries are guided by *boundary structures* and *rule management systems*.

Boundary structures (Petronio, 2000, 2002) determine who is and who is not granted access to private information. Privacy boundaries vary in permeability with closely regulated information having a comparatively rigid boundary and loosely regulated information having a comparatively porous boundary (Petronio, 2002). For example, the more comfortable a person feels with his or her former spouse, the more likely he or she is to reveal information to that person. According to CPM theory, people long to control their private information because of the risks involved and because they believe they have ownership rights to it (Petronio, 2000, 2002). Revealing or withholding information from certain family members can be one way that family members signal ownership of their information (Braithwaite et al., 2001). For instance, choosing to share or not to share sensitive information about a divorce with one's child signals how much information the parent believes the child should co-own.

These boundary structures are guided by a rule management system. Family members dictate the permeability of their privacy boundaries by constructing rules for appropriate disclosure (Petronio, 2000, 2002). More specifically, they create decision rules for what information will be revealed, to whom, and when. As Petronio (2002) notes, these decision rules are based upon numerous criteria, including demographic characteristics of the individuals involved (e.g., the age and gender of the children), the context of the disclosure, cultural norms (e.g., valuing openness in the United States), and individual motivations (disclosing or avoiding for a particular reason). As such, the properties of the rules may vary according to the target and the circumstances of the disclosure.

People often acquire their privacy rules by learning about them through family norms (Petronio, 2002). These rules can then become routinized or habitual in families over time. Family members can become so accustomed to certain topics being avoided or "taboo" in their family that such patterns become second nature (Afifi & Guerrero, 2000). For instance, children in divorced families may learn that talking about one parent in front of the other should be avoided because it makes their other parent sad or angry (Golish & Caughlin, 2002). As Petronio (2000, 2002) also points out, privacy rules can change when triggered by a significant action or life event. Former spouses, for instance, must learn new rules for disclosure with one another and with their children after their separation.

Although numerous attributes may influence post-divorce family members' privacy rules, they must coordinate them through their interaction in order to function effectively. In other words, family members must negotiate appropriate rules for disclosure by communicating about them together. Once this information is shared with others, it becomes co-owned with them (Petronio, 2000, 2002). In families, there may be collective ownership of information when multiple family members have access to private information. Family members may also vary the permeability of their privacy boundaries with others until they reach a particular comfort zone. Parents, for example, often have great difficulty knowing how much information they should reveal to their children about the divorce (Sandler, Tein, & West, 1994). Over time, some parents and children learn to construct explicit privacy rules or guidelines for how they should communicate with one another about the divorce (Afifi et al., 2005a, 2005b).

Simply because families engage in boundary coordination, however, does not mean that it is necessarily an easy or positive experience. Complications can arise in the coordination process, creating what Petronio (2000, 2002) refers to as boundary turbulence. Boundary turbulence or privacy dilemmas can arise when family members' rules for privacy are different from one another (Petronio, 2002). For instance, when one's former spouse decides not to abide by the rules for appropriate disclosure to one's children, it can pose numerous difficulties in the family. Parents and children may have different privacy rules for the amount and type of information they desire about the divorce process. Parents may reveal too much personal information about their personal losses or their negative feelings toward their former spouse to their children (Koerner et al., 2002). Children, in turn, may not know how to respond to such disclosures because it violates how parents and children generally communicate with one another. The privacy dilemmas that can arise in post-divorce families become clear when examining the redefinition of privacy boundaries in former spouses' and parent-child relationships.

Redefining the Boundaries With One's Former Spouse

Even though privacy boundaries are the central feature we are illustrating in this chapter, they are often intertwined with other boundaries in post-divorce families. The interconnectedness among boundaries becomes particularly evident when former spouses transition from marital partners to co-parents. One of the most difficult aspects of the divorce process for former spouses involves the ability to successfully renegotiate their intimacy boundaries with one another (Graham, 2003). Because parents are forever connected to one another through their children, they must establish their relationship with each other in new ways. The persistent and evolving emotional connection with one's former spouse after a separation is often a source of uncertainty, animosity, sadness, and loss (Graham, 1997).

Emotional intensity is believed to be at the core of post-divorce relationships, influencing the renegotiation of interpersonal boundaries (Madden-Derdich et al., 1999). According to Emery (e.g., Emery, 1994; Emery & Dillon, 1994) and others (e.g., Cole & Cole, 1999), two main properties of emotional intensity that underlie the renegotiation of these boundaries are power and intimacy. Redefining these boundaries becomes especially problematic when only one person wants a divorce (Emery & Dillon, 1994). When divorce is not a mutual decision, a pursuer-pursued relationship or demand-withdraw patterns may develop (Afifi & Schrodt, 2003b; Emery, 1994). One person may continue to pursue an emotional relationship with the other, even if that person avoids him or her.

The emotions involved in this type of relationship often reveal themselves in either a preoccupation with one's former spouse or intense anger (Madden-Derdich et al., 1999). As Emery and Dillon (1994) contend, however, intimacy and hate are not polar opposites; rather, they are both indicative of an emotionally intense relationship that is very involved. Partners may be contentious because they have an enmeshed relationship, not an emotionally distant one (Emery, 1994). That is, former spouses may lash out in anger at each other because they are still emotionally attached to one another. These intimacy struggles are often tied to issues of power within the family. In times of conflict, power is typically an attempt to take control over the outcomes of a dispute (Emery, 1994). Often parents focus on content or surface level messages in their conflicts, such as custody rights, finances, and parenting practices. However, power often involves deeper, relational level messages that communicate something about the nature of the parents' relationship. Former spouses, for instance, often threaten to take greater control over the most salient part of their partner's identity (e.g., children, finances) as a way to communicate power (Emery, 1994).

Former spouses' difficulty renegotiating their intimacy boundaries can translate into privacy boundary dilemmas, particularly when there are children involved in the divorce. The intense emotions that underlie intimacy and power boundaries are often conveyed through interparental conflict and inappropriate disclosures (Cole & Cole, 1999). Partners in an acrimonious post-divorce relationship often have difficulty regulating their emotions with one another (Emery, 1994). They may reveal sensitive information and insults as a way to hurt their former partner. In order to adapt effectively, spouses must readjust their privacy rules with each other. Privacy dilemmas ensue when one or both spouses refuse to abide by previously established privacy rules. Parents sometimes feel as if their former spouses' negative behavior is beyond their control, which can foster avoidant coping strategies (Holloway & Machida, 1991).

Even though avoidance is generally an ineffective form of coping when it is persistent and takes the place of other more pro-active forms of coping (Sandler et al., 1994), in highly conflicted relationships, it may be beneficial if former spouses restrict the amount of physical contact they have with one another (Amato & Rezac, 1994). When former spouses engage in a great deal of interparental conflict, it is often more beneficial to children if the parents have less contact with one another and the child primarily resides with one parent (Emery, 1994). In these situations, corresponding by e-mail or the telephone instead of in person could help minimize the emotions involved (Golish, 2003). It also should be noted that the vast majority of the research cited here involves former spouses who have children with one another. When there are no children involved, many former spouses do not have any communication or contact with one another.

Former spouses may also purposefully withhold important information from each other as a way to regain a sense of control over their relationship with their children and perhaps with the other parent. Because of the intense emotions involved in their relationship, partners may refrain from communicating with one another. Instead, they may ask their children to relay information for them or use their children as messengers (Buchanan et al., 1991). While the reluctance to directly communicate information with one's former spouse is not always intentional, there may also be situations in which information is purposefully restricted or revealed as a way to signal ownership of the information. Former spouses may refrain from revealing information regarding visitation, finances, and children's activities and appointments as a way to control this information, and consequently, control their relationship (or manage their boundaries). At the same time, it is important to remember that these privacy boundaries also serve necessary and important functions. The former spouses must maintain some privacy boundaries with one another in order to rebuild their lives, maintain autonomy, and form new romantic attachments (see Graham, 2003). Finding the right balance of privacy boundaries is extremely difficult and is negotiated over time. As Graham (2003) points out, divorce can provide an opportunity for former spouses to learn from the communication patterns that did not work in their marriage and build new privacy boundaries for their future.

How former spouses are able to effectively regulate their privacy boundaries with one another remains a very important question to consider. Researchers and practitioners are aware of the stress that is created by violations of privacy boundaries. However, how former spouses who have children are able to coordinate their privacy boundaries has yet to be discerned. Nevertheless, the research on the communication characteristics of effective co-parenting may shed some light on this process for former spouses who have children together. Research suggests that parents who are able to co-parent together respect the other's privacy and character, monitor their overt displays of emotion, create an open and honest exchange of information to one another about their children, problem-solve together regarding their children, and share responsibility for parenting (Braithwaite et al., 2003). Effective parents realize that in order to regulate their privacy boundaries, they must first redefine their emotional attachment with each other.

Redefining the Boundaries With One's Children

When former spouses are unable to regulate their privacy boundaries with each other, the conflict and stress that often results can be transferred to their children. Just as parents must restructure their privacy boundaries with each other, they must also redefine their privacy boundaries with their children. Divorce often alters the communication patterns between parents and children because the nature of their relationships, as well as their access to outside social networks, has changed. Custodial parents' social networks typically decline after a divorce (Cowen et al., 1989). As a result of a lack of external outlets for their disclosure, custodial parents may confide in their children for support and validation (Biblarz & Gottainer, 2000). Custodial parents' stress is also exacerbated due to the loss of their former spouse, role burden, and financial strain (Larson & Gillman, 1999). The accumulation of these types of stressors can be overwhelming for parents who have little or no assistance with this transition. Children sometimes serve as confidants as a way for parents to release some of this pressure.

Under these circumstances, role reversals or parentification can occur whereby children assume too much of a parental role in the family hierarchy (Alexander, 2003). In addition to taking on too many household responsibilities, children can form peer-like relationships with their parents (Mann et al., 1990). The former is what Jurkovic and his colleagues (Jurkovic, Jessee, & Goglia, 1991) refer to as instrumental parentification, and the latter is referred to as expressive or emotional parentification. Instrumental parentification involves maintaining the physical well-being of the household (e.g., taking care of siblings, cleaning, earning additional income) and emotional parentification revolves around regulating the psychological and social needs of other family members (Jurkovic, Thirkield, & Morrell, 2001). Emotional parentification is especially prominent for custodial mothers and daughters because of the close bond they often form after a divorce due to the disclosive nature of their relationship (Arditti, 1999).

Emotional parentification can occur when parents' privacy boundaries with their children become enmeshed. When parents reveal too much information about divorce-related stressors to their children, children may become what Petronio (2002) refers to as reluctant confidants. Children may become privy to information that is better left unsaid. Parents may disclose sensitive information to their children regarding financial concerns, custody arrangements, negativity toward their former spouse, relational transgressions, work stress, and personal distress (Koerner et al., 2002). While it is acceptable and even desirable for parents to reveal some information about these topics to their children, the question that continues to plague researchers, practitioners, and family members is "How much information is too much?" Moreover, what type of information is appropriate and inappropriate?

As Thomas, Booth-Butterfield, and Booth-Butterfield (1995) contend, parents need to share some information about the divorce process with their children in order to reduce their uncertainty about it. As these scholars found, if young adults believe that their parents are not open with them about the divorce or deceive them about why it happened, it can negatively affect their self-esteem and satisfaction with their relationship with their parents. Indeed, as these authors go on to recognize, some level of permeability in the parents' privacy boundaries must exist in order for children to feel secure in their post-divorce family relationships.

Children are also extremely perceptive of their environment and are cognizant of their parents' conflicted relationship (Westberg, Nelson, & Piercy, 2002). Although children should not be exposed to destructive conflict or be placed in the middle of their parents' disputes, they should not be completely shielded from conflict or the news of an impending divorce. Children often suffer from adjustment difficulties when they are exposed to their parents' negative conflict (Cummings & Davies, 1994). As Amato and DeBoer (2001) discovered, however, children who never saw their parents' divorce coming also experienced difficulties adapting to divorce and committing to their own romantic partners. Children often also remember how their parents disclosed to them that they were getting a divorce and how they reacted to the disclosure (Westberg et al., 2002). What these studies suggest is that some information about the reasons for the divorce and the divorce process itself needs to be provided to children in order for them to legitimize and understand it.

Even though children need to be provided with information about the divorce process in order to adapt effectively, research on parentification and divorce disclosures suggests that revealing too much information about the divorce to children can place them at risk physically and mentally (Koerner et al., 2000). For instance, Koerner and Lehman (e.g., Koerner et al., 2000; Koerner et al., 2002; Lehman & Koerner, 2002) surveyed 62 adolescent daughter-mother dyads two years after divorce. They found that mothers' disclosures about financial difficulties, negativity toward their former spouse, personal concerns, and parenting challenges were related to their daughters' psychological distress, regardless of the daughters' age. Although some research suggests that custodial parents and children become closer after a divorce as a result of experiencing and sharing similar stressors (e.g., Arditti, 1999), these authors found that such disclosures did not foster greater feelings of mother-daughter closeness. To the contrary, they discovered the daughters worried about their mothers' personal welfare as a result of the disclosures and that this mediated the association between maternal disclosure and the daughters' psychological distress.

Even though empirical research on this topic is limited, the research that is available tends to confirm Koerner and Lehman's findings (e.g., Jurkovic et al., 2001). Arditti (1999) offers one of the few exceptions to this work. Based upon retrospective interviews with 58 young adults whose parents divorced, she argues that permeable privacy boundaries between custodial parents and their children after a divorce enhance closeness and are more functional than they are dysfunctional. Arditti (1999) contends that when mothers disclose to their children and rely on them for support, it is largely a positive experience that fosters equality, cohesion, and empathy. While closeness and egalitarianism between custodial mothers and children some-times increase following divorce (see Amato, 2000), along with this enhanced closeness may come greater internalization of the parent's stress. Unfor-tunately, parents are also often unaware that they reveal inappropriate information to their children and that it makes them uncomfortable (Sandler et al., 1994). Thus, while disclosing too much information about divorce-related stressors may foster solidarity in some parent-child relation-ships, it may do so at a cost to the child's health.

Research on communal coping in post-divorce families also points to the privacy dilemmas that can result when rules for appropriate privacy regulation are violated. Communal coping can enhance the coping abilities and efficacy of post-divorce families because family members assume joint responsibility for their stressors (Afifi et al., 2005a). As Coyne and colleagues (Coyne, Wortman, & Lehman, 1988) have found, however, family members can some-times assume too much personal responsibility for other family members' stress. Family members can engage in "protective buffering" (Coyne & Fiske, 1992), where they attempt to protect other family members by absorbing their stress for them. When privacy boundaries become too enmeshed, a type of contagion effect (Coyne, 1976) may result, in which one person's stress is transferred to another. Children, for instance, often worry about their parents' well-being when they are the recipients of too many personal disclosures related to the divorce (Koerner et al., 2000).

Some research also indicates that parents' privacy boundaries may be more permeable with their children in divorced families compared to first-marriage families. Dolgin (1996) found that divorced parents disclosed more about their personal lives and worries with their late-adolescent children than did parents from first-marriage families. In particular, they disclosed more about their personal problems to their children than did parents from non-divorced families. They were also more likely to discuss their romantic involvements and lifestyle changes with their children. In addition, mothers and daughters evidenced the greatest amount of disclosures compared to other familial dyads. As this research indicates, changes in family life that accompany divorce may produce corresponding changes in privacy boundaries within the family.

While custodial parents may create more permeable privacy boundaries with their children following a divorce, noncustodial parents (who are typically fathers) often experience difficulty re-establishing their original levels of disclosure. Noncustodial fathers' parental roles typically undergo severe change after a divorce due to the loss of continual contact with their children (Hetherington & Stanley-Hagan, 1995). A change in contact can be frustrating for parents who desire a more active role in their children's lives (Greif, 1995). This frustration is exacerbated, however, by the ambiguity that shrouds their relationship. More specifically, there is a lack of guidelines for how they should communicate with their children after their relationship with them has been altered (Wallerstein & Corbin, 1986). Noncustodial fathers may find it difficult to penetrate their children's privacy boundaries because of the changes in their family structure and interpersonal roles. As Afifi and Keith (2004) found, children and noncustodial fathers often have difficulty moving beyond a cycle of "baseline disclosures" in their relationship. Because of the interruption in their daily contact, it may take longer for noncustodial parents and their children to disclose at deeper levels.

Little research, however, has investigated noncustodial parents' negotiating of privacy boundaries with their children (see Chapter 9). There are relatively few scientific investigations of divorce and disclosure with fathers and within the population more generally. Most of the research that has been conducted on parents' disclosures to their children about divorce is from clinical populations, case studies, or very small samples (Koerner et al., 2000). Current research has also relied on custodial mothers and their daughters, with very few studies examining custodial fathers and noncustodial parents' communication with their sons and daughters. As a result, researchers know relatively little about the kind of private information that should be revealed, how it should be revealed, potential gender differences in these processes, and the effects of the revealment on children's well-being.

The Privacy Dilemmas of Interparental Conflict and Children's Feelings of Being Caught

Privacy dilemmas can also result when former spouses engage in conflict in front of their children. When parents fail to encapsulate their conflict, children can become triangulated in their disputes (Hetherington, Cox, & Cox, 1982). As the Dear Abby segment at the beginning of this chapter demonstrated, children often "feel caught" between their parents when their parents disclose ongoing marital problems, talk negatively about one another, or attempt to form alliances with them (Buchanan et al., 1991). This phenomenon is often the result of parents' inability to effectively regulate their privacy boundaries with their children. Although it is a psychological construct, it is also largely a communicative one; it reveals itself in, and emanates from, parents' inappropriate boundary constructions. These constructions often include negative disclosures about the other parent, tests of allegiance, using children as messengers or mediators of information, and acquiring private information from children about the other parent (Buchanan et al., 1991).

When parents place their children in the middle of their disputes, children often become reluctant confidantes and may respond by restricting their own privacy boundaries. Children often perceive their parents' conflict as out of their control and avoid talking about it as a way to cope with it (Afifi et al., 2005a). For instance, children in divorced families often avoid talking about one parent in front of the other in order to prevent conflict and being placed in the middle of it (Golish & Caughlin, 2002). They also employ other avoidant and escape strategies such as changing the topic, leaving the room where their parents are arguing, watching television to drown out the noise, and playing with a friend (Afifi et al., 2005a).

Children often respond to their parents' conflict with avoidance because they are unsure how to respond. They have been socialized to respect their parents' authority and may be afraid to disagree with them. Younger children may also not have developed the cognitive complexity or communication competence necessary to know how and what to say to their parents about their conflict (Amato & Afifi, 2005). Avoidance may be an automatic response to choiceless circumstances. Children also respond to their parents' conflict with corresponding acts of aggression or by directly confronting them about their conflict. These more direct strategies, however, may be secondary responses when avoidance is no longer effective.

While avoidance appears to be a common response for children who become reluctant confidantes to their divorcing parents, additional research is necessary to decipher how children of different ages respond to feelings of being caught. Most of the research on this topic has been conducted with adolescents rather than young adults because of increased exposure to conflict due to shared residence with their parents (Buchanan et al., 1991). The results of this research, however, tend to be somewhat mixed. For instance, some research suggests that older adolescents are more likely to feel caught between their parents than are pre-adolescents or young adults (e.g., Buchanan et al., 1991). Yet, other research suggests that young adults may also feel caught between their parents and that these feelings of being caught may carry over into adulthood (e.g., Afifi & Schrodt, 2003b; Amato & Afifi, 2005).

Regardless of the age of the child, feeling caught has been shown to affect children's well-being. Research shows that children in high conflict families tend to form a closer alliance with one parent than another (Mann et al., 1990). Because children typically wish to maintain a cohesive relationship with both parents, being placed in the middle of them is an anxiety-provoking experience (Buchanan & Waizenhofer, 2001). Feelings of being caught have been associated with depression, self-blame, anxiety, and deviance in children (Hetherington, 1999a). For instance, Buchanan et al. (1991) found that interparental conflict was associated with adolescents' depression and deviance, but only through their feelings of being caught.

Feeling caught has also been found to weaken parent-child relationships (Afifi & Schrodt, 2003b; Amato & Afifi, 2005). For instance, Afifi and Schrodt (2003b) discovered that the effects of divorce on adolescents' and young adults' avoidance and satisfaction with their parents was mediated by their feelings of being caught. As a result of feeling caught, children may create more impermeable privacy boundaries when communicating with their parents. In general, these studies illustrate the powerful effect that parents' inability to regulate their personal disputes can have on their children's well-being and parent-child relationships.

Conclusion

While communication in post-divorce families is understudied, it holds considerable promise for helping researchers explain and predict varying levels of family functioning. The negotiation of privacy boundaries is but one important area of research on communication in post-divorce families. A CPM perspective can provide further insight into adaptation in post-divorce families with its focus on how information is regulated in relationships. To date, much research has focused on what constitutes violations in post-divorce relationships, but it is equally important to understand why those violations occur and how they are managed communicatively in order to better comprehend post-divorce family functioning. Although numerous implications can be drawn from this body of literature, two in particular merit attention by scholars, family members, and practitioners: (1) how and why parents and children regulate inappropriate disclosures about the divorce with one another; and (2) how, why, and under what circumstances former spouses develop and maintain privacy rules with one another.

Previous research has shown that parents may not be aware of how disclosures impact their children (Afifi, 2003). In other words, parents often do not see their disclosures as violating parent-child privacy boundaries. Future research might examine how parent and child perceptions of divorce disclosures differ and how these differences affect the boundary coordination process. For instance, when a child thinks the parent's disclosures about the divorce are inappropriate and the parent does not realize this, how does this impact their relationship? How do parents and children resolve this issue? Moreover, how do children's responses to this issue depend upon their age and developmental level?

Researchers must also begin to understand the type of information that is appropriate for parents to reveal to their children and former spouses to reveal to one another during the divorce process. What information should children "co-own" and what information places them in the uncomfortable position of reluctant confidants? As Petronio (2002) notes, however, the management of this boundary likely depends upon numerous contextual factors, such as the age of the child when the parents divorced and the type of relationship the parent and child had with one another prior to the divorce. Former spouses must also redefine their privacy boundaries with one another. For example, how do former spouses who want, and perhaps need, to create new privacy rules (because of their children) do so when avoidance is a common coping strategy they employ? Additionally, how are boundaries renegotiated between former spouses when one spouse is still tightly tied to the relationship and the other would rather relinquish the relationship? By identifying how former spouses establish an effective relationship, post-divorce families will be better able to adapt to the divorce process.

While much is still to be learned about how privacy boundaries and other communication processes are negotiated in post-divorce families, scholars interested in communication play a critical role in deciphering how these patterns of interaction impact family functioning. Divorce transforms a family by forcing its members to acknowledge and confront a number of unanticipated changes. Part of the difficulty in addressing these changes involves how much and what type of information about the divorce family members should disclose to one another. Communication is essential to a family's ability to successfully adapt to these changes.

Commentary on Part C

Beth Le Poire

O nly about one in four (24%) of all families in the United States currently approximate the assumed-to-be-dominant nuclear family form (i.e., one mother, one father, biological children; U.S. Census Bureau, 2003c). This emphasizes that "alternative family forms" are deserving of further study, as they are not, in fact, alternative, but rather are the emerging normative family forms. While it is only possible to estimate that about 4% of all children are adopted (see Chapter 8), we do know that remarriages constitute half of all marriages (National Center for Health Statistics, 1995) and that issues of post-divorce families and stepfamilies are as endemic to family life as are issues of intimacy and conflict to more traditional nuclear families. Thus, it is apparent, as the authors in this section point out, that adoptive, post-divorce, and stepfamilies are rapidly becoming the normative families of the 21st century and are deserving of greater research with less focus on their deficits in comparison to the "normative" nuclear family (e.g., see Chapter 9).

The chapters on adoption, post-divorce families, and stepfamilies compellingly present the heart of the issue all family communication researchers must face: to what extent does "relatedness" define families and to what extent do biological versus legal ties receive preference in how society perceives families and all of their family members? What is striking about all of these chapters is that adoptive families, post-divorce families, and stepfamilies "feel on the edge," or appear to be outside the boundaries of the traditionally constructed family (i.e., through procreation) and may, as a result, be stigmatized family forms. In other words, members of society, in treating adoptive, post-divorce, and stepfamilies as "secrets" or "issues to be managed with privacy," are marginalizing adoptive, post-divorce, and stepfamilies as non-normative.

Adoptive, post-divorce, and stepfamilies all pose challenges to the ways in which families have traditionally been defined in terms of biological and legal relatedness. Adoptive families include legal relatedness but not biological relatedness. One of the reasons adoptive families may be understudied is the inherent secrecy that has historically surrounded this family form (see Chapter 8). In other words, adopting children was seen as a shameful secret (i.e., nonbiological relatedness) to be kept from outside family members and the adoptee alike. The shame associated with legal versus biological ties may be evidenced in post-divorce and stepfamilies as well. Although divorce rates are rising, divorce has been traditionally stigmatized as producing ill effects for society. In other words, there appears to be a strong societal belief that families should endure over time. However, current analysis of the data indicates that families can endure over time with biological ties long after the legal ties have been severed. While the divorce rate is predicted at around 50%, we do know that 32% of men and 34% of women born between 1945 and 1954 (the early baby boomers) are divorced (Kreider & Fields, 2001). Thus, communication in families in our society increasingly surrounds issues related to conflict, relational dissolution, privacy, coping, and child custody arrangements, as pointed out in both Chapter 9 and Chapter 10.

Equally stigmatizing is the notion of "second marriages," even though reality suggests that this family form is increasing in proportion as well. Specifically, about half (46%) of all marriages every year are remarriages (National Center for Health Statistics, 1995), and about one-fifth of men (22%) and one-fourth of women (23%) born between 1945 and 1954 report being married twice. Moreover, 75% of divorcees are predicted to be remarried during their lifetime (Kreider & Fields, 2001). Therefore, communication activities in the family are increasingly surrounding new member integration, with stepparents and stepsiblings attempting to develop new roles within ever-increasingly complex family forms. In fact, blended families are the third most common family form after the single-parent and two-parent household (Davidson & Moore, 1996), and up to one-third of all children will live with a biological and a stepparent for at least one year before they reach 18 (Dainton, 1993). It is also likely that these numbers are underestimates of stepfamily arrangements since up to 33% of single fathers with custody and 11% of single mothers with custody will co-reside with a mate of the opposite sex (U.S. Census Bureau, 2003a). Therefore, it is likely that this mate will act in the role of stepparent, and thus, the numbers of children living in stepfamily situations may be underestimated. This is emphasized in the work by Braithwaite et al. (Chapter 9), who point out that many families begin to "feel like a stepfamily" long before marriage occurs. Intriguingly, this highly established family form is still perceived to be nontraditional and non-normative, which could be due in part to the nonbiological relatedness that exists between stepparents and stepchildren.

Specifically, post-divorce and stepfamilies pose similar challenges as adoptive families with regard to biological and legal relatedness in families. Post-divorce families include biological ties while the legal ties of marriage are being broken. In addition, stepfamilies include biological relatedness between parents and biological children, legal relatedness between spouses, but neither biological nor legal relatedness between stepparents and stepchildren. Stepparents who do not adopt their stepchildren have no legal identity with regard to their stepchildren, and adoption is not possible unless the biological parent is dead or relinquishes all paternal rights (Mahoney, 1994). Thus, these nontraditional family forms present a challenge to those defining families using a criterion of biological and legal relatedness. In addition, severed legal ties and emerging familial ties with no biological or legal basis may pose challenges to family members as they struggle to define their roles within families in the face of no biological or legal relatedness.

The primary way adoptive and stepfamilies are perceived as non-normative is through their methods of procreation. In other words, there appears to be a strong societal assumption that families are procreation organizers, and to that end biological ties are assumed to be a greater definer of family boundaries than are legal ties. This perception is evidenced in stepfamilies where ties are sometimes biological and sometimes legal. Five- to seven-year-olds asked to draw family trees drew representations with biological mothers and fathers even when they co-resided with parents and stepparents across households (Dunn, O'Connor, & Levy, 2002). Thus, for these children, biology defined family more than legal ties did. In addition, many adoptive children still refer to their biological mother as their "birth mother." This distinction made through language is important to them as it recognizes the complexity and the strength of the biological connectedness. Alternatively, Galvin (Chapter 8) provides evidence that adoptive children sometimes rely on their legally defined parents more and refer to them as "mother" while referring to their birth mother by her first name. This provides evidence that experiential processes involved in nurturing and control in the family may be beginning to play a more defining role in who is in, and who is out, of families.

This boundary regulation clearly plays itself out in post-divorce and stepfamilies as well. As Braithwaite et al. point out in their review (Chapter 9), stepchildren report being more satisfied with their stepparents to the extent that their stepparent acts more as a friend than a parent. This emphasizes the invisible boundary that includes the biological mother in the family and excludes the stepparent as being "different from" the biological parent in that the characteristics associated with friendship relations are clearly distinguishable from the characteristics associated with family relations. Thus, as these authors aptly note, boundary distinctions within adoptive, post-divorce, and stepfamilies may be defined outside of traditional definitions of biological relatedness and may be more important than in nuclear families with biological children. There is, therefore, a need to study the relationship between biological and legal definitions of the family and the use of language to define the boundaries within these family forms that find themselves outside the traditional definitional mechanisms associated with families. In this way, as Braithwaite et al. (Chapter 9) request, adoptive, post-divorce, and stepfamilies can be seen "as the same as," yet distinct from, traditional nuclear families.

11

Understudied Relationships in Family Communication Research

Expanding the Social Recipe

Lynn H. Turner and Richard West

D espite the fact that they differ in myriad ways, all the chapters in this book clearly point to a single conclusion: future research in family communication should consider expanding its definition of what constitutes family. These chapters illustrate a great deal of the variety in family relationships that has gone relatively unnoticed by scholars using a definition of family that prioritizes a nuclear configuration. When we're attuned to seeing the family as married parents and their children, it makes sense to investigate marital and parent-child relationships. Of course, in so doing, we neglect aunts, uncles, grandparents, and stepsisters, among many other important familial connections. When we're attuned to seeing the family as consisting of biological relations or kin ties, it makes sense to investigate the relationships that fit this perspective. Yet, in so doing, we neglect families composed of biologically unrelated people such as step-relations, cohabiting couples, and chosen families.

As Stephanie Coontz (2000b) observed, although there are an enormous variety of family experiences in life, we "tend to sift those experiences through the sieve of a social recipe for what 'the Family' ought to be" (p. ix). In the process, we minimize the diversity of family experience and, instead, reify a particular aspect of this diverse landscape as "normal." This process establishes a disconnect between the families we carry around in our heads and the families we actually experience.

This disconnect was aptly stated by John Gillis (1996), a family historian, when he observed that people in the United States value their beliefs about family more than its actual reality. Gillis explains, "It is through the families we live *by* that we achieve the transcendence that compensates for the tensions and frustrations of the families we live *with*" (p. 119). While this process may help us transcend some frustrations, as Gillis states, it also creates myths of what is normal in family life. These myths create frustrations of their own as Judith Stacey (1999) asserts: "this nostalgia does little to improve conditions for the beleaguered families we live *with*, and a great deal to make them even worse" (p. 489).

The authors contributing to this book thoughtfully point out the serious implications of normalizing only one form of family life and maintaining a single recipe for healthy family functioning. Those relationships that are left out fall into a void, making us somewhat unclear as to their worth. Further, as Tara Emmers-Sommer (2005) explains, it is sometimes difficult to ascertain what we mean by labeling something as normal. This difficulty often leaves us wondering how relationships that we experience fit into the definition of "normal." Emmers-Sommer opines that "normative" may have at least two meanings: prevalence or quantity in the culture (as in saying something is the norm because it is common), and appropriateness or acceptability (as in saying something is the norm because it is accepted as the right way to do or be). These two meanings may not always coincide with one another.

For instance, as we have argued elsewhere (Turner & West, 2006), in the United States, marriage rates are declining and same-sex relationships are increasing. Peter Francese (2004) reported that in 2003, heterosexual married couples comprised fewer than 52% of U.S. households. This was down from 1963, when almost 75% of all households consisted of heterosexual married couples. Thus, we might conclude that in the sense of prevalence in the culture, heterosexual married couples are declining. At the same time, same-sex relationships are on the rise in the United States. It is difficult to establish accurate numbers of same-sex couples. The records are fairly unreliable because the U.S. Census has not had a good method for tracking same-sex relationships; nonetheless, conservative figures place their numbers at over a million (Stacey, 2003). Despite these changes in quantity, most people in the U.S. still see marriage as the norm, in the sense of acceptability, and same-sex couples as a deviation from that norm.

The controversy prompted by the Defense of Marriage Act, passed in 1996, and the more recent efforts to pass a constitutional amendment protecting marriage as a heterosexual institution point to some of the tensions between prevalence and acceptance. When we examine the changes in the numbers of married heterosexual couples with children, we see an even more dramatic drop. These families comprised 40% of U.S. households in 1970 and only 24% in 2000 (U.S. Bureau of the Census, 2003a). Yet, these types of families persist in people's minds as the "norm" despite their relatively small size in the population. As Stephanie Coontz (2000a) observes, people refer to this type of family as normal and comfortable and believe that the United States should be composed of these types of families.

Coontz (2000b) also notes that these visions of normal family life "bear a suspicious resemblance to reruns of old television series" (p. 8), and they romanticize a family type that may not have actually existed or, if it did, represented only a very small stratum of the population. Further, Coontz reminds us that abuse, incest, and economic hardship characterized millions of households that formed this family type. Again, the issue of prevalence and acceptability is an issue because, of course, no one is arguing that abuse, for example, is an acceptable family practice, even though as many as 15 out of every 1,000 children in the United States may experience abuse in their families (Barnett, Miller-Perrin, & Perrin, 2005).

In sum, we must conclude, as Emmers-Sommer (2005) does, by saying that "what is considered normative to one is non-normative to another" (p. 2). And it is this very variety that prompts us to push the boundaries in our research as the authors in this collection have done. A family relationship that is critical to many (e.g., parent-child) may be less important to others who might have found another relationship (e.g., grandmother-grandchild) crucial to their definition of family. And the notion that voluntary families—or families of choice—exist further challenges traditional interpretations of the family.

Thus far in this chapter we have been using the terms *family* and *household* as though they were synonymous, but, in fact, as Rayna Rapp (1999) points out, there is a difference between the two. Rapp explains that the entities in which people actually live are households. Households are what census-takers count because "households are the empirically measurable units within which people pool resources and perform certain tasks" (p. 180). Households are "residential units" wherein resources are allocated and exchanged. Finally, as Rapp mentions, households are relatively simple units to define.

Families, however, are much more difficult to define. In large part, this difficulty is due to the enormous variety we mentioned previously. Further, defining family is complicated by the fact that, as Deborah Chambers (2001) observes, the normative sense of the family we have discussed is a discourse subject to infinite revisions. Chambers notes that new research exploring the history of family challenges some of the dominant ideology. She argues that mid-19th-century families, contrary to persistent beliefs, also experienced the same disjuncture between ideology and lived experience that we have discussed with reference to current families. For instance, Chambers asserts that at the same time that the social discourse consolidated around "family values," families of this time often failed to have mothers bring up their biological children, consigning this responsibility instead to aunts, uncles, and older sisters. Additionally, Chambers argues that many families of this period lived in contractual, not biological, arrangements.

Overall, we can see that family is a slippery concept, freighted with social and ideological meaning, often at odds with the empirical enactments people devise. Further, this contradiction is one of long standing and not a contemporary problem caused by a failure to properly live out family relations in the 20th and 21st centuries. Finally, the social construction of a single definition of family poses difficulties for us as family members but provides opportunities for us as family scholars.

The chapters in this volume go a long way toward changing our social recipe and illustrating the complexity of relationships that mean so much to most of us in our lived experience. Kathleen Galvin (2004) notes that it is especially important to examine the social recipe now because we are living in a time when the pace of change is escalating rapidly and this affects every aspect of life, most especially the family. As Galvin states, "family life as we knew it is moving rapidly into history . . . [and] our challenge is to envision, shape, and respond to another half-century of family relationships that are only barely imaginable" (p. 675). She characterizes the climate of change in the future as "permanent white water," following Peter Vaill (1996, cited in Galvin, 2004), remarking that family communication researchers will have to learn to survive and thrive in a fast-changing environment. Scholars will need to negotiate the present while keeping an eye on future changes in the social recipe for family.

These ideas point to at least two dialectic tensions that permeate our task as we work to expand the recipe of family life in our scholarship to more accurately mesh with the family life of our experiences. The first dialectic, which we call concluding/revising, deals with our competing desires as researchers to draw conclusions about family communication while at the same time remaining open to the rapid changes that Galvin (in press) discusses. The second tension we label inclusion/boundaries. This dialectic refers to our desire to be inclusive in exploring family relationships while at the same time recognizing that there are infinite relationships within lived family experiences. Specifically, in this chapter we seek to investigate these tensions and explore some methods for dealing with them. In so doing, we hope to complement the essays in this book and point to future directions for family communication scholars.

Dialectic Tensions

As Leslie Baxter and Barbara Montgomery (1996) have clearly shown us, it is useful to examine communication in relationships through the lens of Mikhail Bakhtin's (1986, 1990) theory of dialogism. Doing so allows us to capture the qualities of social life that make it multivocal and indeterminate. Multivocality and indeterminacy move us away from an either/or perspective toward a conceptualization of both/and. Thus, this theory, framed as dialectics in the communication field, places importance on contradictions. This is the case because Bakhtin (1984) framed dialogue as the simultaneous differentiation from, yet fusion with, another (Baxter & Montgomery, 1996, p. 24). Many researchers have followed these theoretical assertions, applying the notion of contradictions to marital interaction (e.g., Baxter & Braithwaite, 2002; Hoppe-Nagao & Ting-Toomey, 2002), stepfamily communication (e.g., Baxter, Braithwaite, Bryant, & Wagner, 2004), adoption issues (e.g., Krusiewicz & Wood, 2001), and friendship (e.g., Rawlins, 1992).

Bakhtin's argument that social life is characterized by open dialogues where multiple voices come together seems well applied to the research enterprise as well as relational communication. Research itself may be conceived of as an open dialogue where scholars' voices come together, oppose one another, and interpenetrate; in the process, some voices become more dominant while others are marginalized. This dialogue results in contradictions or tensions, creating an interplay that constructs meaning for the scholarly community, much as it does for a family (Baxter, in press).

The two dialectic tensions we have surfaced from the multivocality of this book, co-mingled with our own voices, focus on change and stability and openness and boundaries. The first tension, concluding/revising, hones in on the competing desires for drawing conclusions about family communication while simultaneously staying tentative and respecting the changing family landscape. Rob Anderson, Leslie Baxter, and Kenneth Cissna (2004) speak to this point quite clearly when they ponder how to conclude their edited book on the topic of dialogue. They note,

Although dialogue itself is to a significant extent ongoing and "unfinalizable," as Bakhtin would say, publishing a book about it is a different story. Readers, being human, reasonably expect some sense of clarity as they turn to the final pages. (p. 259)

The very premise of this book on understudied family relationships seems rooted in this tension as it eschews the conclusions of past research on marital couples and parents and their young children, suggesting that examining other, less studied, relationships will prompt different conclusions about family communication. Moving among these various samples reflects some of this dialectic tension.

The second tension, inclusion/boundaries, touches on the desire to map the diversity of family relationships and the recognition of the impossibility of studying every conceivable family association. For every relationship profiled in this book, we can think of several more that still await exploration. Each study seems to beg for another, perhaps allied study to accompany it. For instance, Chapter 1 provides a fascinating glimpse into the mother-adult daughter relationship. Next we need to address the mother-adult son relationship, the father-adult daughter relationship, and so forth. The numbers of relationships are endless (and endlessly fascinating). Yet, we may also want to put boundaries on our explorations in service of generalizing from previous findings. In a way, this tension taps a perennial problem for researchers: how widely to generalize from the observations they make.

In sum, changing the sieve that Stephanie Coontz (1999) referred to, and opening the social recipe to include a wider variety of families, exhilarates and challenges us as researchers. We experience the push and pull of dialectic tensions as we enter the research arena with the goal of expanding our studies and examining the understudied. As we attend to the myriad voices entering the dialogue, we dwell in a state of constructive tension. Yet, this tension requires some response in order to truly provide productive research stimuli. We turn our attention to two main methods for attaining this.

Methods for Dealing With Dialectic Tensions

We suggest two principal methods for confronting the dialectics we have just discussed: (1) actively embrace diversity in your research, and (2) focus on principles of communication. In addition, we address some practical steps to make toward actualizing our research goals. We will describe each method briefly below. Our intent here is to be heuristic. We fully expect that there are many other ways to address the tensions of expanding the social recipe for family. Part of the enduring charm of family communication research will be in the search for them.

Actively Embrace Diversity

How can we honor the complexity of family life, with all its rapid changes, and simultaneously draw some conclusions about the lived experiences of families? Consciously supporting diversity in our research is one way to manage this dialectic.

The 1999 theme of the National Communication Association's annual convention was "Coloring Outside the Lines." To actualize his theme, then Vice President Ray McKerrow programmed panels that articulated the notion that our discipline should be prepared to think differently about the way we teach, research, and provide service to our academic communities. We believe that family communication scholarship should "color outside the lines" with respect to the diversity of our research samples, methods, and theories. We argue that doing so will help us manage the tension between drawing conclusions and revising them. We briefly describe the implications of "thinking differently" with respect to these three areas.

Samples and Sampling. One way to capture the real and varied experiences of families requires expanding the boundaries pertaining to samples and sampling in family communication scholarship. With respect to samples and sampling, one area seems especially opportunistic: sample type. Unequivocally, the first factor to consider in embracing diversity in this area is family type. That is, before embarking upon any research in family communication, we encourage an expansive look at the possibilities of the family in research samples. Anthony Giddens (2005) observes that societies across the world are experiencing a transformation in family relationships. He states that "there is a global revolution going on in how we think of ourselves and how we form ties and connections with others" (p. 26). To this end, family researchers are ethically obligated to understand the family in broad terms. Reflecting on both configurations and characteristics, family communication research would be well served if future scholars—like those in this anthology—considered sampling the unexamined, the overlooked, and the understudied.

This book provides an excellent base through its examination of a number of understudied family relationships. For future scholarship to build on this foundation, we suggest that when we are actively embracing diversity, there are multiple layers of diversity to be considered. One layer that is particularly well represented in this volume we call "family configuration." Diversity in family configuration requires attention to such family forms as stepfamilies (see Chapter 9), families formed through adoption (see Chapter 8), and in-law relationships (see Chapters 6 and 7), as well as nuclear, biological families.

Another layer of diversity we label "family characteristics," and this layer includes variables such as gender, ethnicity, class, ability, religiosity, age, and sexual identity. To understand the import of these characteristics, we turn to feminist theorizing where the concept of social location or standpoint (Hartsock, 1983; Wood, 1992) features the interrelationship of gender, ethnicity, class, and so forth. For instance, Patricia Hill Collins (1999) notes that "motherhood occurs in specific historical situations framed by interlocking structures of race, class, and gender" (p. 197). In making this point, Collins begins to conceptualize how "family characteristics" construct and reconstruct family communication practices. While many scholars agree with the importance of this layer of diversity, research is only just beginning to grapple with the critical questions of how such characteristics as race, ethnicity, class, and gender interact to shape family communication behavior and, in turn, are shaped by communication within the family.

A third layer of diversity we call "contemporary issues in the family," and this includes reproductive technologies, demographic changes such as increasing life spans, healthcare issues, and interracial families, among others. These issues often intersect with the other layers to produce families like two European American gay men who have triplets using the sperm of one of them, an egg donor, and a surrogate mother who is African American. These contemporary issues are a result of technological advances affecting the family as well as rapid changes blurring racial categories such as interracial relationships and transnational adoptions. In 2000, 1.9% of married couples were interracial and 4.3% of cohabiting couples were interracial (U. S. Bureau of the Census, 2000).

The three layers of diversity can be studied alone or combined to help researchers generate understudied samples that deserve study as they reflect many families' reality. For instance, senior citizens who cohabit have been virtually ignored in the literature. Given the aging population and the lack of financial resources for our older population, this family demographic will continue to grow in the future. In addition, gay fathers and lesbian mothers and their children have been only sporadically sampled. The intersection of sexual identity and race with respect to the gay/lesbian family also has lasting importance. Although the difficulty in accessing this population has been established (Turner & West, 2003), efforts to explain such areas as self-disclosure of sexual identity, communication with children, and relationship satisfaction are critical (Peplau & Beals, 2004).

An additional sample to consider is the post-marital relationship (Graham, 2003; see also Chapter 10). Family scholars have an opportunity to examine the friendships following a divorce, the relationships among children, and the effect of the divorce on extended family members. In addition to these family configurations, race, age, ethnicity, religiosity, and other characteristics may play a significant role in family communication and should be explored in tandem with family type. For instance, post-divorce communication in interracial families forms an important, if under-studied, topic for scholarship. Many other family samples exist, each providing family communication scholars with opportunities to tap family relationships that reflect the diversity and reality of family life in society.

Research Methods. Glen Stamp (2004), in his review of family communi-cation scholarship over a 12-year time period, found that 92% of the literature in family communication followed the social scientific method. Stamp states that "as such, the family research within the empirical per-spective reflects such traditional scientific procedures as randomized sam-ples, systematic data collection, objective measurement tools, and orderly theory development" (p. 20). And despite the claim by Patricia Noller and Judith Feeney (2004) that "family communication can be studied using a variety of methodologies" (p. 31), this variability has generally not been the case.

Clearly, a great deal of family communication research is replete with self-report inventories and questionnaires. Yet, additional (and alternative) methods and approaches might be considered that would enhance the prac-ticality of family research. We are not advocating for an abandonment of traditional forms of data collection because they are extremely useful for collecting a certain type of information. Yet, we advance that research can benefit from additional methods that are not default options of family researchers. We understand that every method has its advantages and dis-advantages, but we are aiming to write a social recipe that expands the boundaries of what has been done or what is generally acceptable. As Noller and Feeney (2004) note, "more work is needed that takes full advan-tage of the range of methods available and that combines both insider and outsider data to increase our understanding of family processes" (p. 45).

Family and culture are inextricably linked (Sabourin, 2003), and conse-quently, employing methods that are culturally respectful, sensitive, and applicable seems only reasonable. What types of methods are we suggesting? First, we propose an examination of methods that take into account the communication processes of family members. In other words, we assert that data-based research may benefit from the words spoken by family members in addition to their perceptions. Ethnography, for example, helps us understand not only the words of individuals but the cultures in which they live (Ellis & Bochner, 1996).

Using ethnographic methods to understand family communication has the distinct advantage of bringing the personal to the public and helping one claim a sense of self. In particular, autoethnography allows for what John Fiske (1990) notes as the opening up of "the realm of the interior and the personal and to articulate that which, in the practices of everyday life, lies below any conscious articulation" (p. 90). For example, autoethnographic research in family communication might examine the personal interpretations and reactions to being a single gay father, a grandmother with child custody, or a married couple raising their children to be both Christian and Jewish. Mark Neumann (1996) suggests that autoethnography "stands as a current attempt to, quite literally, *come to terms*, with sustaining questions of self and culture" (p. 193).

In addition to ethnography, the use of observational methods has the potential to help family communication scholars "assess actual behavior rather than individuals' perceptions of their behavior" (Noller & Feeney, 2004, p. 36). Studying family conflict, for instance, from an observational vantage point may help researchers *witness* the conflict patterns rather than review how family members perceive the enactment of such patterns. Since a great deal of self-report research is potentially jeopardized by social desirability bias (Baxter & Babbie, 2004), family research can increase its vitality and applicability with observational methods.

One additional methodological avenue to consider in order to increase the applicability of our research to family life is the use of diaries. Rarely used in family communication research, diaries help scholars better understand the everyday occurrences taking place in families. Diaries permit family members to privately ruminate about mundane, unique, significant, intimate, and conflictual family events. It is worthwhile to consider, for instance, that if a researcher were interested in knowing the effects of unpredictable stress on the family (e.g., winning a lottery, death of a child), the insights the diary method could provide would not be gleaned through traditional scientific means. Further, diaries are unique insofar as they are permanent records and can be retrieved as necessary. In addition to allowing a researcher to gain understanding of a family, diaries also have the potential advantage of helping families, too. The thoughts, words, and feelings of family members—the everyday discursive practices—need to be honored if our scholarship is to make a difference. Diaries help to achieve that scholarly goal.

Theories. Thus far, we have noted that managing the tension between our research and our families is possible by (re)examining our sampling and our methods. We also believe that the theories we employ in our research should be (re)considered as we work toward more realistic reflections of families.

It is clear that the family has theoretical importance (Goode, 2005). Yet, we also understand that family communication scholarship has relied upon theories that have their geneses outside of the communication discipline. Arguably, the scholarly beginnings of family communication began with the formation of the Family Communication Division in the National Communication Association in 1989. Since that time, family scholars have tended to rely upon a core set of theories in their writing, namely attachment, systems, role, and exchange (Stamp, 2004). Although these theories have effectively framed research, the theories are not communicative in nature. That is, they have not been conceptualized nor developed by family communication scholars. The integration of communication theories such as marital types (Fitzpatrick, 1988), relational dialectics (Baxter & Montgomery, 1996), narrative performance theory (Langellier & Peterson, 2004), and communication privacy management theory (Petronio, 1991) provides theoretical presence for communication concepts; however, more diversity in theoretical development seems fruitful.

Theories do not simply appear without thorough and respectable research efforts. Therefore, we temper this call with the understanding that communication theories are not conceptualized overnight and require an ongoing refinement.

Finally, we need to interrogate our theorizing about family communication, unpacking the assumptions within our theories to see if they suit the social recipe of family we are trying to (re)create. In her study of communication in maternal relationships examining grandmothers, mothers, and adult daughters, Michelle Miller-Day (2004) illustrates this questioning approach to theorizing the family. She examines the relational approach, refining it specifically to suit her interpretive, qualitative study. Further, we should approach theorizing, as Karen Sacks (1999) suggests, by critiquing theories that imply norms against which "others" are measured and instead develop theories placing those others at the center. Thus, we need theories that stem directly from the experiences of the families we are interested in studying.

Focus on Communication Processes

How do we capture the variety of families and family relationships and yet acknowledge that by focusing on any one "understudied" relationship we are overlooking many others? One response to this tension is to concentrate on communication processes, examining how they unfold in specific contexts and within particular families. In this endeavor we are looking more for commonalities across different family configurations with different characteristics. By switching our focus to the communication practices of families while consciously choosing a variety of families to study, we can move between the poles of this tension.

Practical Considerations: Changing the Terms of Agreement

In addition to dealing with the tensions brought out by this enterprise, we must take some practical steps to change the social recipe in our research. Elsewhere (Turner & West, 2003) we have argued that family communication scholarship can benefit from looking at the publication process and how it shapes family life. In light of the aforementioned, we suggest the following guidelines as we strive toward reflecting the realities of families. We argue that the "terms of agreement" between family scholars and their research may benefit from modification. Although excellent scholarship exists, we propose a reexamination of thinking and research practices. The present collection of studies is a noteworthy beginning in rethinking family scholarship. Indeed, we embrace scholarly decisions that periodically transcend the traditional routes of investigating families. We support the efforts like those of writers in this anthology who aim to "recast the understudied" as central, significant, and worthy of exploration. In this spirit, we view the following individuals/groups as important change agents for family communication scholarship:

Journal Editors. There is a scholarly reality in communication: journal editors are important gateways to research. We suggest that attention be paid to the editorship of journals. The selection of an editor by either a communication association or a board is of paramount importance to the inclusion of nontraditional samples, sampling, methods, and theories. In the *Journal of Family Communication,* for instance, the preeminent journal devoted to scholarship pertaining to communication in the family, a short, often-ignored statement appears under the "Contributor Information" section: "The journal welcomes diverse theoretical and methodological perspectives." The implications of this statement are far-reaching and suggest an expansive and embracing editorial scope. We support the subtle but important editorial prerogatives that aid in the representation of more realistic portrayals of families and the communication practices that they enact.

Scholarly Book Publishers. Journal editors are one vital change agent; book publishers are also important. Publishers who are willing to publish books that may not draw large adoptions or purchases are rare. Sage, for instance, the publisher of this book, has a rich history of supporting family scholarship that may not necessarily be "mainstream." Other publishers, however, let the "bottom line" take precedence over publishing research which departs from the conventional social recipe. It may be important at times for family communication scholars to educate publishers. This can take place informally (at convention exhibit booths, over coffee, and so forth) or formally (co-participation on convention programs, serving as book reviewers, and so forth). In sum, scholarly books are critical foundations for family communication research, and therefore, communicating the need to "color outside the lines" and support projects that will add to the literature base remains essential.

Granting Agencies. Despite the plethora of family communication research, there is a paucity of knowledge by grantors regarding the area of study. One challenge facing family communication scholars is the legitimization of family communication research through favorable grant dispositions. Many regional and national associations have invited representatives from funding agencies such as the National Science Foundation and the Pew Charitable Trusts. And, some family communication scholars have achieved major and minor grants to fund their research.

Still, many of the granting agencies lack the knowledge or the insight to fund this research. The consequence of this ignorance is far-reaching: if public or private funding does not support family communication research, then the area of study remains isolated. In fact, we suggest that without adequate funding opportunities, family communication research may be limited to its own academic borders. Funding suggests legitimacy and legitimacy enhances visibility. Further, once a grant has been disposed, family scholars should consider offering their expertise as a reviewer, thereby increasing the opportunity of further favorably dispositions. Granting agencies are fundamental links to showcasing the applicability of family communication scholarship to the community.

Conclusion

In summary, the social recipe for family is highly resistant to change despite the fact that social life is buffeted by changes, great and small. People maintain the image of a family that represents a very small percentage of U.S.

families, yet these same people often live within a wide variety of family types. This discrepancy challenges us all because, first, our research is impoverished if it does not represent the lived experiences of families. Second, families that are not represented in the literature (both popular and research) are left to wonder about their normalcy.

This book sounds a call to address this discrepancy by making our studies true to the lived experiences of families, thus expanding the social recipe. Communication researchers' contributions can help create a new, more inclusive social recipe that is more responsive to the families we live in. Consciously choosing diverse samples, examining how communication processes differ or relate across a variety of family configurations, and attending to practical matters, such as persuading gatekeepers to enlarge the sieve and let research about diverse families through, are all concrete steps that follow the foundation set by the essays in this collection.

References

Adams, B. N. (1968). *Kinship in an urban setting.* Chicago: Markham.

Adler, J. (1996, June 17). Building a better dad. *Newsweek, 58–64.*

Adler, L. L., Denmark, F. L., & Ahmed, R. A. (1989). Attitudes toward mother-in-law and stepmother: A cross-cultural study. *Psychological Reports, 65,* 1194.

Adler, R. P. (2001). *Older adults and computers: Report of a national survey.* Retrieved June 9, 2003, from http://www.seniornet.org/php/default.php? PageID=5476

Adoption Learning Partners. (2004). Retrieved March 20, 2004, from http://www .adoptionlearningpartners.org

Afifi, T. D. (2003). "Feeling caught" in stepfamilies: Managing boundary turbulence through appropriate privacy coordination rules. *Journal of Social and Personal Relationships, 20,* 729–756.

Afifi, T. D., & Hamrick, K. (in press). Communication processes that promote risk and resilience in post-divorce families. In M. Fine and J. Harvey (Eds.), *The handbook of divorce and relationship dissolution.* Mahwah, NJ: Lawrence Erlbaum Associates.

Afifi, T. D., Hutchinson, S., & Krouse, S. (2005a). *A context-specific examination of communal coping in post-divorce families.* Manuscript submitted for publication.

Afifi, T. D., Hutchinson, S., & Krouse, S. (2005b). *Communicative ways of coping: Variations in communal, social, and individual coping and resilience in post-divorce families.* Manuscript submitted for publication.

Afifi, T. D., & Keith, S. (2004). A risk and resiliency model of ambiguous loss in post-divorce stepfamilies. *Journal of Family Communication, 4,* 65–98.

Afifi, T. D., & Nussbaum, J. F. (in press). Family career theories: Family stress and adaptation across the lifespan. In D. O. Braithwaite & L. A. Baxter (Eds.), *Engaging theories in family communication. Multiple perspectives.* Thousand Oaks, CA: Sage.

Afifi, T. D., & Schrodt, P. (2003a). Adolescents' and young adults' feelings of being caught between their parents in divorced and non-divorced households. *Communication Monographs, 70,* 142–173.

Afifi, T. D., & Schrodt, P. (2003b). "Feeling caught" as a mediator of adolescents' and young adults' avoidance and satisfaction with their parents in divorced and non-divorced households. *Communication Monographs, 70,* 142–173.

Afifi, T. D., & Schrodt, P. (2003c). Uncertainty and the avoidance of the state of one's family/relationships in stepfamilies, post-divorce single parent families, and first marriage families. *Human Communication Research, 29,* 516–533.

Afifi, W. A., & Guerrero, L. K. (2000). Motivations underlying topic avoidance in close relationships. In S. Petronio (Ed.)., *Balancing the secrets of private disclosures* (pp. 165–180). Mahwah, NJ: Lawrence Erlbaum Associates.

Alexander, P. C. (2003). Parent-child role reversal: Development of a measure and test of an attachment theory model. *Journal of Systemic Therapies, 22,* 31–43.

Allen, G. (1977). Sibling solidarity. *Journal of Marriage and the Family, 39,* 177–184.

Allen, K. R., Blieszner, R., & Roberto, K. (2000). Families in the middle and later years: A review and critique of research in the 1990s. *Journal of Marriage and the Family, 62,* 911–926.

Allport, G. W. (1954). *The nature of prejudice.* Reading, MA: Addison-Wesley.

Altman, I., Brown, B. B., Staples, B., & Werner, C. M. (1992). A transactional approach to close relationships: Courtship, weddings, and placemaking. In W. B. Walsh, K. H. Craik, & R. H. Price (Eds.), *Person-environment psychology: Models and perspectives* (pp. 193–242). Hillsdale, NJ: Lawrence Erlbaum Associates.

Amato, P. R. (1996). Explaining the intergenerational transmission of divorce. *Journal of Marriage and the Family, 58,* 628–640.

Amato, P. R. (2000). The consequences of divorce for adults and children. *Journal of Marriage and the Family, 62,* 1269–1287.

Amato, P. R., & Afifi, T. D. (2005). *Adult children's feelings of being caught between their parents in divorced and nondivorced families: Consequences for parent-child relations and children's well-being.* Manuscript submitted for publication.

Amato, P. R., & DeBoer, D. D. (2001). The transmission of marital instability across generations: Relationship skills or commitment to marriage? *Journal of Marriage and the Family, 63,* 1038–1051.

Amato, P. R., & Rezac, S. J. (1994). Contact with nonresident parents, interparental conflict, and children's behavior. *Journal of Family Issues, 15,* 191–207.

Anderson, K., Harwood, J., & Hummert, M. L. (in press). Age-stereotypes in context: The importance of the grandparent-grandchild relationship in intergenerational communication. *Human Communication Research.*

Anderson, R., Baxter, L. A., & Cissna, K. N. (2004). Concluding voices, conversation fragments, and a temporary synthesis. In R. Anderson, L. A. Baxter, & K. N. Cissna (Eds.), *Dialogue: Theorizing difference in communication studies* (pp. 259–267). Thousand Oaks, CA: Sage.

Angel, R., & Angel, J. (1993). *Painful inheritance: Health and the new generation of fatherless families.* Madison: University of Wisconsin Press.

Arditti, J. A. (1999). Rethinking relationships between divorced mothers and their children: Capitalizing on family strengths. *Family Relations, 48,* 109–119.

Arliss, L. P. (1994). *Contemporary family communication: Meanings and messages.* New York: St. Martin's Press.

Arnett, J. J. (1999). Adolescent storm and stress, reconsidered. *American Psychologist, 54,* 317–326.

Aune, K. S., & Comstock, J. (2001). An exploratory investigation of jealousy in the family. *Journal of Family Communication, 2,* 29–39.

Avioli, P. S. (1989). The social support functions of siblings in later life: A theoretical model. *American Behavioral Scientist, 33,* 45–57.

Avtgis, T. A. (2003). Male sibling social and emotional support as a function of attributional confidence. *Communication Research Reports, 20,* 341–347.

B A Squared, Inc. (2004). *Mother-in-law stories.* Retrieved December 14, 2004, from http://www.motherinlawstories.com

Bach, G. (1946). Father-fantasies and father-typing in father separated children. *Child Development, 38,* 243–250.

Bakhtin, M. M. (1984). *Problems of Dostoevsky's poetics* (C. Emerson, Ed. & Trans.). Minneapolis: University of Minnesota Press.

Bakhtin, M. M. (1986). *Speech genres and other late essays* (C. Emerson & M. Holquist, Eds.; V. McGee, Trans.). Austin: University of Texas Press.

Bakhtin, M. M. (1990). *Art and answerability: Early philosophical essays by M. M. Bakhtin* (M. Holquist & V. Liapunov, Eds.; V. Liapunov & K. Brostrom, Trans.). Austin: University of Texas Press.

Barer, B. M. (2001). The grands and greats of very old black grandmothers. *Journal of Aging Studies, 15,* 1–11.

Barnett, O., Miller-Perrin, C. L., & Perrin, R. D. (2005). *Family violence across the lifespan: An introduction* (2nd ed.). Thousand Oaks, CA: Sage.

Barrett, L. F., & Barrett, D. J. (2001). An introduction to computerized experience sampling in psychology. *Social Science Computer Review, 19*(2), 175–185.

Bartholet, E. (1993). *Family bonds: Adoption and the practice of parenting.* New York: Houghton Mifflin.

Baruch, G. K., & Barnett, R. C. (1996). Consequences of fathers' participation in family work: Parents' role strain and well-being. *Journal of Personality and Social Psychology, 51,* 983–992.

Bastida, E. (2001). Kinship ties of Mexican migrant women on the United States/Mexico border. *Journal of Comparative Family Studies, 32,* 549–569.

Baxter, L. A. (1993). The social side of personal relationships: A dialectical perspective. In S. Duck (Ed.), *Understanding relationship processes, 3: Social context and relationships* (pp. 139–165). Newbury Park, CA: Sage.

Baxter, L. A. (2004). Distinguished scholar article: Relationships as dialogues. *Personal Relationships, 11,* 1–22.

Baxter, L. A. (in press). Relational dialectics: Multivocal dialogues of family communication. In D. O. Braithwaite & L. A. Baxter (Eds.), *Engaging theories in family communication. Multiple perspectives.* Thousand Oaks, CA: Sage.

Baxter, L. A., & Babbie, E. (2004). *The basics of communication research.* Belmont, CA: Wadsworth.

Baxter, L. A., & Braithwaite, D. O. (2002). Performing marriage: The marriage renewal ritual as cultural performance. *Southern Communication Journal, 67,* 94–109.

Baxter, L. A., & Braithwaite, D. O. (2004, July). *Aesthetic love: A third way of love in stepfamilies.* Paper presented at the annual meeting of the International Association for Relationship Research, Madison, WI.

Baxter, L. A., Braithwaite, D. O., & Bryant, L. (2004). *Types of communication triads perceived by young-adult stepchildren in established stepfamilies.* Manuscript submitted for publication.

Baxter, L. A., Braithwaite, D. O., Bryant, L. E., & Wagner, A. (2004). Stepchildren's perceptions of the contradictions in communication with stepparents. *Journal of Social and Personal Relationships, 21,* 447–467.

Baxter, L. A., Braithwaite, D. O., & Nicholson, J. (1999). Turning points in the development of blended family relationships. *Journal of Social and Personal Relationships, 16,* 291–313.

Baxter, L. A., & Montgomery, B. M. (1996). *Relating: Dialogues and dialectics.* New York: Guilford.

Beatty, L. (1995). Effects of paternal absence on male adolescents' peer relations and self-image. *Adolescence, 30,* 873–880.

Beatty, M. J., & Dobos, J. A. (1993). Adult males' perceptions of confirmation and relational partner communication apprehension: Indirect effects of fathers on sons' partners. *Communication Quarterly, 41,* 66–76.

Beaumont, S. L., Vasconcelos, V. C. B., & Ruggeri, M. (2001). Similarities and differences in mother-daughter and mother-son conversations during preadolescence and adolescence. *Journal of Language and Social Psychology, 20,* 419–444.

Beck, A. T., Sethi, B. B., & Tuthill, R. N. (1963). Childhood bereavement and adult depression. *Archives of General Psychiatry, 9,* 295–302.

Bedford, V. H. (1989a). A comparison of thematic apperceptions of sibling affiliation, conflict, and separation at two periods of adulthood. *International Journal of Aging and Human Development, 28,* 53–66.

Bedford, V. H. (1989b). Understanding the value of siblings in old age. *American Behavioral Scientist, 33,* 33–44.

Bedford, V. H. (1990). Predictors of variation in positive and negative affect toward adult siblings. *Family Perspectives, 24,* 245–262.

Bedford, V. H. (1993). Relationships between adult siblings. In A. E. Auhagen & M. von Salisch (Eds.), *Interpersonal relationships* (pp. 119–141). Göttingen, Germany: Hogrefe, Verlage fur Psychologie.

Bedford, V. H. (1995). Sibling relationships in middle and old age. In R. Blieszner & V. H. Bedford (Eds.), *Handbook of aging and the family* (pp. 201–222). Westport, CT: Greenwood Press.

Bengtson, V. L. (1993). Is the "contract across generations" changing? Effects of population aging on obligations and expectations across age groups. In V. L. Bengtson & W. A. Achenbaum (Eds.), *The changing contract across generations* (pp. 3–23). New York: Aldine de Gruyter.

Bengtson, V. L., Rosenthal, C., & Burton, L. M. (1990). Families and aging. In R. Binstock & L. George (Eds.), *Handbook of aging and the social sciences* (pp. 263–287). New York: Academic Press.

Biblarz, T. J., & Gottainer, G. (2000). Family structure and children's success: A comparison of widowed and divorced single-mother families. *Journal of Marriage and the Family, 62,* 533–548.

Biller, H. B. (1993). *Fathers and families: Paternal factors in child development.* Westport, CT: Auburn House.

Block, C. E. (2002). College students' perceptions of social support from grandmothers and stepgrandmothers. *College Student Journal, 36,* 419–432.

Blos, P. (1987). Freud and the father complex. *The Psychoanalytic Study of the Child, 42,* 425–441.

Booth, A., & Amato, P. R. (1994). Parental marital quality, parental divorce, and relations with parents. *Journal of Marriage and the Family, 56,* 21–34.

Booth, A., & Amato, P. R. (2001). Parental predivorce relations and offspring postdivorce well being. *Journal of Marriage and the Family, 63,* 197–212.

Boss, P. (1999). *Ambiguous loss.* New York: Harvard University Press.

Boyum, L. A., & Parke, R. D. (1995). The role of family emotional expressiveness in the development of children's social competence. *Journal of Marriage and the Family, 57,* 593–608.

Braithwaite, D. O., & Baxter, L. A. (Eds.). (2005). *Engaging theories in family communication. Multiple perspectives.* Mahwah NJ: Lawrence Erlbaum Associates.

Braithwaite, D. O., & Baxter, L. A. (in press). "You're my parent but you're not": Dialectical tensions in stepchildren's perceptions about communicating with the nonresidential parent. *Journal of Applied Communication Research.*

Braithwaite, D. O., Baxter, L. A., & Harper, A. (1998). The role of rituals in the management of dialectical tension of "old" and "new" in blended families. *Communication Studies, 48,* 101–120.

Braithwaite, D. O., McBride, M. C., & Schrodt, P. (2003). "Parent teams" and the everyday interactions of co-parenting in stepfamilies. *Communication Reports, 16,* 93–111.

Braithwaite, D. O., Olson, L. N., Golish, T. D., Soukup, C., & Turman, T. (2001). "Becoming a family": Developmental processes represented in blended family discourse. *Journal of Applied Communication Research, 29,* 221–247.

Braithwaite, D. O., Schrodt, P., & Koenig Kellas, J. (in press). Symbolic convergence theory: Communication, dramatizing messages, and rhetorical visions in families. In D. O. Braithwaite & L. A. Baxter (Eds.), *Engaging theories in family communication. Multiple perspectives.* Thousand Oaks, CA: Sage.

Braithwaite, D. O., Toller, P., Daas, K., Durham, W., & Jones, A. (2004, February). *Centered, but not caught in the middle: Stepchildren's perceptions of contradictions of communication of co-parents.* Paper presented at the annual meeting of the Western States Communication Association, Albuquerque, NM.

Brewer, M. (2000). Reducing prejudice through cross-categorization: Effects of multiple social identities. In S. Oskamp (Ed.), *Reducing prejudice and discrimination* (pp. 165–184). Mahwah, NJ: Lawrence Erlbaum Associates.

Brody, G. H. (1998). Sibling relationship quality: Its causes and consequences. *Annual Review of Psychology, 49,* 1–24.

Brody, L. R. (1996). Gender, emotional expression, and parent-child boundries. In R. Kavanaugh, B. Zimmerberg-Glick, & S. Fein (Eds.), *Emotion: Interdisciplinary perspectives* (pp. 139–170). Hillsdale, NJ: Lawrence Erlbaum Associates.

Brodzinsky, D. M., Patterson, C. J., & Varizi, M. (2002). Adoption agency perspectives on lesbian and gay prospective parents: A national study. *Adoption Quarterly, 5,* 5–23.

Brodzinsky, D. M., & Schechter, M. D. (1990). *The psychology of adoption.* New York: Oxford University Press.

Brodzinsky, D. M., Singer, L., & Braff, A. (1984). Children's understanding of adoption. *Child Development, 55,* 869–878.

Brodzinsky, D. M., Smith, D. W., & Brodzinsky, A. B. (1998). *Children's adjustment to adoption: Developmental clinical psychology and psychiatry.* Thousand Oaks, CA: Sage.

Bromberg, P. (1993). Shadow and substance: A relational perspective on clinical process. *Psychoanalytic Psychology, 10,* 147–168.

Brook, J. S., Whitman, M., & Gordon, A. S. (1985). Father absence, perceived family characteristics and stage of drug use in adolescence. *British Journal of Developmental Psychology, 3,* 87–94.

Brooke, J. (2004, May 21). Japan's crown prince complains his wife is stifled by the imperial household. *International Herald Tribune,* p. 4.

Brussoni, M. J., & Boon, S. D. (1998). Grandparental impact in young adults' relationships with their closest grandparents: The role of relationship strength and emotional closeness. *International Journal of Aging and Human Development, 46,* 267–286.

Bryant, C. M., Conger, R. D., & Meehan, J. M. (2001). The influence of in-laws on change in marital success. *Journal of Marriage and the Family, 63,* 614–626.

Bryant, L. E. (2003). *Stepchildren's perceptions of the contradictions in communication with stepfamilies formed post bereavement.* Unpublished doctoral dissertation, University of Nebraska-Lincoln.

Buchanan, C. M., Maccoby, E. E., & Dornbusch, S. M. (1991). Caught between parents: Adolescents' experience in divorced homes. *Child Development, 62,* 1008–1029.

Buchanan, C. M., & Waizenhofer, R. (2001). The impact of interparental conflict on adolescent children: Considerations of family systems and family structure. In A. Booth, A. C. Crouter, & M. Clements (Eds.), *Couples in conflict* (pp. 149–161). Mahwah, NJ: Lawrence Erlbaum Associates.

Burke, L. (2003). The impact of maternal depression on familial relationships. *International Review of Psychiatry, 15,* 243–255.

Burnstein, E., Crandall, C., & Kitayama, S. (1994). Some neo-Darwinian decision rules for altruism: Weighing cues for inclusive fitness as a function of the biological importance of the decision. *Journal of Personality and Social Psychology, 67,* 773–789.

Burton, L. M. (1992). Black grandparents rearing children of drug-addicted parents: Stressors, outcomes, and social service needs. *The Gerontologist, 32,* 744–751.

Burton, L. M., & Bengtson, V. L. (1985). Black grandmothers: Timing and continuity of roles. In V. L. Bengtson & J. F. Robertson (Eds.), *Grandparenthood* (pp. 61–78). Beverly Hills, CA: Sage.

Canary, D. J., Cupach, W. R., & Messman, S. J. (1995). *Relationship conflict: Conflict in parent-child, friendship, and romantic relationships.* Thousand Oaks, CA: Sage.

Canary, D. J., & Stafford, L. (1992). Relational maintenance strategies and equity in marriage. *Communication Monographs, 59,* 243–267.

Canary, D. J., Stafford, L., Hause, K. S., & Wallace, L. A. (1993). An inductive analysis of relational maintenance strategies: Comparisons among lovers, relatives, friends, and others. *Communication Research Reports, 10,* 5–14.

Caron, A. F. (1995). *Strong mothers, strong sons: Raising the next generation of men.* New York: Perennial Books.

Carp, E. W. (1998). *Family matters: Secrecy and disclosure in the history of adoption.* Cambridge, MA: Harvard University Press.

Caughlin, J. P., Golish, T. D., Olson, L. N., Sargent, J. E., Cook, J. S., & Petronio, S. (2000). Intrafamily secrets in various family configurations: A communication boundary management perspective. *Communication Studies, 51,* 116–134.

Caughlin, J. P., & Petronio, S. (2004). Privacy in families. In A. L. Vangelisti (Ed.), *Handbook of family communication* (pp. 319–412). Mahwah, NJ: Lawrence Erlbaum Associates.

Centers for Disease Control and Prevention. (2002a). Deaths: The leading causes for 2000. *National Vital Statistics Reports, 50,* 1–86.

Centers for Disease Control and Prevention. (2002b). Youth risk behavior surveillance system–United States, 2001. *Morbidity and Mortality Weekly Report, 51 (SS-14),* 1–64.

Chambers, D. (2001). *Representing the family.* London: Sage.

Chen, F., Short, S. E., & Entwisle, B. (2000). The impact of grandparental proximity on maternal childcare in China. *Population Research and Policy Review, 19*(6), 571–590.

Cherlin, A. J., & Furstenberg, F. F. (1986). *The new American grandparent: A place in the family, a life apart.* New York: Basic Books.

Cherlin, A. J., & Furstenberg, F. F. (1994). Stepfamilies in the United States: A reconsideration. *Annual Review of Sociology, 20,* 359–381.

Chowdhury, B. (2000). *The last dive: A father and a son's fatal descent into the ocean's depths.* New York: HarperCollins.

Chrisp, J. (2001). That four letter word—sons: Lesbian mothers and adolescent sons. *Journal of Lesbian Studies, 5,* 195–209.

Chudacoff, H. P. (1989). *How old are you? Age consciousness in American culture.* Princeton, NJ: Princeton University Press.

Cicirelli, V. G. (1977). Relationship of siblings to the elderly person's feelings and concerns. *Journal of Gerontology, 32,* 317–322.

Cicirelli, V. G. (1979). *Social services for elderly in relation to the kin network.* Report to the NRTA-AARP Andrus Foundation.

Cicirelli, V. G. (1980). Sibling influence in adulthood: A life span perspective. In L. W. Poon (Ed.), *Aging in the 1980's* (pp. 455–462). Washington, DC: American Psychological Association.

Cicirelli, V. G. (1982). Sibling influence throughout the lifespan. In M. E. Lamb & B. Sutton-Smith (Eds.), *Sibling relationships: Their nature and significance across the lifespan* (pp. 267–284). Hillsdale, NJ: Lawrence Erlbaum Associates.

Cicirelli, V. G. (1985a). The role of siblings as family caregivers. In W. J. Sauer & R. T. Coward (Eds.), *Social support networks and the care of the elderly* (pp. 93–107). New York: Springer-Verlag.

Cicirelli, V. G. (1985b). Siblings relationships thoughout the life cycle. In L. L'Abate (Ed.), *The handbook of family psychology and therapy* (Vol. 1, pp. 177–214). Homewood, IL: Dorsey Press.

Cicirelli, V. G. (1989). Feelings of attachment to siblings and well being in later life. *Psychology and Aging, 4,* 211–216.

Cicirelli, V. G. (1990). Family support in relation to health problems of the elderly. In T. H. Brubaker (Ed.), *Family relationships in later life* (2nd ed., pp. 218–228). Newbury Park, CA: Sage.

Cicirelli, V. G. (1991). Sibling relationships in adulthood. In S. P. Pfeifer & M. B. Sussman (Eds.), *Families: Intergenerational and generational connections* (pp. 291–310). New York: Haworth Press.

Cicirelli, V. G. (1992). *Family caregiving: Autonomous and paternalistic decision-making.* Newbury Park, CA: Sage.

Cicirelli, V. G. (1994). Sibling relationship in cross-cultural perspective. *Journal of Marriage and the Family, 56,* 7–20.

Cicirelli, V. G. (1995). *Sibling relationships across the life span.* New York: Plenum Press.

Cicirelli, V. G., & Nussbaum, J. F. (1989). Relationships with siblings in later life. In J. F. Nussbaum (Ed.), *Life-span communication: Normative processes* (pp. 283–299). Hillsdale, NJ: Lawrence Erlbaum Associates.

Cissna, K. N., Cox, D. E., & Bochner, A. P. (1990). The dialectic of marital and parental relationships within the stepfamily. *Communication Monographs, 37,* 44–61.

Clark, C. (2002). *From father to son: Showing your boy how to walk with Christ.* New York: Navpress Publishing Group.

Clark, R. D., & Shields, G. (1997). Family communication and delinquency. *Adolescence, 32,* 81–92.

Cogswell, C., & Henry, C. (1995). Grandchildren's perceptions of grandparental support in divorced and intact families. *Journal of Divorce & Remarriage, 23,* 127–150.

Cole, C. L., & Cole, A. L. (1999). Boundary ambiguities that bind former spouses together after children leave home in post-divorce families. *Family Relations, 48,* 271–272.

Colarossi, L. G. (2001). Adolescent gender differences in social support: Structure, function, and provider type. *Social Work Research, 25,* 233–241.

Colarossi, L. G., & Eccles, J. S. (2003). Differential effects of support providers on adolescents' mental health. *Social Work Research, 27,* 19–30.

Coleman, M. A., Fine, M. A., Ganong, L. G., Downs, K. M., & Pauk, N. (2001). When you're not the Brady Bunch: Identifying perceived conflicts and resolution strategies in stepfamilies. *Personal Relationships, 8,* 57–73.

Coleman, M., & Ganong, L. H. (1998). Attitudes toward men's intergenerational financial obligations to older and younger male family members following divorce. *Personal Relationships, 5,* 293–309.

Coleman, M., Ganong, L. H., & Fine, M. (2000). Reinvestigating remarriage: Another decade of progress. *Journal of Marriage and the Family, 62,* 1288–1307.

Coleman, M., Ganong, L. H., & Fine, M. (2004). Communication in stepfamilies. In A. L. Vangelisti (Ed.), *Handbook of family communication* (pp. 215–232). Mahwah, NJ: Lawrence Erlbaum Associates.

Coley, R. L. (2001). (In)visible men: Emerging research on low-income, unmarried, and minority fathers. *American Psychologist, 56,* 743–753.

Collins, P. H. (1999). Shifting the center: Race, class, and feminist theorizing about motherhood. In S. Coontz (Ed.), *American families: A multicultural reader* (pp. 197–217). New York: Routledge.

Comstock, J. (1994). Parent-adolescent conflict: A developmental approach. *Western Journal of Communication, 58,* 263–282.

Connidis, I. A. (1989a). Contact between siblings in later life. *Canadian Journal of Sociology, 14,* 429–442.

Connidis, I. A. (1989b). Siblings as friends in later life. *American Behavioral Scientist, 33,* 81–93.

Connidis, I. A. (1992). Life transitions and the adult sibling tie: A qualitative study. *Journal of Marriage and the Family, 54,* 972–982.

Connidis, I. A., & Campbell, L. D. (1995). Closeness, confiding, and contact among siblings in middle and late adulthood. *Journal of Family Issues, 16,* 722–745.

Coontz, S. (2000a). Historical perspectives on family diversity. In D. H. Demo, K. R. Allen, & M. A. Fine (Eds.), *Handbook of family diversity* (pp. 15–31). New York: Oxford University Press.

Coontz, S. (2000b). *The way we never were: American families and the nostalgic trap.* New York: Basic Books.

Corneau, G. (1991). *Absent fathers, lost sons: The search for masculine identity.* Boston: Shambala.

Cousins, S. D. (1989). Culture and self-perception in Japan and the United States. *Journal of Personality and Social Psychology, 56,* 124–131.

Coyne, J. (1976). Toward an interactional description of depression. *Psychiatry, 39,* 28–39.

Coyne, J. C., & Fiske, V. (1992). Couples coping with chronic and catastrophic illness. In T. J. Akiamatsu, M. A. P. Stephens, S. E. Hobfoll, & J. H. Crowther (Eds.), *Family health psychology* (pp. 129–149). Washington, DC: Publishing Corp.

Coyne, J. C., Wortman, C. B., & Lehman, D. R. (1988). The other side of social support: Emotional overinvolvement and miscarried helping. In B. H. Gottlieb (Ed.), *Marshalling social support: Formats, processes, and effects* (pp. 305–330). Newbury Park, CA: Sage.

Creswell, J. W. (1998). *Qualitative inquiry and research design: Choosing among five traditions.* Thousand Oaks, CA: Sage.

Csikszentmihalyi, M., & Rochberg-Halton, E. (1981). *The meaning of things.* Cambridge, MA: Cambridge University Press.

Cummings, E. M., & Davies, P. (1994). *Children and marital conflict: The impact of family dispute and resolution.* New York: Guilford Press.

Cupach, W. R., & Metts, S. (1991). Sexuality and communication in close relationships. In. K. McKinney & S. Sprecher (Eds.), *Sexuality in close relationships* (pp. 93-110). Hillsdale, NJ: Lawrence Erlbaum.

Cushman, L. F., Kalmuss, D., & Namerow, P. B. (1997). Openness in adoption: Experiences and social psychological outcomes among birth mothers. *Marriage and Family Review, 25,* 7–18.

Cutrona, C. E. (1996). The interplay of negative and supportive behaviors in marriage. In G. Pierce, B. Sarason, & I. Sarason (Eds.), *Handbook of social support and the family* (pp. 173–194). New York: Plenum.

Dainton, M. (1993). The myths and misconceptions of the stepmother identity: Descriptions and prescriptions for identity management. *Family Relations, 42,* 93–98.

Daley, J. (1999). Progressive ed's war on boys. *City Journal, 9,* 26–32.

Datta, P., Poortinga, Y. H., & Marcoen, A. (2003). Parent care by Indian and Belgian caregivers in their roles of daughter/daughter-in-law. *Journal of Cross-Cultural Psychology, 34,* 736–749.

Daum, J. (1983). Father's absence and moral development of male delinquents. *Psychological Reports, 54,* 223–228.

Davidson, B. (1997). Service needs of relative caregivers: A qualitative analysis. *Families in Society, 78,* 502–510.

Davidson, J. K., & Moore, N. B. (1996). *Marriage and family: Change and continuity.* Boston: Allyn & Bacon.

Davis, L. (1997). Having something in common. In J. Wells (Ed.), *Lesbians raising sons.* Los Angeles: Alyson Books.

Day, R. D., & Lamb, M. E. (Eds.). (2004). *Conceptualizing and measuring father involvement.* Mahwah, NJ: Lawrence Erlbaum Associates.

de Beauvoir, S. (1974). *Memoirs of a dutiful daughter.* Middlesex, UK: Penguin.

Deacon, S. A. (1997). Intercountry adoption and the family life cycle. *The American Journal of Family Therapy, 25,* 245–260.

DeKlyen, M., Speltz, M. L., & Greenberg, M. T. (1998). Fathering and early onset conduct problems: Positive and negative parenting, father-son attachment, and the marital context. *Clinical Child and Family Psychology Review, 1,* 3–21.

Dellman-Jenkins, M., Blankenmeyer, M., & Pinkard, O. (2000). Young adult children and grandchildren in primary caregiver roles to older relatives and their service needs. *Family Relations, 49,* 177–187.

Derlega, V. J., Metts, S., Petronio, S., & Margulis, S. T. (1993). *Self-disclosure.* Newbury Park, CA: Sage.

Diamond, M. J. (1997). Boys to men: The maturing of male identity through paternal watchful protectiveness. *Gender Psychoanalysis, 2,* 443–468.

Diamond, M. J. (2004). The shaping of masculinity: Revisioning boys turning away from their mothers to construct male gender identity. *International Journal of Psychoanalysis, 85,* 359–379.

Dick, G. (2004). Men's relationships with their fathers: Comparing men who batter women with non-violent men. *Journal of Emotional Abuse, 4*, 61–84.

Dill, B. T. (1998). Fictive kin, paper sons, compadrazgo: Women of color and the struggle for family survival. In K. V. Hansen & A. I. Garey (Eds.), *Families in the U.S.: Kinship and domestic politics* (pp. 431–445). Philadelphia: Temple University Press.

Dindia, K., & Baxter, L. A. (1987). Strategies for maintaining and repairing personal relationships. *Journal of Social and Personal Relationships, 10*, 163–173.

Dodson, J. (2003). *Final rounds: A father, a son, the golf journey of a lifetime.* New York: Bantam Books.

Doherty, W. J., Kouneski, E. F., & Erikson, M. F. (1998). Responsible fathers: An overview and conceptual framework. *Journal of Marriage and the Family, 60*, 277–292.

Dolgin, K. G. (1996). Parents' disclosure of their own concerns to their adolescent children. *Personal Relationships, 3*, 159–169.

Dolgin, K. G., & Lindsay, K. R. (1999). Disclosure between college students and their siblings. *Journal of Family Psychology, 13*, 393–400.

Downs, V. C. (1989). The grandparent-grandchild relationship. In J. F. Nussbaum (Ed.), *Lifespan communication: Normative processes* (pp. 257–281). Hillsdale, NJ: Lawrence Erlbaum Associates.

Dressel, P. L., & Barnhill, S. K. (1994). Reframing gerontological thought and practice: The case of grandmothers with daughters in prison. *The Gerontologist, 34*, 685–691.

Drew, L. M., & Smith, P. K. (2002). Implications for grandparents when they lose contact with their grandchildren: Divorce, family feud, and geographical separation. *Journal of Mental Health and Aging, 8*(2), 95–119.

Duck, S. W., & Wright, P. (1993). Reexamining gender differences in same-sex friendships: A close look at two kinds of data. *Sex Roles, 28*, 709–727.

Duncan, D. F. (1996). Growing up under the gun: Children and adolescents coping with violent neighborhoods. *Journal of Primary Prevention, 16*, 343–356.

Duncan, G. J., Hill, M., & Yeung, J. (1996, April). *Fathers' activities and child attainments.* Paper presented at the NICHD Family and Child Well-Being Network's Conference on Father Involvement, Bethesda, MD.

Dunn, J., Bretherton, L., & Munn, P. (1987). Conversations about feeling states between mothers and their young children. *Developmental Pschology, 23*, 132–139.

Dunn, J., O'Connor, T. G., & Levy, I. (2002). Out of the picture: A study of family drawings by children from step-, single-parent, and non-step families. *Journal of Clinical Child and Adolescent Psychology, 31*, 505–512.

Duran-Aydintug, C. (1993). Relationships with former in-laws: Normative guidelines and actual behavior. *Journal of Divorce and Remarriage, 19*, 69–81.

DuRant, R. H., Getts, A., Cadenhead, C., Emans, S. J., & Woods, E. R. (1995). Exposure to violence and victimization and depression, hopelessness, and purpose in life among adolescents living in and around public housing. *Developmental and Behavioral Pediatrics, 16*, 233–237.

Duvall, E. M. (1954). *In-laws: Pro and con.* New York: Association Press.

Eberstadt, M. (2000, July 9). Boys under siege. *Washington Times,* p. B8.

Ellingson, L. L., & Sotirin, P. J. (in press). Exploring nieces/nephews' perspectives on communication with aunts. *Journal of Social and Personal Relationships.*

Ellis, C., & Bochner, A. P. (1996). Talking over ethnography. In C. Ellis & A. P. Bochner (Eds.), *Composing ethnography: Alternative forms of qualitative writing* (pp. 13–45). Walnut Creek, CA: Alta Mira.

Elmhorst, J. (2003, February). *Communication privacy management theory and international adoption.* Paper presented at the annual conference of the Western States Communication Association, Salt Lake City, UT.

Emery, R. E. (1994). *Renegotiating family relationships: Divorce, child custody, and mediation.* New York: Guilford Press.

Emery, R. E., & Dillon, P. (1994). Conceptualizing the divorce process: Renegotiating boundaries of intimacy and power in the divorce family system. *Family Relations, 43,* 374–379.

Emmers-Sommer, T. M. (2005). Non-normative relationships: Is there a norm of (non)normativity? *Western Journal of Communication, 69,* 1–4.

Erbert, L. A., & Floyd, K. (2004). Affectionate expressions as face-threatening acts: Receiver assessments. *Communication Studies, 55,* 230–246.

Essock-Vitale, S. M., & McGuire, M. T. (1985). Women's lives viewed from an evolutionary perspective, II. Patterns of helping. *Ethology and Sociobiology, 6,* 155–173.

Evan B. Donaldson Adoption Institute. (1997). *Benchmark adoption survey: Report on findings.* New York: Author.

Evans, K. (2000). *The lost daughters of China: Abandoned girls, their journey to America, and the search for a missing past.* New York: Jeremy P. Tarcher/Putnam.

Falk, U. A., & Falk, G. (2002). *Grandparents: A new look at the supporting generation.* Prometheus, NY: Amherst.

Faludi, S. (1999). *Stiffed: The betrayal of the American man.* New York: William Morrow.

Farmer, S. (1991). *The wounded male.* New York: Ballantine.

Fields, P. (2001). Living arrangements of children 1996. In *Current Population Reports* (pp. 70–74). Washington, DC: U.S. Bureau of the Census.

Findler, L. S. (2000). The role of grandparents in the social support system of mothers of children with a physical disability. *Families in Society: The Journal of Contemporary Human Services, 81,* 370–381.

Fine, M. A., Coleman, M., & Ganong, L. H. (1998). Consistency in perceptions of the step-parent role among step-parents, parents, and stepchildren. *Journal of Social and Personal Relationships, 15,* 811–829.

Fine, M. A., & Kurdek, L. A. (1995). Relation between marital quality and (step)parent-child relationships quality for parents and stepparents in stepfamilies. *Journal of Family Psychology, 9,* 216–223.

Fingerman, K. L. (2001). *Aging mothers and their adult daughters: A study in mixed emotions.* New York: Springer.

Fingerman, K. L., & Griffiths, P. C. (1999). Season's greetings: Adults' social contact at the holiday season. *Psychology and Aging, 14,* 192–205.

Fingerman, K. L., & Hay, E. L. (2002). Searching under the streetlight? Age biases in the personal and family relationships literature. *Personal Relationships, 9,* 415–433.

Fischer, L. R. (1981). Transitions in the mother-daughter relationship. *Journal of Marriage and the Family, 43,* 613–622.

Fischer, L. R. (1983a). Married men and their mothers. *Journal of Comparative Family Studies, 14,* 393–402.

Fischer, L. R. (1983b). Mothers and mothers-in-law. *Journal of Marriage and the Family, 45,* 187–192.

Fischer, L. R. (1986). *Linked lives.* New York: Harper and Row.

Fischer, L. R. (1991). Between mothers and daughters. *Marriage and Family Review, 16,* 237–248.

Fisher, A. P. (2003). A critique of the portrayal of adoption in college textbooks and readers on families, 1998-2001. *Family Relations, 52,* 154–160.

Fisher, C. L. (2004). *Mothers' and daughters' perceptions of turning points that affected closeness in the relationship over time.* Unpublished master's thesis, Arizona State University West.

Fiske, J. (1990). Ethnosemiotics: Some personal and theoretical reflections. *Cultural Studies, 4,* 85–99.

Fitness, J., & Duffield, J. (2004). Emotion and communication in families. In A. L. Vangelisti (Ed.), *Handbook of family communication* (pp. 473–494). Mahwah, NJ: Lawrence Erlbaum Associates.

Fitzpatrick, K., & Boldizar, J. P. (1993). The prevalence and consequences of exposure to violence among African-American youth. *Journal of the American Academy of Child and Adolescent Psychiatry, 32,* 424–430.

Fitzpatrick, M. A. (1988). *Between husbands and wives: Communication in marriage.* Newbury Park, CA: Sage.

Fitzpatrick, M. A., & Badzinski, D. M. (1994). All in the family: Interpersonal communication in kin relationships. In M. L. Knapp & G. R. Miller (Eds.), *Handbook of interpersonal communication* (2nd ed., pp. 726–771). Thousand Oaks, CA: Sage.

Floyd, K. (1995). Gender and closeness among friends and siblings. *Journal of Psychology, 129,* 193–202.

Floyd, K. (1996a). Brotherly love I: The experience of closeness in the fraternal dyad. *Personal Relationship, 3,* 369–385.

Floyd, K. (1996b). Communicating closeness among siblings: An application of the gendered closeness perspective. *Communication Research Reports, 13,* 27–34.

Floyd, K. (1997). Brotherly love II: A developmental perspective on liking, love, and closeness in the fraternal dyad. *Journal of Family Psychology, 11,* 196–209.

Floyd, K., Hess, J. A., Miczo, L. A., Halone, K. K., Mikkelson, A. C., & Tusing, K. J. (2005). Human affection exchange VIII: Further evidence of the benefits of expressed affection, independent of the benefits of received affection. *Communication Quarterly, 53,* 285–303.

Floyd, K., & Morman, M. T. (2000). Affection received from fathers as a predictor of men's affection with their own sons: Tests of the modeling and compensation hypotheses. *Communication Monographs, 67,* 347–361.

Floyd, K., & Morman, M. T. (2002). Human affection exchange III: Discriminative parental solicitude in men's affectionate communication with their biological and nonbiological sons. *Communication Quarterly, 49,* 310–327.

Floyd, K., & Morman, M. T. (2003). Human affection exchange II: Affectionate communication in father-son relationships. *Journal of Social Psychology, 143,* 599–613.

Floyd, K., & Morr, M. C. (2003). Human affection exchange VII: Affectionate communication in the sibling/spouse/sibling-in-law triad. *Communication Quarterly, 51,* 247–261.

Folwell, A. L., Chung, L. C., Nussbaum, J. F., Bethea, L. S., & Grant, J. A. (1997). Differential accounts of closeness in older adult sibling relationships. *Journal of Social and Personal Relationships, 14,* 843–849.

Francese, P. (2004). Marriage drain's big cost. *American Demographics, 26,* 40–41.

Fravel, D. L., McRoy, R. G., & Grotevant, H. D. (2000). Birthmother perceptions of the psychologically present adopted child: Adoption openness and boundary ambiguity. *Family Relations, 49,* 425–433.

Freud, S. (1917/1966). *The complete introductory lectures on psychoanalysis.* New York: Norton.

Freud, S. (1923). The ego and the id. In J. Strachey (Trans.), *Standard edition of the complete psychological works of Sigmund Freud* (Vol. 19, pp. 12–68). New York: Norton.

Freundlich, M. (2002). "Embryo adoption": Are we ready for this new frontier? *Adoption Quarterly, 6,* 1–5.

Frey, C. U., & Rothlisberger, C. (1996). Social support in healthy adolescents. *Journal of Youth and Adolescence, 25,* 17–31.

Friedlander, M. L. (1999). Ethnic identity development of internationally adopted children and adolescents: Implications for family therapists. *Journal of Marital and Family Therapy, 25,* 43–60.

Friel, B. (1999). *Brian Friel: Plays two:* Dancing at Lughnasa, Fathers and Sons, Making History, Wonderful Tennessee, Molley Sweeney. New York: Faber & Faber.

Fujimoto, E. (2001, November). *South Korean adoptees growing up in white America: Negotiating race, ethnicity and multivocality.* Paper presented to the annual meeting of the National Communication Association, Atlanta, GA.

Fuligni, A. S., & Brooks-Gunn, J. (2004). Measuring mother and father shared caregiving: An analysis using the panel study of income dynamics-child development supplement. In R. D. Day & M. E. Lamb (Eds.), *Conceptualizing and measuring father involvement* (pp. 341–357). Mahwah, NJ: Lawrence Erlbaum Associates.

Funk & Wagnalls new international dictionary of the English language. (2001). Chicago: Ferguson Publishing.

Furman, W., & Lanthier, R. P. (1996). Personality and sibling relationships. In G. H. Brody (Ed.), *Sibling relationships: Their causes and consequences* (pp. 127–246). Westport, CT: Ablex Publishing.

Furstenberg, F. (1988). Good dads-bad dads: Two faces of fatherhood. In A. Cherlin (Ed.), *The changing American family and public policy* (pp. 193–218). Washington, DC: Urban Institute Press.

Gaertner, S. L., & Dovidio, J. F. (2000). *Reducing intergroup bias: The common ingroup identity model.* Philadelphia, PA: Psychology Press.

Galvin, K. M. (2000, October). *Girls are exportable: The paradoxical issues of gender identity and cultural socialization in parent-child discussions of transnational adoption.* Paper presented at the meeting of the Organization for Language, Communication and Gender, Milwaukee, WI.

Galvin, K. M. (2003). International and transracial adoption: A communication research agenda. *Journal of Family Communication, 3*, 237–353.

Galvin, K. M. (2004). The family of the future: What do we face? In A. Vangelisti (Ed.), *Handbook of family communication* (pp. 675–697). Mahwah, NJ: Lawrence Erlbaum Associates.

Galvin, K. M. (in press). Discourse-dependency: Diversity's impact on defining the family. In R. West & L. H. Turner (Eds.), *Family communication: A reference of theory and research.* Thousand Oaks, CA: Sage.

Galvin, K. M., Bylund, C. L., & Brommel, B. J. (2004). *Family communication: Cohesion and change* (6th ed.). Boston: Allyn & Bacon.

Galvin, K. M., & Fonner, K. (2003, April). *"The Mailman" as family defense strategy: International/transracial adoption and mixed sibling communication strategies.* Paper presented at the annual meeting of the Central States Communication Association Conference, Omaha, NE.

Ganong, L. H., & Coleman, M. (1993). An exploratory study of stepsibling subsystems. *Journal of Divorce & Remarriage, 19*(3/4), 125–141.

Ganong, L. H., & Coleman, M. (1994). *Remarried family relationships.* Thousand Oaks, CA: Sage.

Ganong, L. H., & Coleman, M. (1998). An exploratory study of grandparents' and stepgrandparents' financial obligations to grandchildren and stepgrandchildren. *Journal of Social and Personal Relationships, 15*, 39–59.

Ganong, L. H., Coleman, M., Fine, M., & Martin, P. (1999). Stepparents' affinity-seeking and affinity-maintaining strategies with stepchildren. *Journal of Family Issues, 20*, 299–327.

Ganong, L. H., & Coleman, M. (2004). *Stepfamily relationships: Development, dynamics, and interventions.* New York: Kluwer Academic/Plenum.

Gao, G. (1996). Self and other: A Chinese perspective on interpersonal relationships. In W. B. Gudykunst, S. Ting-Toomey, & T. Nishida (Eds.), *Communication in personal relationships across cultures* (pp. 81–101). Thousand Oaks, CA: Sage.

Garrett, P., & Williams, A. (2004, July). *Adolescents' perceptions of communication with elders, young adults, and peers.* Paper presented at the International Conference on Language and Social Psychology, University Park, PA.

Gerrold, D. (2003). *The martian child: A novel about a single father adopting a son.* New York: Tor Books.

Gerstel, N., & Gallagher, S. K. (1993). Kinkeeping and distress: Gender, recipients of care, and work-family conflict. *Journal of Marriage and the Family, 55*, 598–607.

Giarruso, R., Silverstein, M., & Bengston, V. (1996, Spring). Family complexity and the grandparent role. *Generations*, 17–23.

Gibbons, F. X., Gerrard, M., Cleveland, M. J., Wills, T. A., & Brody, G. (2004). Perceived discrimination and substance use in African American parents and their children: A panel study. *Journal of Personality and Social Psychology*, 86, 517–529.

Gibson, D., & Mugford, S. (1986). Expressive relations and social support. In H. L. Kendig (Ed.), *Aging and families: A social network perspective* (pp. 63–84). Boston: Allen & Unwin.

Giddens, A. (1984). *The constitution of society: Outline of the theory of structuration*. Berkeley: University of California Press.

Giddens, A. (2005). The global revolution in family and personal life. In A. S. Skolnick & J. H. Skolnick (Eds.), *Family in transition* (pp. 26–32). Boston: Pearson/Allyn & Bacon.

Gilbertson, J., Dindia, K., & Allen, M. (1998). Relational continuity, constructional units and maintenance of relationships. *Journal of Social and Personal Relationships*, 15, 774–790.

Giles-Sims, J., & Crosbie-Burnett, M. (1989). Adolescent power in stepfather families: A test of normative-resource theory. *Journal of Marriage and the Family*, 51, 1065–1078.

Gillis, J. R. (1996). *A world of their own making: Myth, ritual, and the quest for family values*. New York: Basic Books.

Gladstone, J. W. (1988). Perceived changes in grandmother-grandchild relations following a child's separation or divorce. *The Gerontologist*, 28, 66–72.

Glenn, N. D., & Weaver, C. N. (1981). The contribution of marital happiness to global happiness. *Journal of Marriage and the Family*, 42, 161–168.

Glueck, S., & Glueck, E. (1950). *Unraveling juvenile delinquency*. Cambridge, MA: Harvard University Press.

Goetting, A. (1986). The developmental tasks of siblingship over the life cycle. *Journal of Marriage and the Family*, 48, 703–714.

Gold, D. T. (1989a). Generational solidarity. *American Behavioral Scientist*, 33, 19–32.

Gold, D. T. (1989b). Sibling relationships in old age: A typology. *International Journal of Aging and Human Development*, 28, 37–51.

Goetting, A. (1990). Patterns of support among in-laws in the United States. *Journal of Family Issues*, 11, 67–90.

Golish, T. D. (2000). Changes in closeness between adult children and their parents: A turning point analysis. *Communication Reports*, 13, 79–98.

Golish, T. D., & Caughlin, J. (2002). I'd rather not talk about it: Adolescents' and young adults' use of topic avoidance in stepfamilies. *Journal of Applied Communication Research*, 30, 78–106.

Golish, T. D. (2003). Stepfamily communication strengths: Examining the ties that bind. *Human Communication Research*, 29, 41–80.

Goode, W. J. (2005). The theoretical importance of the family. In A. S. Skolnick & J. H. Skolnick (Eds.), *Family in transition* (pp. 14–25). Boston: Pearson.

Gottlieb, A. R. (2003). *Sons talk about their gay fathers: Life curves*. New York: Harrington Park Press.

Gottman, J. M. (1982). Emotional responsiveness in marital conversations. *Journal of Communication, 32,* 108–120.

Gottman, J. M. (1994). *What predicts divorce? The relationship between marital processes and marital outcomes.* Hillsdale, NJ: Lawrence Erlbaum Associates.

Gottman, J. M. (2000). *The seven principles for making marriage work.* Pittsburgh, PA: Three Rivers Press.

Graham, E. E. (1997). Turning points and commitment in post-divorce relationships. *Communication Monographs, 64,* 351–367.

Graham, E. E. (2003). Dialectical contradictions in postmarital relationships. *Journal of Family Communication, 3,* 193–214.

Greeff, A. P., & Roux, M. C. (1999). Parents' and adolescents' perceptions of a strong family. *Psychological Reports, 84,* 1219–1224.

Greif, G. L. (1995). When divorced fathers want no contact with their children: A preliminary analysis. *Journal of Divorce and Remarriage, 23,* 75–85.

Grinwald, S. (1995). Communication-family characteristics: A comparison between stepfamilies (formed after death or divorce) and biological families. *Journal of Divorce & Remarriage, 24*(1/2), 183–196.

Grotevant, H. D. (2000). Openness in adoption: Research with the adoption kinship network. *Adoption Quarterly, 4,* 45–65.

Grotevant, H. D., Dunbar, N., Kohler, J., & Esau, A. L. (2000). Adoptive identity: How contexts within and beyond the family shape developmental pathways. *Family Relations, 49,* 379–38.

Grotevant, H. D., Perry, Y. V., & McRoy, R. G. (in press). Openness in adoption: Outcomes for adolescents within their adoptive kinship networks. In D. Brodzinsky & J. Palacios (Eds.), *Psychological issues in adoption: Theory, research and application.* Westport, CT: Greenwood Publishing.

Gullan, H. (2004). *First fathers: The men who inspired our presidents.* New York: Wiley.

Gurian, M. (1997). *The wonder of boys: What parents, mentors, and educators can do to raise boys into exceptional men.* New York: Jeremy P. Tarcher/Putnam.

Hagestad, G. O. (1986). Adult intergenerational relationships: Parents and children. In L. E. Troll (Ed.), *Review of human development* (pp. 191–226). New York: Wiley-Interscience.

Hartsock, N. (1983). The feminist standpoint: Developing the ground for a specifically feminist historical materialism. In S. Harding & M. B. Hintikka (Eds.), *Discovering reality* (pp. 283–310). Boston: Ridel.

Harwood, J. (2000a). Communication media use in the grandparent-grandchild relationship. *Journal of Communication, 50*(4), 56–78.

Harwood, J. (2000b). Communicative predictors of solidarity in the grandparent-grandchild relationship. *Journal of Social and Personal Relationships, 17,* 743–766.

Harwood, J. (2004). Relational, role, and social identity as expressed in grandparents' personal web sites. *Communication Studies, 55,* 268–286.

Harwood, J., Hewstone, M., Paolini, S., & Voci, A. (2005). Grandparent-grandchild contact and attitudes towards older adults: Moderator and mediator effects. *Personality and Social Psychology Bulletin, 31,* 393–406.

Harwood, J., & Lin, M-C. (2000). Affiliation, pride, exchange and distance in grandparents' accounts of relationships with their college-age grandchildren. *Journal of Communication, 50*(3), 31–47.

Harwood, J., Raman, P., & Hewstone, M. (2004, July). *Communicative dynamics of age salience.* Paper presented at the International Conference on Language and Social Psychology, University Park, PA.

Hays, D., & Hays, D. (1995). *My old man and the sea: A father and son sail around Cape Horn.* Chapel Hill, NC: Algonquin Books.

Hays, S. (1996). *The cultural contradictions of motherhood.* New Haven, CT: Yale University Press.

Heinemann, G. D. (1985). Interdependence in informal support systems: The case of elderly, urban widows. In W. A. Peterson & J. Quadagno (Eds.), *Social bonds in later life* (pp. 165–186). Beverly Hills: Sage.

Hendrick, S. S., & Hendrick, C. (1992). *Romantic love.* Newbury Park, CA: Sage.

Hess, J. A. (2000). Maintaining nonvoluntary relationships with disliked partners: An investigation into the use of distancing behaviors. *Human Communication Research, 26,* 458–488.

Hetherington, E. M. (1999a). *Coping with divorce, single parenting, and remarriage: A risk and resiliency perspective.* Mahwah, NJ: Lawrence Erlbaum Associates.

Hetherington, E. M. (1999b). Family functioning and the adjustment of adolescent siblings in diverse types of families. *Monographs of the Society for Research in Child Development, 64,* 1–25.

Hetherington, E. M., Cox, M., & Cox, R. (1982). Effects of divorce on parents and children. *Nontraditional families: Parenting and child development* (pp. 233–259). Hillsdale, NJ: Lawrence Erlbaum Associates.

Hetherington, E. M., & Stanley-Hagan, M. S. (1995). Parenting in divorced and remarried families. In M. Bornstein (Ed.), *Handbook of parenting.* Hillsdale, NJ: Lawrence Erlbaum Associates.

Hetherington, E. M., Stanley-Hagan, M., & Anderson, E. R. (1989). Marital transitions: A child's perspective. *American Psychologist, 44,* 303–312.

Hetzel, L., & Smith, A. (2001, October). *The 65 years and over population: 2000.* Census 2000 Brief. Retrieved April 9, 2004, from http://www.census.gov/prod/2001pubs/c2kbr01-10.pdf

Hirschi, T. (1969). *Causes of delinquency.* Berkeley: University of California Press.

Holladay, S., Lackovich, R., & Lee, M. (1998). (Re)constructing relationships with grandparents: A turning point analysis of granddaughters' relational development with maternal grandmothers. *International Journal of Aging and Human Development, 46,* 287–303.

Holladay, S., & Seipke, H. L. (2003, November). *Communication between grandparents and grandchildren in geographically dispersed relationships.* Paper presented at the annual meeting of the National Communication Association, Miami, FL.

Hollenstein, T., Leve, L. D., Scaramella, L. V., Milfort, R., & Neiderhiser, J. M. (2003). Openness in adoption, knowledge of birthparent information, and adoptive family adjustment. *Adoption Quarterly, 7,* 43–52.

Hollingsworth, L. D. (2003). When an adoption disrupts: A study of public attitudes. *Family Relations, 52,* 161–166.

Holloway, S. D., & Machida, S. (1991). The relationship between divorced mothers' perceived control over child rearing and children's post-divorce development. *Family Relations, 40,* 272–295.

Holmes, T. H., & Rahe, R. H. (1967). The social readjustment rating scale. *Journal of Psychosomatic Research, 11,* 213–218.

Hoover, S. M., Clark, L. S., & Alters, D. F. (2004). *Media, home, and family.* New York: Routledge.

Hoppe-Nagao, A., & Ting-Toomey, S. (2002). Relational dialectics and management strategies in marital couples. *Southern Communication Journal, 67,* 142–159.

Horsfall, J. (1991). *The presence of the past: Male violence in the family.* Sydney: Allen & Unwin.

Hummert, M. L., Garstka, T. A., Shaner, J. L., & Strahm, S. (1994). Stereotypes of the elderly held by young, middle-aged and elderly adults. *Journal of Gerontology: Psychological Sciences, 49,* 240–249.

Hwang, S. (2004, September 28). U.S. Adoptions get easier. *Wall Street Journal,* p. D1.

Ilardo, J. (1993). *Father-son healing: An adult son's guide.* New York: New Harbinger.

Immigrant visas issued to orphans coming to the U.S. (2004). Retrieved June 15, 2004, from http://travel.state.gov/orphan_numbers.html

Ingersoll-Dayton, B., Neal, M. B., Ha, J. H., & Hammer, L. B. (2003). Redressing inequity in parent care among siblings. *Journal of Marriage and the Family, 65,* 201–212.

Irwin, M., Daniels, M., Smith, T. L., Bloom, E., & Weiner, H. (1987). Impaired natural killer cell activity during bereavement. *Brain, Behavior, and Immunity, 1,* 98–104.

Jackson, C., Henriksen, L., & Foshee, V. A. (1998). The authoritarian parenting index: Predicting health risk behaviors among children and adolescents. *Health Education and Behavior, 25,* 319–337.

Jackson, J., & Berg-Cross, L. (1988). Extending the extended family: The mother-in-law and daughter-in-law relationship of black women. *Family Relations, 37,* 293–297.

Jampolsky, G. G., & Jampolsky, L. L. (1998). *Listen to me: A book for women and men about father-son relationships.* New York: Celestial Arts.

Jendrek, M. P. (1993). Grandparents who parent their grandchildren: Effects on lifestyle. *Journal of Marriage and the Family, 55,* 609–621.

Jendrek, M. P. (1994). Grandparents who parent their grandchildren: Circumstances and decisions. *The Gerontologist, 34,* 206–216.

Jessor, R., & Jessor, S. L. (1977). *Problem behavior and psychosocial development: A longitudinal study of youth.* San Diego, CA: Academic Press.

Johnson, K., Banghan, H., & Liyao, W. (1999). Infant abandonment and adoption in China. *Population and Development Review, 24,* 469–510.

Jones, K. A., Kramer, T. L., Armitage, T., & Williams, K. (2003). The impact of father absence on adolescent separation-indviduation. *Genetic, Social, and General Psychology Monographs, 129,* 73–95.

Jones, S., & Nissenson, M. (1997). *Friends for life.* New York: William Morrow.

Jordan, J. (1993). The relational self: A model of women's development. In J. van Mens-Verhulst, J. Schreurs, & L. Woertman (Eds.), *Daughtering and mothering: Female subjectivity reanalysed* (pp. 135–144). New York: Routledge.

Jorgenson, J. (1989). Where is the "family" in family communication?: Exploring families' self-definitions. *Journal of Applied Communication Research, 17,* 27–41.

Jorgenson, J. (1994). Situated address and the social construction of "in-law" relationships. *Southern Communication Journal, 55,* 196–204.

Juby, H., & Farrington, D. (2001). Distinguishing the link between disrupted families and delinquency. *British Journal of Criminology, 41,* 22–40.

Julian, T. W., McKenry, P. C., & Arnold, K. (1990). Psychosocial predictors of stress associated with the male midlife transition. *Sex Roles, 22,* 707–722.

Jung, C. G., & Kerenyi, C. (1969). *Essays on a science of mythology: The myths of the divine child and the mysteries of Eleusis.* Princeton, NJ: Princeton University Press.

Jurkovic, G. J., Jessee, E. H., & Goglia, L. R. (1991). Treatment of parental children and their families: Conceptual and technical issues. *American Journal of Family Therapy, 19,* 302–314.

Jurkovic, G. J., Thirkeild, A., Morrell, R. (2001). Parentification of adult children of divorce: A multidimensional analysis. *Journal of Youth and Adolescence, 30,* 245–258.

Kamo, Y. (1998). Asian grandparents. In M. E. Szinovacz (Ed.), *Handbook on grandparenthood* (pp. 97–112). Westport, CT: Greenwood Press.

Kaye, K., & Warren, S. (1988). Discourse about adoption in adoptive families. *Journal of Family Psychology, 1,* 406–433.

Kemper, S., & Harden, T. (1999). Experimentally disentangling what's beneficial about elderspeak from what's not. *Psychology and Aging, 14,* 656–670.

Kemper, S., Kynette, D., Rash, S., O'Brien, K., & Sprott, R. (1989). Lifespan changes to adults' language: Effects of memory and genre. *Applied Psycholinguistics, 10,* 49–66.

Kerig, P. K., Cowan, P. A., & Cowan, C. P. (1993). Marital quality and gender differences in parent-child interaction. *Developmental Psychology, 29,* 931–939.

Kiecolt-Glaser, J. K., Kennedy, S., Malkoff, S., Fisher, L., Speicher, C. E., & Glaser, R. (1988). Marital discord and immunity in males. *Psychosomatic Medicine, 50,* 213–229.

Kim, U. (1994). Individualism and collectivism: Conceptual clarification and elaboration. In U. Kim, H. C. Triandis, C. Kagitcibasi, S.-C. Choi, & G. Yoon (Eds.), *Individualism and collectivism: Theory, method, and applications* (pp. 19–40). Thousand Oaks, CA: Sage.

Kindlon, D., & Thompson, M. (1999). *Raising Cain: Protecting the emotional life of boys*. New York: Ballantine.

King, V. (2003). The legacy of a grandparent's divorce: Consequences for ties between grandparents and grandchildren. *Journal of Marriage and the Family*, 65, 170–183.

King, V., & Elder, G. H. (1997). The legacy of grandparenting: Childhood experiences with grandparents and current involvement with grandchildren. *Journal of Marriage and the Family*, 59, 848–859.

King, V., Elder, G. H., & Conger, R. D. (2000). Church, family, and friends. In G. H. Elder & R. D. Conger (Eds.), *Children of the land: Adversity and success in rural America* (pp. 151–163). Chicago: University of Chicago Press.

Kirby, E. L., Golden, A. G., Medved, C. E., Jorgenson, J., & Buzzanell, P. M. (2003). An organizational communication challenge to the discourse of work and family research: From problematics to empowerment. In P. J. Kalbfleisch (Ed.), *Communication yearbook 27* (pp. 1–43). Mahwah, NJ: Lawrence Erlbaum Associates.

Kite, M. E., & Johnson, B. T. (1988). Attitudes toward older and younger adults: A meta-analysis. *Psychology and Aging*, 3, 233–244.

Kivett, V. R. (1985). Consanguinity and kin level: Their relative importance to the helping network of older adults. *Journal of Gerontology*, 40, 228–234.

Kleinfeld, J. (1998). *The myth that schools shortchange girls: Social science in the service of deception*. Washington, DC: Women's Freedom Network.

Koerner, A. F., & Fitzpatrick, M. A. (2002). Toward a theory of family communication. *Communication Theory*, 12, 70–91.

Koerner, S. S., Jacobs, S. L., & Raymond, M. (2000). When mothers turn to their adolescent daughters: Predicting daughters' vulnerability to negative adjustment outcomes. *Family Relations*, 49, 301–309.

Koerner, S. S., Wallace, S., Lehman, S. J., & Raymond, M. (2002). Mother-to-daughter disclosure after divorce: Are there costs and benefits? *Journal of Child and Family Studies*, 11, 469–483.

Koltyk, J. A. (1998). *New pioneers in the heartland: Hmong life in Wisconsin*. New Immigrant Series (N. Foner, Ed.). New York: Allyn & Bacon.

Kornhaber, A. (1985). Grandparenthood and the "new social contract". In V. L. Bengtson & J. F. Robertson (Eds.), *Grandparenthood* (pp. 159–172). Beverly Hills, CA: Sage.

Kornhaber, A., & Woodward, K. L. (1981). *Grandparents/grandchildren: The vital connection*. Garden City, NY: Anchor Press/Doubleday.

Kraus, S. J. (1989). On adult daughters and their mothers: A peripatetic consideration of developmental tasks. *Journal of Feminist Family Therapy*, 1, 27–35.

Kreider, R. M. (2003, October). *Adopted children and stepchildren: 2000* (CENSR-6RV). Census 2000, Special Reports. Washington, DC: U.S. Bureau of the Census. Retrieved April 9, 2004, from http://www.census.gov/prod/2003pubs/censr-6.pdf

Kreider, R. M., & Fields, J. M. (2001). *Number, timing, and duration of marriages and divorces: Fall 1996* [Current population reports, P70–80]. Washington, DC: U.S. Bureau of the Census.

Kreider, R. M., & Simmons, T. (2003). *Marital status: 2000* [U.S. Census Bureau Brief Number C2KBR-30]. Washington, DC: U.S. Bureau of the Census. Retrieved August 9, 2004, from http://www.census.gov/prod/2003pubs/c2kbr-30.pdf

Kroger, J. (2000). *Identity development: Adolescence through adulthood*. Thousand Oaks, CA: Sage.

Kroll, M. L. (2000). My name is . . . In M. W. Lustig & J. Koester (Eds.), *Among us: Essays on identity, belonging, and intercultural competence* (pp. 18–23). New York: Longman.

Krusiewicz, E. S., & Wood, J. T. (2001). "He was our child from the moment we walked into that room": Entrance stories of adoptive parents. *Journal of Social and Personal Relationships, 18*, 785–803.

Lamb, E. N. (2004, November). *Communication privacy management of stepsiblings*. Paper presented at the annual meeting of the National Communication Association, Chicago.

Lamb, M. E. (1987). *The father's role: Applied perspectives*. New York: Wiley.

Lamb, M. E. (1997). *The role of the father in child development*. New York: Wiley.

Lambe, M. (2004). *Growing up adopted*. Retrieved April 1, 2004, from www.adoptivefamilies.com

Landry, L. (1999). Research into action: Recommended intervention strategies for grandparent caregivers. *Family Relations, 48*(4), 381–390.

Langellier, K. M. (2002). Performing family stories, forming cultural identity: Franco American Memere stories. *Communication Studies, 53*, 56–73.

Langellier, K. M., & Peterson, E. E. (2004). *Storytelling in daily life: Performing narrative*. Philadelphia: Temple University Press.

Larson, R. W., & Gillman, S. (1999). Transmission of emotions in the daily interactions of single-mother families. *Journal of Marriage and the Family, 61*, 21–37.

Larson, R., & Richards, M. (1994). *Divergent realities: The emotional lives of mothers, fathers, and adolescents*. New York: Basic Books.

Laursen, B. (1995). Conflict and social interaction in adolescent relationships. *Journal of Research on Adolescence, 5*, 55–70.

Laursen, B., Coy, K. C., & Collins, W. A. (1998). Reconsidering changes in parent-child conflict across adolescence: A meta-analysis. *Child Development, 69*, 817–832.

Leach, M. S., & Braithwaite, D. O. (1996). A binding tie: Supportive communication of family kinkeepers. *Journal of Applied Communication Research, 24*, 200–216.

Leaper, C., Anderson, K. J., & Sanders, P. (1998). Moderators of gender effects on parents' talk to their children: A meta-analysis. *Developmental Psychology, 34*, 3–27.

Lee, J. (1987). *The flying boy: Healing the wounded man.* Deerfield Beach, FL: Health Communications.

Lee, J. (1991). *At my father's wedding: Reclaiming our true masculinity.* New York: Bantam Books.

Lee, T. R., Mancini, F. A., & Maxwell, J. W. (1990). Sibling relationships in adulthood: Contact patterns and motivations. *Journal of Marriage and the Family, 52,* 431–440.

Lehman, S. J., & Koerner, S. S. (2002). Family financial hardship and adolescent girls' adjustment: The role of maternal disclosure of financial concerns. *Merill-Palmer Quarterly, 48,* 1–15.

Leigh, G. (1982). Kinship interaction over the family life span. *Journal of Marriage and the Family, 44,* 197–208.

Levine, B. (1999, December 13). How boys lost out to girl power. *New York Times,* p. 3.

Li, J., Precht, D. H., Mortensen, P. B., & Olsen, J. (2003). Mortality in parents after death of a child in Denmark: A nationwide follow-up study. *Lancet, 361,* 363–367.

Li, X., Stanton, B., & Feigelman, S. (2000). Impact of perceived parental monitoring on adolescent risk behavior over 4 years. *Journal of Adolescent Health, 27,* 49–56.

Lillard, L. A., & Waite, L. J. (1995). 'Til death do us part: Marital disruption and mortality. *American Journal of Sociology, 100,* 1131–1156.

Lin, M.-C., & Harwood, J. (2003). Predictors of grandparent-grandchild relational solidarity in Taiwan. *Journal of Social and Personal Relationships, 20,* 537–563.

Lin, M.-C., Hummert, M. L., & Harwood, J. (2004). Age identity representation in on-line discourse. *Journal of Aging Studies, 18,* 261–274.

Lind, R. (1993). *Pedaling northwards: A father and son's bicycle adventure from Virginia to Canada.* New York: Hope Springs Press.

Lindlof, T. R., & Taylor, B. C. (2002). *Qualitative communication research methods* (2nd ed.). Thousand Oaks, CA: Sage.

Lindsey, E. W., Lewis, C. M., Campbell, J., Frabutt, J. M., & Lamb, M. E. (2002). Marital conflict and boys' peer relationships: The mediating role of mother-son emotional reciprocity. *Journal of Family Psychology, 16,* 466–477.

Lino, M. (2005). *Expenditures on children by families, 2004.* U.S. Department of Agriculture, Center for Nutrition Policy and Promotion. Miscellaneous Publication No. 1528-2004.

Lipschitz, D. S., Winegar, R. K., Hartnick, E., Foote, B., & Southwick, S. M. (1999). Post-traumatic stress disorder in hospitalized adolescents: Psychiatric co-morbidity and clinical correlates. *Journal of the American Academy of Child and Adolescent Psychiatry, 38,* 385–392.

Litke, M. (2003). *Undesirable girls: China combats problem of baby girls being left for dead.* Retrieved August 25, 2003, from http://www.abcnews.com

Lott, B. (2000). *Fathers, sons, and brothers: The men in my family.* New York: Washington Square Press.

Lyons, R. F., Mickelson, K., Sullivan, J. L., & Coyne, J. C. (1998). Coping as a communal process. *Journal of Social and Personal Relationships, 15*, 579–607.

Maccoby, E. E., & Martin, J. A. (1983). Socialization in the context of the family: Parent-child interaction. In E. M. Hetherington (Ed.), *Handbook of child psychology: Vol. 4. Socialization, personality, and social development* (pp. 1–101). New York: Wiley.

Madden-Derdich, D. A., Leonard, S. A., & Christopher, F. S. (1999). Boundary ambiguity and coparental conflict after divorce: An empirical test of a family systems model of the divorce process. *Journal of Marriage and the Family, 61*, 588–598.

Mahler, M. S., Pine, F., & Bergman, A. (1975). *The psychological birth of the human infant.* New York: Basic Books.

Mahoney, M. (1994). *Stepfamilies and the law.* Ann Arbor: University of Michigan.

Mann, B. J., Borduin, C. M., Henggeler, S. W., & Blaske, D. M. (1990). An investigation of systemic conceptualizations of parent-child coalitions and symptom change. *Journal of Consulting and Clinical Psychology, 58*, 336–344.

Manning, L. D. (2000, November). *Mapping the journey: A narrative study of the transition to adoptive parenthood.* Paper presented at the annual meeting of the National Communication Association, Seattle, WA.

Manning, L. D. (2001). International adoption and bi-cultural identity development: A case study of a Chinese cultural school. *Journal of Intergroup Relations, 28*, 17–30.

Marchese, J. (2002). *Renovations: A father and son rebuild a house and rediscover each other.* New York: Riverhead Books.

Mares, M. L. (1995). The aging family. In M. A. Fitzpatrick & A. L. Vangelisti (Eds.), *Explaining family interactions* (pp. 344–374). Thousand Oaks, CA: Sage.

Marotz-Baden, R., & Cowan, D. (1987). Mothers-in-law and daughters-in-law: The effects of proximity on conflict and stress. *Family Relations, 36*, 385–390.

Marsiglio, W. (1992). Stepfathers with minor children living at home: Parenting perceptions and relationship quality. *Journal of Family Issues, 13*, 195–214.

Martin, M. M., Anderson, C. M., & Mottet, T. P. (1997). The relationship between perceived understanding and self-disclosure in the sibling relationship. *Communication Research Reports, 14*, 331–338.

Mason, C. A., Cauce, A. M., Gonzales, N., & Hiraga, Y. (1994). Adolescent problem behavior: The effect of peers and the moderating role of father absence and the mother-child relationship. *American Journal of Community Psychology, 22*, 723–743.

Matthews, K. A., Woodall, K. L., Kenyon, K., & Jacob, T. (1996). Negative family environment as a predictor of boys' future status on measures of hostile attitudes, interview behavior, and anger expression. *Health Psychology, 15*, 30–37.

Matthews, S. H. (1987). Provision of care to old parents: Division of care among adult children. *Research on Aging, 9*, 45–60.

McGhee, J. L. (1985). The effects of siblings on the life satisfaction of the rural elderly. *Journal of Marriage and the Family, 49*, 85–95.

McGraw, D. (2000). *First and last seasons: A father, a son, and Sunday afternoon football.* New York: Doubleday Books.

McKeen, W., & McKeen, G. (2003). *Highway 61: A father and son journey through the middle of America.* New York: W.W. Norton.

Melina, L. R. (1998). *Raising adopted children.* New York: Harper Perennial.

Melosh, B. (2002). *Strangers and kin: The American way of adoption.* Cambridge, MA: Harvard University Press.

Meyerstein, I. (1996). A systemic approach to in-law dilemmas. *Journal of Marital and Family Therapy, 22,* 469–480.

Miedzian, M. (1992). Father hunger: Why soup kitchen fathers are not good enough. In K. Hagen (Ed.), *Women respond to the men's movement.* San Francisco: Harper.

Mikkelson, A. C. (2004, May). *The role of physical separation in the sibling relationship.* Paper presented at the annual meeting of the International Communication Association, New Orleans, LA.

Miller, R. J., & Boon, S. D. (2000). Trust and disclosure of sexual orientation in gay males' mother-son relationships. *Journal of Homosexuality, 38,* 41–63.

Miller, T. (1984). Paternal absence and its effects on adolescent self-esteem. *International Journal of Social Psychiatry, 30,* 293–296.

Miller-Day, M. A. (2004). *Communication among grandmothers, mothers, and adult daughters: A qualitative study of maternal relationships.* Mahwah, NJ: Lawrence Erlbaum Associates.

Miller-Day, M. (2005). Effective parent-child communication: A preventive measure. *Counselor, 6,* 70–71.

Miller-Rassulo, M. (1992). The mother–daughter relationship: Narrative as a path to understanding. *Women's Studies in Communication, 15,* 1–21.

Min, P. G. (1998). *Changes and conflicts: Korean immigrant families in New York.* New York: Allyn & Bacon.

Minuchin, S. (1974). *Family and family therapy.* Cambridge, MA: Harvard University Press.

Mitchell, D., & Wilson, W. (1967). Relationship of father absence to masculinity and popularity of delinquent boys. *Psychological Reports, 20,* 1173–1174.

Mittino, V. C. (2004). *Common themes for couples of open adoption.* Unpublished manuscript, Northwestern University.

Montemayor, R. (1983). Parents and adolescents in conflict: All families some of the time and some families most of the time. *Journal of Early Adolescence, 3,* 83–103.

Montgomery, B. M., & Baxter, L. A. (Eds.). (1998). *Dialectical approaches to studying personal relationships.* Mahwah, NJ: Lawrence Erlbaum Associates.

Morman, M. T., & Floyd, K. (1998). "I love you, man": Overt expressions of affection in male-male interaction. *Sex Roles, 38,* 871–881.

Morman, M. T., & Floyd, K. (2002). A "changing culture of fatherhood": Effects on affectionate communication, closeness, and satisfaction in men's relationships with their fathers and their sons. *Western Journal of Communication, 66,* 395–411.

Morman, M. T., & Floyd, K. (2003, November). *Good fathering: Men's perceptions of quality fatherhood behaviors.* Paper presented at the annual meeting of the National Communication Association, New Orleans, LA.

Morr, M. C. (2003, February). *Private disclosure in a family membership transition: Focus group investigation of in-laws' disclosures to newlyweds.* Paper presented at the annual meeting of the Western States Communication Association, Salt Lake City, UT.

Murphy, S. A., Johnson, L. C., Chung, I., & Beaton, R. D. (2003). The prevalence of PTSD following the violent death of a child and predictors of change 5 years later. *Journal of Traumatic Stress, 16*(1), 17–25.

Myers, S. A. (1998). Sibling communication satisfaction as a function of interpersonal solidarity, individualized trust, and self-disclosure. *Communication Research Reports, 15,* 309–317.

Myers, S. A., Cavanaugh, E. K., Dohmen, L. M., Freeh, J. L., Huang, V. W., Kapler, M., et al. (1999). Perceived sibling use of relational communication messages and sibling satisfaction, liking, and love. *Communication Research Reports, 16,* 339–352.

Myers, S. A., & Knox, R. L. (1998). Perceived sibling use of functional communication skills. *Communication Research Reports, 15,* 397–405.

Myers, S. A., & Members of COM 200. (2001). Relational maintenance behaviors in the sibling relationship. *Communication Quarterly, 49,* 19–34.

National Adoption Information Clearinghouse. (2004). *Openness in adoption: A fact sheet for families.* Retrieved March 20, 2004, from http://naic.acf.hhs.gov/pubs/f_openadopt.cfm

National Center for Health Statistics. (1995). Births, marriages, divorce, and death for September, 1994. *Monthly Vital Statistics Report, 43*(9) (DHHS Publication No. 94-1120). Hyattsville, MD: Public Health Service.

National Center for Health Statistics. (2003a). Table 2. Live births by age of mother, live-birth order, and race of mother: United States, 2002. *National Vital Statistics Report, 52.* Retrieved August 9, 2004, from http://www.cdc.gov/nchs/fastats/pdf/nvsr52_10t2.pdf

National Center for Health Statistics. (2003b). *Table 27. Life expectancy at birth, at 65 years of age, and at 75 years of age, according to race and sex: United States, selected years 1900–2001.* Retrieved August 9, 2004, from http://www.cdc.gov/nchs/data/hus/tables/2003/03hus027.pdf

National Opinion Research Center. (1998). General Social Survey, 1998 [data file]. Available from the GSS 1998 Codebook Web site, hytp://www.icpsr.umich.edu:8080/GSS/homepage.htm

Neil, E. (2003). Understanding other people's perspectives: Tasks for adopters in open adoption. *Adoption Quarterly, 6,* 3–30.

Neumann, M. (1996). Collecting ourselves at the end of the century. In C. Ellis & A. P. Bochner (Eds.), *Composing ethnography: Alternative forms of qualitative writing* (pp. 172–200). Walnut Creek, CA: Alta Mira.

Newcomb, M. D. (1990). Social support and personal characteristics: A developmental and interactional perspective. *Journal of Social and Clinical Psychology,* *9,* 54–68.

Ng, S. H., & He, A. (2004). Code-switching in tri-generational family conversations among Chinese immigrants in New Zealand. *Journal of Language and Social Psychology, 23,* 28–48.

Noller, P., & Feeney, J. A. (2004). Studying family communication: Multiple methods and multiple sources. In A. Vangelisti (Ed.), *Handbook of family communication* (pp. 31–52). Mahwah, NJ: Lawrence Erlbaum Associates.

Nussbaum, J. F., & Bettini, L. (1994). Shared stories of the grandparent-grandchild relationship. *International Journal of Aging and Human Development, 39,* 67–80.

Nussbaum, J. F., & Coupland, J. (2004). *Handbook of communication and aging research* (2nd ed.). Mahwah, NJ: Lawrence Erlbaum Associates.

Nydegger, C. N. (1991). The development of paternal and filial maturity. In K. Pillemer (Ed.), *Parent-child relations throughout life* (pp. 93–113). Hillsdale, NJ: Lawrence Erlbaum Associates.

O'Brien, M., & Schmilt, I. (2003). *Working fathers: Earning and caring.* London: Equal Opportunities Commission.

Ogletree, M. D., Jones, R. M., & Coyl, D. D. (2002). Fathers and their adolescent sons: Pubertal development and paternal involvement. *Journal of Adolescent Research, 17,* 418–424.

Papernow, P. L. (1993). *Becoming a stepfamily: Patterns of development in remarried families.* San Francisco: Jossey-Bass.

Parish, T., & Taylor, J. C. (1979). The impact of divorce and subsequent father absence on children's and adolescents' self-concepts. *Journal of Youth and Adolescence, 8,* 427–432.

Parsons, T., & Bales, R. F. (1955). *Family, socialization, and interaction process.* Glencoe, IL: Free Press.

Paschall, M. J., Ringwalt, C. L., & Flewelling, R. L. (2003). Effects of parenting, father absence, and affiliation with delinquent peers on delinquent behavior among African American male adolescents. *Adolescence, 38,* 15–34.

Pastore, D. R., Fisher, M., & Friedman, S. B. (1996). Violence and mental health problems among urban high school students. *Journal of Adolescent Health, 18,* 320–324.

Patton, M. Q. (1999). *Grand Canyon celebration: A father-son journey of discovery.* New York: Prometheus Books.

Patton, S. (2000). *Birth marks: Transracial adoption in contemporary America.* New York: New York University Press.

Paxton, K. C., Robinson, W. L., Shah, S., & Schoeny, M. E. (2004). Psychological distress for African-American adolescent males: Exposure to community violence and social support as factors. *Child Psychiatry and Human Development, 34,* 281–295.

Pease, B. (2000). Beyond the father wound: Memory-work and the deconstruction of the father-son relationship. *Australia and New Zealand Journal of Family Therapy, 21,* 9–15.

Pecchioni, L. L., & Croghan, J. M. (2002). Young adults' stereotypes of older adults with their grandparents as the targets. *Journal of Communication, 52*(4), 715–730.

Peplau, L. A., & Beals, K. P. (2004). The family lives of lesbians and gay men. In A. L. Vangelisti (Ed.), *Handbook of family communication* (pp. 233–248). Mahwah, NJ: Lawrence Erlbaum Associates.

Pertman, A. (2000). *Adoption nation.* New York: Basic Books.

Peters, H. E., & Day, R. D. (Eds.). (2000). Fatherhood: Research, interventions, and policies, Parts 1 & 2. *Marriage and the Family Review, 29,* 1–322.

Peterson, J. L., & Zill, N. (1986). Marital disruption, parent-child relationships, and behavioral problems in children. *Journal of Marriage and the Family, 48,* 295–307.

Petronio, S. (1991). Communication boundary management: A theoretical model of managing disclosure of private information between marital couples. *Communication Theory, 1,* 311–335.

Petronio, S. (2000). The boundaries of privacy: Praxis in everyday life. In S. Petronio (Ed.), *Balancing the secrets of private disclosure* (pp. 37–50). Mahwah, NJ: Lawrence Erlbaum Associates.

Petronio, S. (2002). *Boundaries of privacy: Dialectics of disclosure.* Albany: State University of New York Press.

Pettys, G. L., & Balgopal, P. R. (1998). Multigenerational conflicts and new immigrants: An Indo-American experience. *Families in Society: The Journal of Contemporary Human Services, 79,* 410–423.

Pew Project on the Internet and American Life. (2000). *Tracking online life: How women use the Internet to cultivate relationships with family and friends.* Retrieved April 10, 2004, from http://www.pewinternet.org/reports/index.asp

Pfeifer, S. K. (1989). *Mothers'-in-law and daughters'-in-law perceptions of interpersonal interaction.* Unpublished doctoral dissertation, University of Delaware.

Pinquart, M. (2003). Loneliness in married, widowed, divorced, and never-married older adults. *Journal of Social and Personal Relationships, 20,* 31–54.

Pleck, J. H., & Masciadrelli, B. P. (2004). Paternal involvement by U.S. residential fathers: Levels, sources, and consequences. In M. E. Lamb (Ed.), *The role of the father in child development* (4th ed., pp. 222–271). New York: Wiley.

Plummer, W. (2000). *Wishing my father well: A memoir of fathers, sons, and fly fishing.* New York: Overlook Press.

Pollack, W. S. (1998). *Real boys: Rescuing our sons from the myths of boyhood.* New York: Random House.

Ponzetti, J. J., & James, C. M. (1997). Loneliness and sibling relationships. *Journal of Social Behavior and Personality, 12,* 103–112.

Popenoe, D. (1993). American family decline, 1960-1990: A review and appraisal. *Journal of Marriage and the Family, 55,* 527–542.

Poulter, S. B. (2004). *Father your son: How to become the father you've always wanted to be*. New York: McGraw-Hill.

Powell, K. A., & Afifi, T. D. (2005). Uncertainty management and adoptees' ambiguous loss of their birth parents. *Journal of Social and Personal Relationships, 22,* 129–151.

Pruett, K. D. (1989). The nurturing male: A longitudinal study of primary nurturing fathers. In S. H. Cath, A. Gurwitt, & L. Gunsberg (Eds.), *Fathers and their families* (pp. 389–405). Hillsdale, NJ: Analytic Press.

Pulakos, J. (1989). Young adult relationships: Siblings and friends. *Journal of Psychology, 123,* 237–245.

Pulakos, J. (1990). Correlations between family environment and relationships of young adult siblings. *Psychological Reports, 67,* 1283–1286.

Raffaelli, M., & Green, S. (2003). Parent-adolescent communication about sex: Retrospective reports by Latino college students. *Journal of Marriage and the Family, 65,* 474–495.

Rapp, R. (1999). Family and class in contemporary America: Notes toward an understanding of ideology. In S. Coontz (Ed.), *American families: A multicultural reader* (pp. 180–196). New York: Routledge.

Rastogi, M., & Wampler, K. S. (1999). Adult daughters' perception of the mother-daughter relationship: A cross-cultural comparison. *Family Relations, 48,* 327–336.

Rawlins, W. K. (1992). *Friendship matters: Communication, dialectics, and the life course*. New York: Aldine de Gruyter.

Reagan, M., & Hyams, J. (1988). *Michael Reagan: On the outside looking in*. New York: Zebra Books.

Register, C. (1991). *Are those kids yours? American families with children adopted from other countries*. New York: The Free Press.

Reitz, M., & Watson, K. W. (1992). *Adoption and the family system*. New York: Guilford Press.

Rich, A. (1977). *Of woman born: Motherhood as experience and institution*. New York: Bantam Books.

Richmond, L. S., & Christensen, D. H. (2000). Coping strategies and postdivorce health outcomes. *Journal of Divorce and Remarriage, 34,* 41–59.

Riggio, H. R., & Desrochers, S. (2004). Maternal employment and the work and family attitudes and expectations of young adults. In D. Halpern & S. E. Murphy (Eds.), *From work-family balance to work-family interaction: Changing the metaphor* (pp. 202–238). Mahwah, NJ: Lawrence Erlbaum Associates.

Rindfuss, R. R. (1991). The young adult years: Diversity, structural change, and fertility. *Demography, 28,* 493–512.

Robins, R. W., John, O. P., & Caspi, A. (1994). Major dimensions of personality in early adolescence: The big five and beyond. In C. F. Halverson, Jr. & G. A. Kohnstamm (Eds.), *The developing structure of temperament and personality from infancy to adulthood* (pp. 267–291). Hillsdale, NJ: Lawrence Erlbaum Associates.

Rocca, K. A., & Martin, M. M. (1998). The relationship between willingness to communicate and solidarity with frequency, breadth, and depth of communication in the sibling relationship. *Communication Research Reports, 15*, 82–90.

Romberger, B. V. (1986). 'Aunt Sophie always said. . .': Oral histories of the commonplaces women learned about relating to men. *American Behavioral Scientist, 29*, 342–367.

Rosenberg, E. B., & Hajal, F. (1985). Stepsibling relationships in remarried families. *Social Casework: The Journal of Contemporary Social Work, 66*, 287–292.

Rosenthal, C. S. (1985). Kinkeeping in the familial division of labor. *Journal of Marriage and the Family, 47*, 965–974.

Ross, H. G., & Milgram, J. I. (1982). Important variables in adult sibling relationships: A qualitative study. In M. E. Lamb & B. Sutton-Smith (Eds.), *Sibling relationships: Their nature and significance across the lifespan* (pp. 225–249). Hillsdale, NJ: Lawrence Erlbaum Associates.

Rothbaum, F., & Weisz, J. R. (1994). Parental caregiving and child externalizing behavior in nonclinical samples: A meta-analysis. *Psychological Bulletin, 116*, 55–74.

Russert, T. (2004). *Big Russ and me: Father and son—lessons of life*. New York: Miramax Books.

Ryan, E. B., Kwong See, S., Meneer, W. B., & Trovato, D. (1994). Age-based perceptions of conversational skills among younger and older adults. In M. L. Hummert, J. M. Wiemann, & J. F. Nussbaum (Eds.), *Interpersonal communication in older adulthood: Interdisciplinary perspectives* (pp. 15–39). Thousand Oaks, CA: Sage.

Sabourin, T. C. (2003). *The contemporary American family: A dialectical perspective on communication and relationships*. Thousand Oaks, CA: Sage.

Sachs, L. (1999). Knowledge of no return: Getting and giving information about genetic risk. *Acta Ontologica, 38*, 735–740.

Sacks, K. B. (1999). Toward a unified theory of class, race, and gender. In S. Coontz (Ed.), *American families: A multicultural reader* (pp. 218–229). New York: Routledge.

Salmon, C. A., & Daly, M. (1996). On the importance of kin relations to Canadian women and men. *Ethology and Sociobiology, 17*, 289–297.

Saltzburg, S. (2004). Learning that an adolescent child is gay or lesbian: The parent experience. *Social Work, 49*, 109–118.

Sandler, I. N., Tein, J. Y., Mehta, P., Wolchik, S., & Ayers, T. (2000). Coping efficacy and psychological problems of children of divorce. *Child Development, 71*, 1099–1118.

Sandler, I. N., Tein, J., & West, S. G. (1994). Coping, stress and the psychological symptoms of children of divorce: A cross-sectional and longitudinal study. *Child Development, 65*, 1744–1763.

Sangree, W. H. (1992). Grandparenthood and modernization: The changing status of male and female elders in Tiriki, Kenya, Irigwe, Nigeria. *International Journal of Aging and Human Development, 7*(4), 331–361.

Sault, N. L. (2001). Godparenthood ties among Zapotec women and the effects of Protestant conversion. In J. W. Dow & A. R. Sandstrom (Eds.), *Holy saints and fiery preachers: The anthropology of Protestantism in Mexico and Central America* (pp. 117–146). Westport, CT: Praeger.

Scheirer, L. M., & Botvin, G. J. (1997). Psychological correlates of affective distress: Models of male and female adolescents in a community. *Journal of Youth and Adolescence, 26,* 89–115.

Schilmoeller, G. L., & Baranowski, M. D. (1998). Intergenerational support in families with disabilities: Grandparents' perspectives. *Families in Society, 79,* 465–476.

Schrodt, P. (2003). *A typological examination of stepfamily communication schemata.* Unpublished doctoral dissertation, University of Nebraska-Lincoln.

Schrodt, P. (in press). The stepfamily life index: Development and validation of a new measure for stepfamily relationship research. *Journal of Social and Personal Relationships.*

Schrodt, P., Baxter, L. A., McBride, C., Braithwaite, D. O., & Fine, M. A. (2004). *The divorce decree, communication, and the structuration of co-parenting relationships in stepfamilies.* Manuscript submitted for publication.

Schumm, W. R., Barnes, H. L., Bollman, S. R., Jurich, A. P., & Milliken, G. A. (1985). Approaches to the statistical analysis of family data. *Home Economics Research Journal, 14,* 112–122.

Scott, J. P. (1983). Siblings and other kin. In T. H. Brubaker (Ed.), *Family relationships in later life* (pp. 47–62). Beverly Hills, CA: Sage.

Seligman, E. (1974). The effects of earlier parental loss in adolescence. *Archives of General Psychiatry, 31,* 475–499.

Serewicz, M. C. M. (2004). *Private disclosure from in-laws to newlyweds: Relationships among disclosure, family privacy orientations, and relational quality.* Manuscript submitted for publication.

Serewicz, M. C. M. (in press). The difficulties of in-law relationships. In D. C. Kirkpatrick, S. Duck, & M. Foley (Eds.), *Difficult relationships.* Mahwah, NJ: Lawrence Erlbaum Associates.

Serovich, J. M., Price, S. J., & Chapman, S. F. (1991). Former in-laws as a source of support. *Journal of Divorce and Remarriage, 17*(1/2), 67–90.

Sheehy, G. (2002, May 12). It's about pure love. *Parade Magazine,* pp. 6–7.

Shelley-Sireci, L. M., & Ciano-Boyce, C. (2002). Becoming lesbian adoptive parents: An exploratory study of lesbian adoptive, lesbian birth and heterosexual adoptive parents. *Adoption Quarterly, 6,* 33–43.

Shenitz, B., & Holleran, A. (2002). *The man I might become: Gay men write about their fathers.* New York: Marlowe & Company.

Shepard, C., Giles, H., & Le Poire, B. A. (2001). Communication accommodation theory. In W. P. Robinson & H. Giles (Eds.), *The new handbook of language and social psychology* (pp. 33–56). Chichester, England: Wiley.

Shields, C. (1987). *Swann.* New York: Viking.

Shinder, J. (1984). *Divided light: Father and son poems: A 20th century American anthology.* New York: Sheep Meadow Press.

Sillars, A. L. (1995). Communication and family culture. In M. A. Fitzpatrick & A. L. Vangelisti (Eds.), *Explaining family interactions* (pp. 375–399). Thousand Oaks, CA: Sage.

Silverman, A. R., & Feigelman, W. (1990). Adjustment in interracial adoptees: An overview. In D. M. Brodzinsky & M. D. Schechter (Eds.), *The psychology of adoption* (pp. 187–200). New York: Oxford University Press.

Silverstein, D. R., & Demick, J. (1994). Toward an organizational-relational model of open adoption. *Family Process, 33*, 111–124.

Silverstein, J. L. (1990). The problem with in-laws. *Journal of Family Therapy, 14*, 399–412.

Silverstein, M., & Chen, X. (1999). The impact of acculturation in Mexican American families on the quality of adult grandparent-grandchild relationships. *Journal of Marriage and the Family, 61*, 188–198.

Silverstein, M., & Marenco, A. (2001). How Americans enact the grandparent role across the family life course. *Journal of Family Issues, 22*, 493–522.

Silverstein, M., & Parrott, T. M. (1997). Attitudes toward public support of the elderly: Does early involvement with grandparents moderate generational tensions? *Research on Aging, 19*, 108–132.

Simmons, R. L., Beaman, J., Conger, R. D., & Chao, W. (1993). Gender differences in the intergenerational transmission of parenting beliefs. *Journal of Marriage and the Family, 54*, 823–836.

Simmons, T., & Dye, J. L. (2003). *Grandparents living with grandchildren: 2000.* Census 2000 Brief. Retrieved April 9, 2004, from http://www.census.gov/prod/2003pubs/c2kbr-31.pdf

Simon, R., & Alstein, H. (2000). *Adoption across borders.* Lanham, MD: Rowman & Littlefield.

Singer, A. T. B., & Weinstein, R. S. (2000). Differential parental treatment predicts achievement and self-perception in two cultural contexts. *Journal of Family Psychology, 14*, 491–509.

Skemp, S. L. (1994). *Benjamin and William Franklin: Father and son, patriot and loyalist.* New York: Bedford Books.

Smith, M. S., Kish, B. J., & Crawford, C. B. (1987). Inheritance of wealth as human kin investment. *Ethology and Sociobiology, 8*, 171–182.

Soliz, J. (2004). *Shared family identity, age salience, and intergroup contact: Investigation of the grandparent-grandchild relationship.* Unpublished doctoral dissertation, University of Kansas, Lawrence.

Soliz, J., & Harwood, J. (2003). Communication in a family relationship and the reduction of intergroup prejudice. *Journal of Applied Communication Research, 31*, 320–345.

Sommers, C. H. (2000). *The war against boys: How misguided feminism is harming our young men.* New York: Simon & Schuster.

Sotirin, P., & Ellingson, L. L. (2004, November). *Rearticulating the aunt in popular culture.* Paper presented at the annual meeting of the National Communication Association, Chicago.

Stacey, J. (1993). Good riddance to "the family": A response to David Popenoe. *Journal of Marriage and the Family, 55*, 545–547.

Stacey, J. (1999). The family values fable. In S. Coontz (Ed.), *American families: A multicultural reader* (pp. 487–490). New York: Routledge.

Stacey, J. (2003). Toward equal regard for marriages and other imperfect intimate affiliations. *Hofstra Law Review, 32,* 331–348.

Stack, C. (1974). *All our kin.* New York: Basic Books.

Stack, C. B., & Burton, L. M. (1998). Kinscripts. In K. V. Hansen & A. I. Garey (Eds.), *Families in the U.S.: Kinship and domestic politics* (pp. 405–415). Philadelphia: Temple University Press.

Stamp, G. H. (2004). Theories of family relationships and a family relationships model. In A. Vangelisti (Ed.), *Handbook of family communication* (pp. 1–30). Mahwah, N J: Lawrence Erlbaum Associates.

Stanton, T. (2001). *The final season: Fathers, sons, and one last season in a classic American ballpark.* New York: Thomas Dunn Books.

Stocker, C. M., & McHale, S. M. (1992). The nature and family correlates of preadolescents' perceptions of their sibling relationships. *Journal of Social and Personal Relationship, 9,* 179–195.

Stone, E. (1988). *Black sheep and kissing cousins: How our family stories shape us.* New York: Penguin Books.

Stone, L. (2000). *Kinship and gender: An introduction* (2nd ed.). Boulder, CO: Westview Press.

Strauss, A., & Corbin, J. (1990). *Basics of qualitative research: Grounded theory procedures and techniques.* Newbury Park, CA: Sage.

Sturgis, I. (Ed.). (2004). *Aunties: Thirty-five writers celebrate their other mother.* New York: Ballantine Books.

Surrey, J. (1993). The mother–daughter relationship: Themes in psychotherapy. In J. van Mens-Verhulst, J. Schreurs, & L. Woertman (Eds.), *Daughtering and mothering: Female subjectivity reanalysed* (pp. 114–124). New York: Routledge.

Sussman, M. B., & Burchinal, L. (1962). Kin family network: Unheralded structure in current conceptualizations of family functioning. *Marriage and Family Living, 24,* 231–240.

Szinovacz, M. E. (1998). *Handbook on grandparenthood.* Westport, CT: Greenwood Press.

Tajfel, H., & Turner, J. C. (1986). The social identity theory of intergroup behavior. In S. Worchel & W. Austin (Eds.), *Psychology of intergroup relations* (pp. 7–24). Chicago: Nelson-Hall.

Takiff, M. (2003). *Brave men, gentle heroes: American fathers and sons in World War II and Vietnam.* New York: William Morrow.

Tam, T., Hewstone, M., Harwood, J., & Voci, A. (2004). *Intergroup contact and grandparent-grandchild communication: Do self-disclosure, anxiety, and empathy improve implicit and explicit attitudes toward the elderly?* Unpublished manuscript, University of Oxford.

Teachman, J. D., Tedrow, L. M., & Crowder, K. D. (2000). The changing demography of America's families. *Journal of Marriage and the Family, 62,* 1234–1246.

Tessler, R., Gamache, G., & Liu, L. (1999). *West meets East: Americans adopt Chinese children.* Westport, CT: Bergin & Garvey.

Teven, J. J., Martin, M. M., & Neupauer, N. C. (1998). Sibling relationships: Verbally aggressive messages and their effect on relational satisfaction. *Communication Reports, 11,* 179–186.

Thomas, C. E., Booth-Butterfield, M., & Booth-Butterfield, S. (1995). Perceptions of deception, divorce disclosures, and communication satisfaction with parents. *Western Journal of Communication, 59,* 228–242.

Thibaut, J. W., & Kelley, H. H. (1959). *The social psychology of groups.* New York: Wiley.

Thomas, C. E., Booth-Butterfield, M., & Booth-Butterfield, S. (1995). Perceptions of deception, divorce disclosures, and communication satisfaction with parents. *Western Journal of Communication, 59,* 228–242.

Thompson, R. A., & Amato, P. R. (1999). The postdivorce family: An introduction to the issues. In R. A. Thompson & P. R. Amato (Eds.), *The postdivorce family: Children, parenting, and society* (pp. xi–xxiii). Thousand Oaks, CA: Sage.

Timmer, S. G., & Veroff, J. (2000). Family ties and the discontinuity of divorce in black and white newlywed couples. *Journal of Marriage and the Family, 62,* 349–361.

Titus, J. J. (2004). Boy trouble: Rhetorical framing of boys' underachievement. *Discourse: Studies in the Cultural Politics of Education, 25,* 145–169.

Tracy, K. (2002). *Everyday talk: Building and reflecting identities.* New York: Guilford.

Traeder, T., & Bennett, J. (1998). *Aunties: Our older, cooler, wiser friends.* Berkeley, CA: Wildcat Canyon Press.

Trees, A. R. (2000). Nonverbal communication and the support process: Interactional sensitivity in interactions between mothers and young adult children. *Communication Monographs, 67,* 239–262.

Trenholm, S., & Jensen, A. (2000). *Interpersonal communication* (4th ed.). Belmont, CA: Wadsworth.

Troll, L. E. (1975). *Early and middle adulthood.* Monterey, CA: Brooks/Cole.

Troll, L. E. (1985). *Early and middle adulthood* (2nd ed.). Pacific Grove, CA: Brooks/Cole.

Tugend, T. (2004, December 2). Woody Guthrie's Jewish legacy. *The Jerusalem Post,* Arts Section, p. 24.

Turner, L. H., & West, R. (2003). Breaking through the silence: Increasing voice for diverse families in communication research. *Journal of Family Communication, 3,* 181–186.

Turner, L. H., & West, R. (2006). *Perspectives on family communication* (3rd ed.). New York: McGraw-Hill.

Uhlenberg, P., & Kirby, J. B. (1998). Grandparenthood over time: Historical and demographic trends. In M. E. Szinovacz (Ed.), *Handbook on grandparenthood* (pp. 23–39). Westport, CT: Greenwood Press.

U.S. Bureau of the Census. (1996). *Statistical abstract of the United States 1996.* Washington, DC: U.S. Government Printing Office.

U.S. Bureau of the Census. (1998). *Statistical abstract of the United States 1998.* Washington, DC: U.S. Government Printing Office.

U.S. Bureau of the Census. (2000). *Statistical abstract of the United States 2000.* Washington, DC: U.S. Government Printing Office.

U.S. Bureau of the Census. (2002). *U.S. population report* [data file]. Available at http://www.dof.ca.gov/HTML/DEMOGRAP/USCPS-2002.pdf

U.S. Bureau of the Census. (2003a). *Children's living arrangements and characteristics: March 2002* (Current population reports, Series P-20, No. 547). Washington, DC: U.S. Government Printing Office.

U.S. Bureau of the Census. (2003b). *Table 2. Estimated median age at first marriage, by sex: 1890 to present.* Retrieved August 9, 2004, from http://www.census .gov/population/socdemo/hh-fam/tabMS-2.pdf

U.S. Bureau of the Census. (2003c). *Two married parents the norm.* Retrieved August 21, 2004, from http://www.census.gov/Press-Release/www/2003/ cb03-97.html

U.S. Department of Justice. (2002). *Victim characteristics.* Retrieved September 1, 2004, from http://www.ojp.usdoj.gov/bjs/cvict_v.htm

Usdansky, M. L. (1994, August 20). Blended, extended, now all in the family. *USA Today,* pp. 1A, 3A.

van Mens-Verhulst, J., Schreurs, J., & Woertman, L. (Eds.). (1993). *Daughtering and mothering: Female subjectivity reanalysed.* New York: Routledge.

Vangelisti, A. L. (1994). Family secrets: Forms, functions and correlates. *Journal of Social and Personal Relationships, 11,* 113–135.

Vangelisti, A. L., Caughlin, J. P., & Timmerman, L. (2001). Criteria for revealing family secrets. *Communication Monographs, 68,* 1–27.

Veerman, D. R., & Barton, B. B. (2003). *When your father dies: How a man deals with the loss of his father.* New York: Nelson Books.

Visher, E. B., & Visher, J. S. (1979). *Stepfamilies: A guide to working with stepparents and stepchildren.* New York: Brunner/Mazel.

Waldrop, D. P., & Weber, J. A. (2001). From grandparent to caregiver: The stress and satisfaction of raising grandchildren. *The Journal of Contemporary Human Services, 82,* 461–472.

Wallerstein, J. S. (1984). Children of divorce: Preliminary report of a 10-year follow-up of young children. *American Journal of Orthopsychiatry, 54,* 444–458.

Wallerstein, J. S., & Corbin, S. B. (1986). Father-child relationships after divorce: Child support and educational opportunity. *Family Law Quarterly, 20,* 109–128.

Walsh, F. (1993). Conceptualization of normal family processes. In F. Walsh (Ed.), *Normal family processes* (2nd ed., pp. 3–69). New York: Guilford Press.

Walsh, W. M. (1992). Twenty major issues in remarriage families. *Journal of Counseling and Development, 70,* 709–715.

Walters, S. D. (1992). *Lives together, worlds apart.* Berkeley: University of California Press.

Wegar, K. (1997). *Adoption identity and kinship: The debate over sealed birth records*. New Haven: Yale University Press.

Wegar, K. (1998). Adoption and kinship. In K. V. Hansen & A. I. Garey (Eds.), *Families in the U.S.: Kinship and domestic politics* (pp. 41–51). Philadelphia: Temple University Press.

Wellman, B. (1998). The place of kinfolk in personal community networks. In K. V. Hansen & A. I. Garey (Eds.), *Families in the U.S.: Kinship and domestic politics* (pp. 231–239). Philadelphia: Temple University Press.

Wellman, B., & Wortley, S. (1989). Brother's keepers: Situating kinship relations in broader networks of social support. *Sociological Perspectives, 32*, 273–306.

Westberg, H., Nelson, T. S., & Piercy, K. W. (2002). Disclosure of divorce plans to children: What the children have to say. *Contemporary Family Therapy, 24*, 525–542.

Whalen, C. K., Henker, B., Hollingshead, J., & Burgess, S. (1996). Parent-adolescent dialogues about AIDS. *Journal of Family Psychology, 10*, 343–357.

Whitchurch, G. G., & Dickson, F. C. (1999). Family communication. In M. Sussman, S. K. Stinmetz, & G. W. Peterson (Eds.), *Handbook of marriage and the family* (pp. 687–704). New York: Plenum Press.

White, L. K., & Riedman, A. (1992a). Ties among adult siblings. *Social Forces, 71*, 85–102.

White, L. K., & Riedman, A. (1992b). When the Brady bunch grows up: Step/half- and full sibling relations in adulthood. *Journal of Marriage and the Family, 54*, 197–208.

Wilkinson, H. S. P. (1985). *Birth is more than once*. Bloomfield Hills, MI: Sunrise Ventures.

Williams, A., & Giles, H. (1996). Intergenerational conversations: Young adults' retrospective accounts. *Human Communication Research, 23*, 220–250.

Williams, A., & Harwood, J. (2004). Intergenerational communication: Intergroup, accommodation, and family perspectives. In J. F. Nussbaum & J. Coupland (Eds.), *Handbook of communication and aging research* (2nd ed., pp. 115–138). Mahwah, NJ: Lawrence Erlbaum Associates.

Williams, A., & Nussbaum, J. F. (2001). *Intergenerational communication across the lifespan*. Mahwah, NJ: Lawrence Erlbaum Associates.

Wilmot, W. (1995). The relational perspective. In W. Wilmot (Ed.), *The relational communication reader* (4th ed., pp. 1–12). New York: McGraw-Hill.

Wiscott, R., & Kopera-Frye, K. (2000). Sharing the culture: Adult grandchildren's perceptions of intergenerational relations. *International Journal of Aging & Human Development, 51*, 199–215.

Wood, J. J., & Repetti, R. L. (2004). What gets dad involved? A longitudinal study of change in parental child caregiving involvement. *Journal of Family Psychology, 18*, 237–249.

Wood, J. T. (1992). Gender and moral voice: Moving from woman's nature to standpoint epistemology. *Women's Studies in Communication, 15*, 1–24.

Wood, J. T. (1999). *Gendered lives: Communication, gender, and culture.* Belmont, CA: Wadsworth.

Wood, J. T. (2000). *Relational communication: Continuity and change in personal relationships* (2nd ed.). Belmont, CA: Wadsworth.

Wood, J. T. (2002). What's a family, anyway? In J. Stewart (Ed.), *Bridges not walls: A book about interpersonal communication* (pp. 375–383). Columbus, OH: McGraw-Hill.

Workman, L, & Reader, W. (2004). *Evolutionary psychology: An introduction.* New York: Cambridge University Press.

Wright, K. (2000). The communication of social support within an on-line community for older adults: A qualitative analysis of the SeniorNet community. *Qualitative Research Reports in Communication, 1,* 33–43.

Xuan, V.-T. J., & Rice, P. L. (2000). Vietnamese-Australian grandparenthood: The changing roles and psychological well-being. *Journal of Cross-Cultural Gerontology, 15,* 265–288.

Yoshimura, C. G. (2005). *Envy is a family matter.* Manuscript submitted for publication.

Index

About the Editors

Kory Floyd is Associate Professor of Human Communication, Director of the Communication Sciences Laboratory, and Director of the graduate M.A. program in Human Communication at Arizona State University. He holds a Ph.D. from the University of Arizona, an M.A. from the University of Washington, and a B.A. from Western Washington University. His research focuses on the communication of affection in families and other intimate relationships and on the interplay between communication, physiology, and health. He has written or edited five books and more than 60 journal articles and book chapters, is currently chair of the family communication division of the National Communication Association, and is currently editor of *Journal of Family Communication.*

Mark T. Morman is Associate Professor of Communication Studies at Baylor University, where he serves as faculty advisor for the Lambda Pi Eta communication honor society. He received his M.A. and Ph.D. degrees from the University of Kansas and his B.S. from Southern Utah University. His research focuses on affectionate communication within families and close relationships and on persuasive messages relevant to men's health issues. He has published several articles in both regional and national communication journals, is currently vice chair of the family communication division of the National Communication Association, and serves on the editorial boards of *Journal of Family Communication* and *Journal of Social and Personal Relationships.*

About the Contributors

Tamara D. (Golish) Afifi (Ph.D., University of Nebraska-Lincoln) is Assistant Professor in the Department of Communication Arts and Sciences at Penn State University. Her research interests include information regulation (e.g., privacy, avoidance, secrets) in families and communication processes in families experiencing difficult life transitions. In particular, she is interested in communication characteristics that promote risk and resilience in post-divorce families.

Karen Anderson (Ph.D., University of Kansas) is Assistant Professor and Basic Course Director of Communication Studies at the University of North Texas. Her primary research area is intergenerational communication with a particular focus on age stereotypes, media representations of older adults, and the grandparent-grandchild relationship. Her recent work appears in *Human Communication Research*, *Communication Reports*, and *Journal of Family Communication*.

Leslie A. Baxter (Ph.D., University of Oregon) is F. Wendell Miller Distinguished Professor of Communication Studies at the University of Iowa. She has published four books and close to 100 articles and book chapters on family communication, relational communication, and research methods. Her scholarly awards include the Berscheid-Hatfield Award for Mid-Career Achievement (INPR), the Gerald R. Miller Book Award (NCA), the Franklin H. Knower Article Award (NCA), and the Legacy Theory Award (CSCA).

Dawn O. Braithwaite (Ph.D., University of Minnesota) is Professor of Communication Studies at University of Nebraska-Lincoln. Her research focuses on communication in personal and family relationships. She studies relational dialectics, rituals, and social support in the context of stepfamilies, elderly couples, and people with disabilities. She has published three books and 50 articles and chapters. She is past president of the Western

States Communication Association and is the director of the Research Board of the National Communication Association.

Fran C. Dickson (Ph.D., Bowling Green State University) is Associate Professor and Chair of Human Communication Studies at the University of Denver. Her research focuses on communication and intimacy within later-life couples, communication and aging, and the later-life family member. She has published over 25 journal articles and book chapters and is a past chair of the Family Communication Division for the National Communication Association.

Laura L. Ellingson (Ph.D., University of South Florida) is Assistant Professor of Communication at Santa Clara University. Her research interests include health care provider-patient communication, interdisciplinary communication, health care teamwork, communication and gender, and feminist theory and methodology. She is the author of *Communicating in the Clinic: Negotiating Frontstage and Backstage Teamwork* (Hampton Press) and has published articles in *Health Communication, Journal of Aging Studies, Journal of Applied Communication Research, Women's Studies in Communication*, and *Communication Studies*. Currently, she is conducting an ethnography of team communication in a dialysis clinic.

Carla Fisher (M.A., Arizona State University West) is a doctoral student in communication arts and sciences at the Pennsylvania State University. Her primary research interests are in family communication with focuses on how communication in intergenerational relationships evolves over the life span and how families respond to change. A pilot study of the research discussed herein was presented at the 2004 Western Communication Association Conference in Albuquerque, NM.

Kathleen M. Galvin (Ph.D., Northwestern University) is Professor of Communication Studies at Northwestern University. Her research focuses on the communication patterns in adoptive families and the role of discourse in the identity development of families not fully formed through biological or adult legal ties. She is the senior author of *Family Communication: Cohesion and Change*, currently in its sixth edition. She has authored seven other books, developed a PBS teleclass in family communication, and serves on the editorial board of *Journal of Family Communication*.

Jake Harwood (Ph.D., University of California, Santa Barbara) is Professor of Communication and Chair of the Gerontology Program at the University of Arizona. His research focuses on intergroup communication with a particular focus on age groups and grandparent-grandchild relationships. He has published more than 50 articles in professional journals, with recent articles in *Personality and Social Psychology Bulletin, Journal of Communication, Journal of Applied Communication Research,* and *Journal of Social and Personal Relationships.*

Beth Le Poire (Ph.D., University of Arizona) is Professor of Communication at the University of California, Santa Barbara. She has published more than 40 journal articles and book chapters cutting across various areas of applied interpersonal research in the family, including the communication of stigma, early parental and subsequent romantic attachment, and the effects that partners of substance abusers can have on continued substance abuse. Recently, she has completed an editorship of *Communication Reports,* and she is currently the chair of the interpersonal division of the International Communication Association.

Mei-Chen Lin (Ph.D., University of Kansas) is Assistant Professor in the School of Communication Studies at Kent State University. Her research and teaching interests are in aging; group and intercultural communication, specifically communication and aging across cultures; age identity; intergenerational communication; and grandparent-grandchild relationships. Her research has appeared in *Communication Monographs, Journal of Communication, Journal of Social and Personal Relationships,* and *Journal of Aging Studies.*

Tara McManus (M.A., University of Cincinnati) is a doctoral candidate in the Department of Communication Arts and Sciences at Penn State University. Her primary area of research is family communication, with an emphasis on relational maintenance during times of stress and uncertainty.

Alan C. Mikkelson (M.A., Arizona State University) is Assistant Professor of Communication Studies at Whitworth College. He holds an M.A. in human communication from Arizona State University and a B.A. in speech communication and religion from Whitworth College, and is currently completing his Ph.D. in human communication at Arizona State University. His current research focuses on the communication of closeness in adult sibling relationships.

Michelle Miller-Day (Ph.D., Arizona State University) is Associate Professor of Communication Arts and Sciences at the Pennsylvania State University. Her research focuses on interpersonal and family communication processes related to problem behaviors such as drug use and suicide. She has authored two books, the most recent titled *Communication Among*

Grandmothers, Mothers, and Adult Daughters: A Qualitative Study of Maternal Relationships (Lawrence Erlbaum).

Mary Claire Morr Serewicz (Ph.D., Arizona State University) is Assistant Professor of Human Communication Studies at the University of Denver. Her research focuses on in-law relationships, privacy, and the initiation of romantic relationships. Her work has been published in journals including *Communication Monographs*, *Communication Research*, and *Communication Quarterly*.

Paul Schrodt (Ph.D., University of Nebraska-Lincoln) is Assistant Professor of Communication at the University of Kansas. He specializes in family and relational communication and instructional communication. His research explores communication cognitions and behaviors that facilitate family functioning, specifically examining co-parenting and stepparenting relationships in stepfamilies and the associations among family communication schemata and family functioning. His research has appeared in *Human Communication Research*, *Communication Monographs*, and *Communication Education*.

Jordan Eli Soliz (Ph.D., University of Kansas) is Assistant Professor of Communication Studies at the University of Nebraska-Lincoln. His teaching and research interests are in interpersonal and family communication, with an emphasis on intergenerational interactions, intergroup and intercultural dynamics within the family, group differences in supportive interactions, and communication and intergroup prejudice. His research has appeared in the *Journal of Applied Communication Research*.

Patricia J. Sotirin (Ph.D., Purdue University) is Associate Professor of Communication at Michigan Technological University. Her research focuses on relational communication, gender, and work. She has published in such journals as *Women & Language, Text and Performance Quarterly*, and *Organization*.

Lynn H. Turner (Ph.D., Northwestern University) is Professor of Communication Studies at Marquette University. Her research areas of interest include interpersonal, gendered, and family communication. She is the coauthor or co-editor of more than 10 books as well as several articles and book chapters. She has served in a number of different positions: director of graduate studies for the College of Communication at Marquette University; president of the Organization for the Study of Communication, Language, and Gender; president of Central States Communication Association; and chair of the Family Communication Division for the National Communication Association.

Anita L. Vangelisti (Ph.D., University of Texas at Austin) is Professor in the Department of Communication Studies at the University of Texas at Austin.

She is interested in interpersonal communication among family members and between romantic partners. She is co-editor of the Cambridge University Press book series on advances in personal relationships, was associate editor of *Personal Relationships*, and has served on the editorial boards of numerous journals. Dr. Vangelisti has coauthored and edited several books and is presently working on two more volumes.

Richard West (Ph.D., Ohio University) is Professor and Chair of the Department of Communication and Media Studies at the University of Southern Maine. His research seeks to understand the intersection of family communication, classroom communication, and culture. Rich is the coauthor of several book chapters, articles, and books, and he serves as an editorial board member for a number of communication journals. He has served as chair of the Instructional Development Division and is director-elect of the Educational Policies Board for the National Communication Association. He is also the president-elect of the Eastern Communication Association. Rich is the recipient of the Outstanding Alumni Awards from both Illinois State University and Ohio University.

Christina G. Yoshimura (Ph.D., Arizona State University) is Adjunct Assistant Professor of Interpersonal Communication at the University of Montana. Her research interests address the communication behaviors used by families in response to challenging dynamics such as maintenance of the work/family tension and the entrance or exit of family members.